Teaching foreign languages

Exploration Series in Education
under the
Advisory Editorship of
JOHN GUY FOWLKES

FRANK M. GRITTNER

State Supervisor of
Foreign Languages with
the Wisconsin Department of
Public Instruction

Teaching

foreign languages

Harper & Row, Publishers
New York,
Evanston,
and London

To Rilla

Teaching Foreign Languages
Copyright © 1969 by Frank M. Grittner

Library of Congress catalog card number: 69-10547

Contents

Editor's introduction

This field-tested work is a systematic, objective, presentation of methods of teaching foreign languages in the American school. Much more than a mere list of pedagogical techniques, this book presents hundreds of practical examples, each in the context of an underlying rationale, and supports them, where possible, with research. The various schools of methodology are discussed objectively, including the limitations and failures as well as the advantages and successes of each.

This is a unified text; each succeeding chapter is built upon the preceding ones. The first chapter traces the origin and history of the teaching of foreign language in America and identifies the historical causes of many problems which face every present-day foreign language teacher. The second chapter deals with the values to be derived from the study of foreign language and establishes a rationale for the offering of foreign language studies in the contemporary curriculum. Chapter 3 focuses upon those aspects of linguistics which have practical application to the teaching of foreign language in the classroom. The limitations which are imposed upon the American foreign language teacher by such factors as school organization, local traditions, age at which foreign language study is begun, etc. are presented in Chapter 4. Ways of overcoming the difficulties created by these limitations are suggested. Chapter 5 provides detailed instructional goals for each year of French, German, and Spanish four-level programs (a true help to teachers who are developing local curriculum guides). Chapter 6 treats the psychological aspects of foreign language learning, with particular attention to motivation and method. Chapter 7 deals with programmed learning and other self-instructional techniques. Chapter 8 explains the theory and use of pattern drills and includes models that can aid in the construction of all commonly used drill types. Also included is a criteria sheet for evaluating commercially produced drill tapes. Chapter 9 discusses the steps to be followed in teaching the four basic skills. Chapter 10 makes practical suggestions on how to match language laboratory equipment with the instructional program. Included is a manual for writing technically correct specifications for the language laboratory and the electronic classroom. The final chapter deals with test construction and with techniques for evaluating the overall foreign language program.

Teaching Foreign Languages is written clearly, simply, and concisely, with explanations provided for technical terms. While it is aimed at the undergraduate student, the book will also be of great value to high school teachers, curriculum directors, and school administrators. All those interested in the teaching of foreign language will find this volume informative and stimulative as well as specifically helpful.

JOHN GUY FOWLKES

Preface

This book is an attempt to bring together in a unified fashion the chief areas of knowledge which are directly relevant to the teaching of foreign languages and to present that knowledge in a readily comprehensible form. Too often in the past foreign language educators have expected the teacher-trainee to digest large, unmodified readings dealing with pure psychology, pure linguistics, and pure pedagogy, assuming all the while that the student would somehow have the ability to relate these disparate chunks of information to his function as a foreign language teacher.

Several hundred classroom visitations (including visits to elementary, secondary, and college foreign language classrooms) have convinced the author that nothing can be taken for granted where transfer of knowledge is concerned. The FLES teacher who expects small children to respond to philological lectures has failed to profit from his theoretical training in human development. The high school teacher who explains foreign language syntax as being "backwards" has missed the cultural significance of his linguistics course. And the college teacher who insists that "students can't understand the foreign language unless they translate" may not have examined closely enough the philosophical justification for his existence as a teacher of foreign languages.

In view of the above it appears that most teachers and prospective teachers of foreign language can benefit from a methods book which decompartmentalizes the learning process by focusing only upon those aspects of each relevant discipline which apply quite directly to the individual's role as an active member of the profession. A number of these cross-disciplinary aspects were identified in a report issued by the Modern Language Association of America entitled *The Education of the Modern Foreign Language Teacher for American Schools* by Joseph Axelrod. This report, published in 1966, was based upon a study of the NDEA Foreign Language Institute program during the summer of 1965. A team of 23 foreign language educators (including this author) submitted recommendations concerning those aspects of the NDEA Summer Institute Program which, in their opinion, should be carried over into the education of the foreign language teacher in the normal undergraduate program. Among the items from this study used by the author in determining the content and focus of the book were the following: (1) The history and function of education in American society and the place of foreign language in that framework; (2) the nature of learning in general and the psychology of language learning in particular; (3) the differences which exist in learners at elementary, secondary, college, and adult levels and the implications which those differences have for foreign language instruction; (4) the use of instructional media in foreign language learning, and criteria for evaluating such media; (5) the evaluation of student learning in foreign languages; (6) the elimination of myths about language in general and about foreign languages in particular; (7) the need to view knowledge in the field of foreign languages as tentative and continuously developing rather than as static and absolute; (8) the ability to help students gain progressive control of the four language skills; and (9) the ability to identify all relevant similarities and differences between the structure of the target language and the structure of English.

Thus, the content of this book is based on recommendations of a team which included state supervisors of foreign language; college professors of Germanic, Slavic, and Romance languages; a foreign language consultant for a large metropolitan school district; a city superintendent; a state director of certification and a college dean.

Madison, Wisconsin   FRANK M. GRITTNER

A note on bibliographies

The bibliographies in this book consist mainly of items which are likely to be available in the average college library or which can be obtained at nominal cost from the MLA Materials Center, 62 Fifth Avenue, New York City 10011. It is assumed that the foreign language methods instructor will direct all prospective teachers to the *Selective List of Materials* (or SLOM) bulletin and to supplements available from this address. SLOM is an annotated listing of books and materials available for use in the classroom. It also includes evaluative criteria which can be used in making decisions about tapes, texts, and audiovisual materials. In the author's opinion there was no good reason for duplicating the efforts of the SLOM committee.

More recently a bibliography of significant professional publications has been developed under the sponsorship of the American Council on the Teaching of Foreign Languages (ACTFL) It was written by Emma Marie Birkmaier and Dale L. Lange and was published under the title "A Selective Bibliography on the Teaching of Foreign Languages," 1920–1966, *Foreign Language Annals*, Volume One, Number Four, May 1968, pages 318–353. In the words of the authors, "This bibliography may be considered the prologue to the ACTFL *Bibliography*, an annual listing which began in *Foreign Language Annals* 1, i (October 1967)."

Also worthy of note is the Educational Resources Information Center (ERIC). *Foreign Language Annals* contains the ERIC Clearinghouse on the Teaching of Foreign Languages. This section of the journal deals with the teaching of the commonly taught languages—French, German, Italian, Russian, Spanish—and the classical languages, Latin and Ancient Greek. Abstracts of selected ERIC accessions appear in *Annals*; a complete listing of accessions appears in the regular ACTFL Bibliography mentioned above. In view of the availability of such bibliographies with their built-in policy of updating, the author chose to limit his bibliographical selections to the most basic items.

He who does not learn from the past is condemned to relive it.
SANTAYANA

The historical roots of foreign language teaching in America

1 The new "American Method" did not come into existence by spontaneous generation. Much of what is happening in our foreign language classes today is closely tied to the past. However, a large proportion of present-day methodology is a deliberate renunciation of goals and practices which were long held sacred. Over a period of several decades, the proponents of change have created a whole new school of thought regarding how languages should be taught and what should be learned. The ideas of the new school have, in a relatively short time, brought drastic changes in teaching procedures and objectives. What was the old? How does the new differ from the old? What changes in language instruction have taken place through the centuries? What brought about the changes, past and present? These are a few of the questions which must first be answered if the present is to be viewed in the proper perspective.

The classical language heritage

Hear how learn'd Greece her useful rules indites,
When to repress, and when indulge our flights. . . .

. . . .

Those rules of old discovered, not devised
Are Nature still, but Nature methodized. . . .

. . .

Learning and Rome alike in empire grew;
And Arts still followed where her Eagles flew;
From the same foes, at last, both felt their doom,
And the same age saw Learning fall, and Rome.

ALEXANDER POPE (1688–1744)

It is often said that western civilization began with the Greeks;
yet they are only indirectly responsible for the creation of foreign
language study as a separate discipline. The Greeks themselves
attached little value to any language but their own. It was the
Romans who first established knowledge of a foreign language—
the language of the conquered Greeks—as the mark of an educated
gentleman. The magnificence of Greek letters apparently over-
whelmed the Romans. In fact, so great was their enthusiasm that
they eventually set up Hellenic literary forms as the only models
worth imitating. In their emulation of the Greeks, Roman poets came
to create a great literature of their own in Latin. In addition, centuries of Roman rule produced a vast legacy of practical writings
in such areas as law, engineering, architecture, medicine, and military tactics. And so it was that long after the collapse of Roman political power, Latin continued on as the language of philosophy and
religion; as the repository of significant knowledge; as the means
of communication of the educational elite of Europe. Throughout
the middle ages, Greek was largely eclipsed by Latin, a language
whose conquest of the educational world was to continue on into the
present century.

A thousand years after the fall of Rome, a surprising number
of Greek and Latin manuscripts were still extant. By that time, of
course, the languages themselves were "dead." That is, almost no
one was learning Latin or classical Greek from childhood on as the
means of everyday oral communication. By the sixteenth century,
national tongues such as English, French, German, and Spanish had
taken shape, and men who spoke them were producing significant
writings in the vernacular. Yet European men of letters and science
continued to draw heavily, if not exclusively, upon the Greek and

Roman classics for knowledge and for literary models. This process of extracting knowledge from ancient writings was not without its critics. Montaigne, the famous sixteenth-century French essayist, had learned Latin as a child by a "natural" conversational method. Nevertheless, he was impelled to say: "No doubt but Greek and Latin are very great ornaments, and of very great use, but we buy them too dear."[1] In reference to bookish studies in Latin grammar and composition to which many a boy was subjected Montaigne added: "Men are quick to inquire, 'Does he know Greek or Latin? Does he write in verse or in prose?' But whether he has become better or more prudent, which is the principal thing, this receives not the least notice. . . . If his soul be not put into better rhythm, if the judgment be not better settled, I would rather have him spend his time at tennis."[2]

Yet, despite Montaigne's dissatisfaction with the teaching methodology of his day, there were few who challenged either the practical or the cultural value of knowing Latin and Greek. The term "Renaissance" itself is a form of tribute to the study of the classical writings. For without such study a major portion of the knowledge upon which western civilization is based could not have been transmitted to later generations of Europeans and Americans. The great figures of the Renaissance realized the incalculable importance of the ancient languages. Erasmus went so far as to say, "When I have money I will first buy Greek books and then clothes." Rabelais indicated his respect for classical learning by having his hero, Gargantua, study ancient languages. Like Erasmus, Rabelais favored Greek, which had fallen into discredit in the middle ages. "Now all disciplines are restored, and the languages reinstated," he writes. "Greek (without which it is a shame for a person to call himself learned), Hebrew, Chaldean, Latin."[3]

The Renaissance established classical languages in a position of preeminence which they were to hold for centuries. Yet it was during this period that forces were set in motion which would lead to the ultimate decline of Latin and Greek. One force was the great

[1] Michel de Montaigne, *Essays*, Book I, chap. 25.
[2] *Ibid.*, chap. 24.
[3] Gabriel Compayre, *The History of Pedagogy*, Boston, Heath, 1886, p. 95.

The historical roots of foreign language teaching in America

literature being produced in the vulgar languages which would later serve as the base for the establishment of competing disciplines. A still greater force was the protestant reformation. As one writer expressed it.:

In making man responsible for his own faith, and in placing the source of that faith in the Holy Scriptures, the Reform contracted the obligation to put each one in a condition to save himself by the reading and understanding of the Bible. . . . The necessity of explaining the Catechism, and making comments on it, was for teachers an obligation to learn how to expound a thought, and to decompose it into its elements. The study of the mother tongue and of singing, was associated with the reading of the Bible (translated into German by Luther) and with religious services.[4]

Acceptance of the belief that a Christian should read the Bible in his own language set up a chain of circumstances which profoundly influenced education in the western world. It provided a powerful motive for commoners to become literate in the vernacular languages. It established a reason for the creation of primary schools. Ultimately, it led to the belief—in twentieth-century America—that a man could be ignorant of foreign languages and still consider himself adequately educated; a view which had been rejected by educated men in the western world since the early days of the Roman empire.

Foreign languages in America before the Civil War

The brief historical outline of foreign language learning in Europe can only hint at the educational traditions which the colonists had brought with them to the New World. For the field of foreign languages, two aspects of that tradition are of central importance. First, the link between literacy and salvation helped to establish the need for general primary education with particular emphasis upon the ability to read English. Second, the need for professional men—particularly clergymen and lawyers—led to the establishment of secondary and higher education. For education beyond the three

[4] *Ibid.*, p. 113.

Rs, the traditions of past centuries dictated that Greek and Latin were indispensable. English and other modern spoken languages were still considered as unsuitable subjects for serious scholarship. The situation at Harvard University in the early 1800s typifies the shaky position of modern languages in the pre-Civil War period. "The course of study was designed to turn out right-thinking members of a New England society, and for the most part it did just that. Latin and Greek were the languages that were considered important. Modern foreign languages were tolerated."[5]

Ticknor, one of Harvard's first great professors of modern language (Spanish and French), was highly critical of the shabby treatment accorded to his field. Shortly before his resignation, he issued a sweeping condemnation of the entire institution: "We are neither a university—which we call ourselves, nor a respectable high school—which we ought to be."[6]

Aside from the University of Virginia, it is difficult to find an institution of higher learning in the first half of the nineteenth century which placed heavy emphasis on modern language study. Under the guidance of Thomas Jefferson, Virginia adopted a program of studies which included French, Italian, Spanish, German, and Anglo-Saxon. So successful was the program that, in 1825, modern language enrollment equalled that of mathematics and exceeded that of the ancient languages.[7]

Another of the founding fathers, Benjamin Franklin, had also been a strong advocate of modern language study. As early as 1749 he had proposed that the trustees of the Charity School of Philadelphia should "with all convenient speed endeavor to engage Persons capable of teaching the French, German and Spanish languages."[8]

It appears, however, that Franklin and Jefferson were not as

[5] Sturgis E. Leavitt, *The Teaching of Spanish in the United States,* Modern Language Association, 1961, p. 311.
[6] *Ibid.*
[7] *Ibid.,* p. 315.
[8] Reprinted by permission of the Modern Language Association from *The Teaching of German in the United States* by Edwin H. Zeydel, Modern Language Association, 1961, p. 288.

The historical roots of foreign language teaching in America

successful in swaying the educational policies of the time as they were in effecting political changes. For it was not until after the Civil War that modern foreign languages—specifically French and German—began to establish themselves as part of the American educational system. Spanish made little progress until well into the twentieth century.

If we review the history of the teaching of Spanish in the colleges and universities in the nineteenth century, it is clear that the language seldom formed part of the curriculum. In some cases, provision was made for studying it outside the classroom and no credit was given. . . . The usual salary of the instructors was $500 (yearly), hardly a living wage.[9]

French and German did not gain a respectable place in the curriculum without a struggle. Much of the teaching of modern languages before the nineteenth century was done by self-appointed professors who advertised their services in the local newspapers. Such teachers might serve as tutors either in their own homes or in the residence of the student. Sometimes the instructor would set up a contract with a small group of students from whom he demanded payment in advance. In other instances, instruction was carried on in foreign language boarding schools. In general, modern language instruction in colonial America and in the early years of the Republic was viewed as a frill which, if needed, could be acquired outside of the educational establishment. However, as the nineteenth century progressed and the public high schools began to replace the earlier forms of secondary education, French and German found an increasingly more prominent place in the regular course of studies.

Foreign languages from 1880 to World War I—the years of promise

In the first hundred years of American history (roughly from 1780 to 1880), opposition to modern languages had come from professors of the classical languages. English and other living languages were considered too easy and too utilitarian to serve the high purpose of developing the intellectual faculties. Yet despite the resistance of the educational elite, German, French, and English gradually in-

[9] Leavitt, *op. cit.*, p. 316.

filtrated the college and secondary curriculum. By 1883, these forces had grown strong enough to found the Modern Language Association, an organization which has survived and flourished down to the present. However, to gain academic respectability, the modern language forces felt compelled in the beginning to adopt the methods and objectives of the more highly regarded classical languages. The resulting emphasis upon grammatical analysis and the translation of prestige literature is manifested in the teaching of modern languages even today. The first major change in language teaching, then, came in the form of an alliance between the classical humanists and teachers of the modern languages. By the end of the eighteenth century, English had become firmly established as the common language of the colonies. French had become known world-wide as the language of diplomacy. This, coupled with the popularity of French enlightenment authors and Revolutionary sympathy for France, made a compelling case for the study of the French language. German established itself as the most popular modern foreign language for somewhat different reasons. It had survived the first mild setback after the revolution when public reaction against the Hessian mercenaries caused the discontinuance of several established programs.[10] However, the large influx of German immigrants during the nineteenth century resulted in the existence of many communities and sections of larger cities in which German was the native tongue; English the foreign language. As late as 1857, the school reports in Pennsylvania and Indiana were published in both English and German; in New Jersey this practice persisted until 1888. And in 1870 the U.S. Commissioner of Education reported that "the German language has actually become the second language of our Republic, and a knowledge of German is now considered essential to a finished education."[11] As a further impetus, the highly regarded German Universities of the late 1880s drew thousands of American students who brought back a zeal for German idealism as reflected in the writings of the great seventeenth- and eighteenth-century German authors and philosophers. France

[10] Zeydel, *op. cit.*, p. 289.
[11] *Ibid.*, p. 294. Note: The 1960 U.S. census reported that German was still the language spoken by more Americans than any except English.

The historical roots of foreign language teaching in America

and England too had produced great literatures, and on this basis a compromise with the classical humanists was possible. Literary monuments of the past could all be studied in the same way whether modern or classical. Grammars based on the Latin and Greek models could be written, and the fortress of high intellectual standards could thus be held against the onslaught of the sciences, technology, and other useful subjects.

The voices of those who saw modern languages as "useful" subjects went unheeded as had the suggestions of Ben Franklin and Thomas Jefferson in an earlier period. In the compromise with the classics, modern languages lost much of their modernity while Latin ultimately lost in comparative enrollments. For several decades, modern languages claimed an ever-larger share of the growing high-school enrollments as the following statistics indicate.

1

Foreign language enrollment trends prior to World War I

| Year | Total enrollment | Latin | Modern language | | | |
			Total	French	German	Spanish
1890	202,963	34.7%	16.3%	5.8%	10.5%	
1895	350,099	43.9	17.9	6.5	11.4	
1900	519,251	50.6	22.1	7.8	14.3	
1905	679,702	50.2	29.3	9.1	20.2	
1910	915,061	49.0	34.3	9.9	23.7	0.7%
1915	1,328,984	37.3	35.9	8.8	24.4	2.7

SOURCE: William R. Parker, *The National Interest and Foreign Languages,* 3rd ed., Department of State Publication 7324, 1961, p. 85.

While these enrollment increases are impressive, they tell only part of the story. Equally as important as a head count of high-school students are the answers to the following questions:

1. At what age did the students begin their study of the foreign language?
2. How long did students continue the study of the language in an uninterrupted sequence?
3. What was the total number of exposure hours to the language?

4. How well coordinated were the programs from year to year?
5. What methods were being used?
6. How well prepared were the foreign language teachers?

Reports and surveys from this era provide some of the answers to these questions. Considerable progress was made, for example, toward establishing an earlier beginning and a longer sequence of foreign language study. Tens of thousands of grade-school youngsters were studying foreign languages in the early part of this century in Toledo, New York City, Milwaukee, Buffalo, Cincinnati, San Francisco, and many other cities and towns.[12] Some of the elementary programs became well established, while others were dropped after a few years of experimentation. Buffalo, for example, was unable to cope with the problem of setting up a sequential course of study.

... instruction in the elementary schools was poorly administered and badly given. It consisted mainly of reading a given pensum, without regard to control or teaching of vocabulary. Drill in pronunciation and speaking was haphazard, and a syllabus non-existent. After six years of this type of hit-or-miss instruction, the children took a uniform examination covering as much as might be achieved in an ordinary one-year high school course. ... Of the 10,000 enrolled ... fewer than 400 took an examination for advanced credit. As the report points out: "Measured by these results, nearly 10,000 pupils are taught by 67 teachers in 43 schools in order that approximately 400 may get what they would have been able to obtain under two or three teachers in one year of the high school course."[13]

Also during this period, a number of modern language teachers had begun to break with the grammar-reading-translation syndrome inherited from the alliance with the classics. The famous *Committee of Twelve Report* published in 1899 by the National Education Association, described some teaching techniques then in use which sound strikingly like the methods that gained currency in the 1960s. Also mentioned in this report were the so-called "natural" and "direct" methods. These two approaches were doomed to limited

[12] Zeydel, *op. cit.*, pp. 295–298.
[13] *Ibid.*, p. 298.

The historical roots of foreign language teaching in America

success because of the fourth variable mentioned above—the teacher.

These methods require a native teacher with great energy, enthusiasm, and skill, almost exclusive use of the foreign language by teacher and pupil, much repetition, and an approach to the written word not by means of grammar but through oral-aural means. The method had many opponents from the start; they claimed that it is too time-consuming, that it encourages glibness, rather than depth, and treats adolescent and adult as though they were children.

In spite of the drawbacks of the system, it left its mark upon modern-language teaching in the United States once it had been developed into the Direct Method. Insofar as they stress the spoken word and the oral-aural approach and represent a reaction to the grammar translation method . . . the Natural and Direct method are similar. But the latter is less radical. It exploits the methodology of its predecessors eclectically, does not throw grammar overboard yet never teaches it for its own sake, and follows a well constructed plan of presentation.[14]

According to a contemporary observer, an ever-growing number of teachers had realized the need for a change of method.

Even if reading the foreign language is held to be the legitimate aim of teaching, the need was felt by progressive teachers for a more active control of the vocabulary and grammar than could ever be won through the mere learning of rules, paradigms and translation. The Direct Method suggested that this could be accomplished by developing language material, usually a connected passage, by means of questions and answers. This procedure had long been utilized in the elementary schools, but now began to grow important in high school classes.[15]

A canvass of eighty high schools in 1894 also revealed a development favorable to the improvement of foreign language instruction. Two-thirds of them were offering a three- or four-year sequence of instruction in at least one foreign language.[16]

In an attempt to solve the problems of changing methods, lengthening sequences of study, and college entrance requirements, The National Educational Association Committee of Ten, in 1893,

[14] *Ibid.*
[15] *Ibid.*, p. 298.
[16] *Ibid.*, p. 296.

set down a series of recommendations. The ideal program was designated as four years of elementary school plus four years of high school. If the elementary program were not feasible, then four years of high school study were recommended for certain types of secondary schools while two years were considered adequate for other types. This, according to Zeydel, was a fatal weakness of the *Committee of Ten Report:*

. . . in order not to interfere unduly with the courses in Latin and Greek, it provided for the notorious two-year modern foreign language course, which has been the bane of foreign-language teachers ever since. As the number of subjects and courses offered in the American high school increased by leaps and bounds in the next few generations, soon mounting to well over four hundred, and with the expansion of the high school into areas never dreamed of in the nineteenth century, less and less room remained in the curriculum for so "academic" a subject as modern languages. Hence the schedule makers, overlooking the fact that the two-year course was only an expedient suggested for exceptional cases, so as not to interfere unduly with the vested interests of Latin and Greek, treated the two-year course as the norm, which it was never meant to be. The final step, then, was to discredit the teachers of the languages because they could not accomplish in two years what requires at least four (in England, France, Germany, and almost any other country six or more).[17]

In all fairness it should be pointed out that the Committee actually went on record in favor of a four-year program for those students who stayed in high school through to graduation. In fact, the Committee went so far as to recommend that more than one language should be included in certain courses of study.[18] The "Classical" course called for four years of Latin *plus* three years of either French or German *plus* another two years of Greek. In the "Latin-Scientific course the student was to study four years of Latin plus two years of either French or German. The "Modern Languages" course included French and German one of which was

[17] *Ibid.*, p. 295.
[18] Edward A. Krug (ed.), *Charles W. Elliot and Popular Education,* Classics in Education No. 8, New York, Teachers College, Columbia University, 1961, pp. 90–93.

The historical roots of foreign language teaching in America

to be studied for four years the other for three. Finally, in the "English" course the student was to study Latin, German, or French for four full years.[19] Thus, in their intentions, the Committee of Ten was highly favorable to the study of foreign language, listing it among "the principal fields of knowledge" and suggesting that most youngsters could profit from such study.[20]

A report by the Committee of Twelve which appeared in 1899 was perhaps more thorough and helpful than the *Committee of Ten Report*. However, the method of teaching advocated was the same: extensive reading-translation of graded texts and the study of grammatical principles with some oral drill work. It approved elementary foreign language study, but only if a truly competent teacher were available. On the whole, the *Committee of Twelve Report* exercised a great deal of influence upon foreign language study in America.

Its proposals were widely discussed and adopted, and even the less well prepared teachers did their best to modify their soul-deadening translation procedures in accordance with it. For it also proved to be, and was used as, a handbook of method. . . Most of the universities and colleges soon adopted the recommendations of the Committee, especially that of the establishment of three national grades of preparatory instruction, and in 1901, when the College Entrance Examination Board was set up, they were put into effect.[21]

Yet, despite its positive influence, this report also tended to fortify the notion that foreign language study should be a short-sequence affair. As Professor Zeydel expresses it: "So far as the pernicious over-emphasis of the two-year course and its gradual acceptance as the standard are concerned, this report was no better than its predecessor."[22] Yet, when everything is considered, the two reports *had* recommended the four-year course of study; and, in spite of their shortcomings, they had suggested alternative methods and had, in other ways, allowed sufficient breadth for positive development. One can only guess what their ultimate influence might have been

[19] *Ibid.*
[20] *Ibid.*, p. 89.
[21] Zeydel, *op. cit.*, p. 296.
[22] *Ibid.*, p. 296.

had the climate for foreign language study remained favorable. But, unfortunately, the climate was about to change.

From U-Boat to Sputnik—the bleak years

On May 7, 1915, a German submarine sank the Lusitania off the coast of England. Among the 1198 people who went to the bottom with the British liner were 128 Americans. Submarine warfare and the subsequent American participation in World War I were to have a disastrous effect upon the study of foreign languages in the United States. In the years between 1910 and 1915, as high as 80 percent of all high-school students were in Latin; one-fourth in German. French was holding its own and Spanish was beginning to catch on. Latin still outnumbered all modern languages by a few percentage points. Then came 1917, and:

> . . . in the spring of that year, when the United States declared war on Germany, all hell broke loose. The propaganda, which had concentrated upon the German emperor, his army and submarines, with many allegations of atrocities, turned immediately, now that we were at war, against the language, its literature as a whole and, in some cases, even against its teachers who were confronted with the sweeping accusation of being "pro-German." Groups of vigilantes visited the libraries and removed German books; other came to the departmental offices in the universities and confiscated textbooks containing pictures of Emperor William II or equally "subversive" material. . . .
>
> State legislatures (twenty-two in number . . .) and a score of cities vied with one another in forbidding the teaching of German in the public elementary and high schools, or even in prohibiting the speaking of German.[23]

But German did not suffer by itself. Like noncombatant passengers on a torpedoed ship, French and Latin went down with German. Forty years later, when the downward plunge finally ended, only Spanish had improved its percentage of enrollments over the year 1917. This was small consolation; it meant only that Spanish had won the largest share of a very small slice of pie. For in the mid-

---

[23] *Ibid.*, p. 298.

1950s, a little more than 20 percent of all students were now electing foreign languages as compared with 80 percent before World War I. Again, let the enrollments tell their own story.

2

Foreign language enrollment trends after World War I

| Year | Total enrollment | Latin | Modern language | | | |
			Total	French	German	Spanish
1915	1,328,984	37.3%	35.9%	8.8%	24.4%	2.7%
1922	2,230,000	27.5	27.4	15.5	.6	11.3
1928	3,354,473	22.0	25.2	14.0	1.8	9.4
1934	5,620,625	16.0	19.5	10.9	2.4	6.2
1949	5,399,452	7.8	13.7	4.7	.8	8.2
1954	6,582,300	6.9	14.2	5.6	.8	7.3

SOURCE: William R. Parker, *The National Interest and Foreign Languages,* 3rd ed., Department of State Publication 7324, 1961, p. 86.

The zeal and energy with which Americans attacked the problems of World War I quickly turned sour when the fighting was over. Not only did this country reject the League of Nations; everything "foreign" was held in contempt. Apparently the process of anglicizing the many disparate groups from non-English-speaking lands had not been completed satisfactorily. The norm for "true-blue" Americans had been stated in an old slogan: "To be Americanized is to be anglicized." And this meant speaking the "American language" with no trace of an accent. Certainly, the ability to use a foreign language of any kind was no very great or worthwhile accomplishment. A visiting evangelist at Peoria, Arizona summed up the prevailing attitude in a 1926 sermon: "If I had my way there would be no language taught in the United States except English, and any foreigner coming here would be immediately sent back if he could not speak our language. I am 100% American."[24] Vituperation was not limited to language and national background

[24] Quoted by H. L. Mencken (ed.), *Americana 1926,* New York, Knopf, 1926, p. 9.

alone. Even entertainment had to be Americanized if one can judge from an editorial in the New York *American Standard*, 1926.

The Metropolitan Opera House is the most thoroughly foreign institution in this country. Standing at the back of the house and surveying an operatic audience, one can scarcely find an Anglo-Saxon face. Jews and Italians predominate, with a liberal proportion of Germans, Slavs, and miscellaneous dregs of the Mediterranean and Levantine races. . . . Genuine Americans have no real feeling for it (Opera), and can neither produce operas nor act in them. To imagine George Washington, Benjamin Franklin, Thomas Jefferson, or any other such representative American pay to witness the horrors and sensualities of grand opera, is to imagine the impossible. . . .[25]

Students at the University of Arkansas were somewhat more tolerant of Germans and Slavs. In voting for "the world's greatest musician of all times" they assigned second place to Beethoven. Paderewski tied for third with Henry J. Tovey, Director of the Musical Department of Arkansas University. The title of the "world's greatest musician of all time" was awarded to Paul Whiteman.[26]

Some have blamed isolationism, super-Americanism, and anti-intellectualism for the decline in foreign language study. Whatever the causes, the decline took place. Not only did enrollments shrink, but elementary-school courses and advanced study programs vanished. Research in the 1920s showed that 83 percent of all high schools offered only two years of foreign language instruction.[27] To the language teachers of the day, one thing was clear: With so little exposure to language instruction it was futile to attempt to teach students how to understand, read, write, and speak a foreign language. Or at least, this was the conclusion reached by the most famous of a series of investigations conducted by grants from the Carnegie Corporation. Known as the "Coleman Report," this publication had a profound effect upon the teaching of foreign languages. According to Parker, ". . . it is a fact that from 1929 until World War II most modern language instruction in American schools and colleges stressed the 'reading aim' and produced a gen-

[25] *Ibid.*, p. 147.
[26] *Ibid.*, pp. 11–12.
[27] William R. Parker, *The National Interest and Foreign Languages*, p. 87.

The historical roots of foreign language teaching in America

eration largely unable to speak French, German, or Spanish, or even to read a newspaper or magazine article in these languages beyond the ability of a fifth-grade pupil in English.[28]

Between the two world wars the climate grew increasingly inhospitable to foreign language study. The causes for the antilanguage trend are difficult to trace and harder to prove. Among the reasons often cited are anti-intellectualism in American society, utilitarianism in education, isolationism in politics, and the immigrant's tendency to reject the culture of the "old country" and (in the second generation) the non-English language of the parents. Also, the rather narrow objectives and limited methodology employed by many foreign language teachers of the period may have contributed greatly to the deterioration. Further, the absence of any strong, organized group representing the interests of the foreign language profession at the secondary level, as well as the resulting inability of many scattered and isolated language teachers to contend with a changing high-school curriculum, may partly explain the downfall. But, whatever the causes, the decline continued even beyond World War II, reaching such catastrophic proportions by the 1950s that over half the high schools in America offered no modern language during the postwar decade. In these bleak years, foreign languages tended to be referred to as "peripheral" subjects or were simply ignored. As late as 1950 a book on secondary education contained the following statement:

It is difficult to justify languages for all youth. True, languages can help students understand various cultures. A great deal of instruction in language, however, is concerned with reading and speaking skills, and in face of so many urgent needs, use of the time and effort necessary to master these skills is questionable. . . . The time saved might be used for study of the current social problems completely overlooked by the classical curriculum. . . . Actually, about the only valid justification the authors can find for inclusion of foreign languages in the high school curriculum is that of satisfying the intellectual curiosity of a few students who are interested in developing their linguistic interests and abilities.[29]

[28] *Ibid.*, p. 87.
[29] J. G. Saylor, *Secondary Education: Basic Principles and Practices,* 1950, quoted by Parker, *op. cit.*, p. 90.

16

With the exception of a few notable programs, such as the "Cleveland Plan" in Ohio, elementary school foreign language and the teaching of listening and speaking skills went by the board after World War I. The few programs which remained were not sufficient to maintain continuity of development within the profession and, as a result, a total rebuilding program was subsequently necessary. Although the actual reconstruction did not start in earnest until the late 1950s, the foundations for it were laid well before America's involvement in World War II.

World War II—the army method

Few laymen and a surprisingly small number of language teachers have a clear conception of either the origin or nature of the misnamed "Army Method." When Pearl Harbor suddenly wrenched America loose from its isolationism and the need for foreign languages became associated with the war effort, a group of Army officers—so it seemed—had put their heads together and had devised a miraculous way of converting monolingual GIs into fluent speakers of Japanese, Chinese, Russian, German, or any other language for which there was a need. What is more, these skills could be acquired with only nine months of instruction! By contrast, the graduates of our schools and colleges, after two to six years of study, could only stammer hesitantly in language which was loaded with incorrect forms and antiquated vocabulary. A professor of languages visiting abroad once received a dubious compliment: "You speak very well," he was told, "for a character out of a nineteenth-century novel." The story is also told of an American professor of French who refused to speak that language with a visiting French woman. When she persisted in using her native tongue, the Professor is said to have replied testily, "Madame, I told you I *teach* French; I did not say that I *speak* French." It seemed clear that our schools and universities had failed to provide even the rudiments of genuine language learning. How was it, then, that boys from the corn belt could, in less than a year, be trained to interrogate prisoners, carry on espionage, and even successfully monitor low-fidelity radio transmissions in a foreign language?

The historical roots of foreign language teaching in America

The answer to this question can be summarized by describing four main characteristics of the Army Method:

Selection. The young men were selected on the basis of intelligence, aptitude, and willingness to participate in the program. In short, a group of bright young men with the proper attitudes could receive special recognition for doing something they liked and come away with the feeling that they were serving their country in time of need in the process. Motivation could hardly have been better.

Time. The "nine months" of training was in reality a dawn-to-dark schedule of intensive study. If equated in terms of exposure hours, the time was more than equivalent to two years of high school plus four years of college.

Teaching conditions. Instruction was carried on in small groups by native or near-native instructors. The entire program was under the close surveillance of specially trained linguists who made adjustments in the program as it went along. Moreover, the language was used as the means of communication from breakfast to bedtime. A native "informant" was usually at hand to supply the correct expression when it was needed. Then too, the program was blessed with a liberal wartime budget which allowed for the latest in instructional materials and facilities.

Well-defined objectives. Rapid and perfect comprehension of the spoken language plus the ability to speak with a good accent were the chief objectives of the program. Reading and writing were secondary in importance, and the literary and cultural objectives were largely replaced by an emphasis upon contemporary customs and the way-of-life of the people whose language was being studied. The college student had read poems by Villon or the prose of Cervantes. The military trainee learned to relate oral messages about gun emplacements, to convert miles into kilometers, or to eat holding his fork in the left hand.

It should be quite apparent to anyone that the course of instruction described above could not be applied directly and in toto to the college or high-school program. Quite predictably, the first attempts to do so met with disappointment and frustrations. For more than a decade following the war, efforts were made to adapt the intensive Army Method to the nonintensive academic programs.

By 1960 texts, tapes, and other audio-visual materials had been developed and were ready to market on a large scale. *Modern Spanish,* developed by the Modern Language Association, was the first major college text which was fully representative of the new American Method. The so-called "Audio-Lingual Materials" developed in Glastonbury, Connecticut with a federal grant from the U.S. Office of Education became the prototype for the new direction in secondary instruction. In the early 1960s, a commercial publisher acquired the rights to the materials and began publishing versions in French, German, Italian, Russian, and Spanish. Soon other publishers began producing their own audiolingual textbooks in the commonly taught modern languages. The more skeptical publishing houses made gestures in the direction of the new methodology by slightly revamping their old grammar-reading texts and providing tapes to accompany them. "Change comes slowly," ran the old adage, "it takes at least twenty years for a new educational idea to take hold once it has become widely known." But this time the adage did not hold true. Within three years, millions of students were being taught by one or the other of the new texts. More than $30,000,000 had been expended for 6,000 high school language laboratories. Tens of thousands of teachers had been run through a pedagogical version of the intensive military programs in the form of summer training institutes financed by the federal government. And where there had been only three states with foreign language supervisors in 1957, by 1964 the number had grown to 70 supervisors in 40 states, most of them sympathetic to the objectives of the American Method.[30] It seemed that a small group of Army officers had really started something big; or had they?

In plain truth, the main credit, as far as the military men are concerned, lay in their willingness to accept and apply a theory of linguistic analysis and language instruction that had lain dormant for several decades. Edward Sapir and Otto Jespersen had written books in 1923 which pointed the direction. C. C. Fries and a Frenchman, Joseph Vendryes, had also done pioneer work later

[30] Frank Grittner, "The Influence of the State Foreign Language Supervisor upon Foreign Language Instruction in America," *Modern Language Journal,* *XLIX* (February 1965), 91–94.

The historical roots of foreign language teaching in America

in the twenties, as had Leonard Bloomfield in the thirties, and Bernard Bloch and George Trager in the forties. However, the real catalytic agent behind the Army Method was the American Council of Learned Societies (ACLS). Even before the war, ACLS had put a number of linguists to work analyzing certain neglected foreign languages and developing methods for teaching them with the greatest efficiency. In addition to advocating longer exposure to the language, utilization of electronic equipment, use of native speakers, and emphasis upon speaking and listening skills, the ACLS theorists rejected the age-old practice of organizing language study around conventional Latinizing grammar. A new way of identifying points of grammar was suggested, and the points were to be learned functionally by drill in the foreign language rather than by analysis in English. It was these two aspects of the Army Method —the new linguistic analysis and the view of grammar as habit formation—which were to have an important influence in shaping the American Method.

For more than a decade after the war the ideas continued to incubate. The development of the wire recorder and then the tape recorder made it possible to store spoken-language material effectively and to reproduce the voices of native speakers inexpensively and with good fidelity. This appeared to solve one of the blocks to implementing the new ideas. Where the Army Method had called for expensive native informants to work with small groups of students, native voices could now be provided on tape at relatively low cost. The first full-fledged language laboratory was developed in 1947 at Louisiana State University. By 1957, 240 institutions of higher learning had some sort of language laboratory. (Significantly, there were only about 60 high-school language laboratories in 1957, one year before the federal government had passed a law appropriating funds for the purchase of such equipment. Five years later, with federal aid, this number had exploded to 6000.)

Many colleges and universities continued experimenting with the less-technological applications of the new linguistic theory. Meanwhile, conditions outside the profession began to change in favor of modern languages. Well-known personalities such as Mrs. Roosevelt, General Eisenhower, and Mr. Dulles, as well as important people in business and education began to speak out in favor of language study. Within the Modern Language Association a well-organized group had already formulated the basic tenets of reform. By 1956, these rebels had written up specific proposals for turning their cause into a movement; all that was lacking was adequate support. Then, in 1957, the Russians shot their first Sputnik into orbit, and support for foreign language study was quick in coming. The bleak years, which had begun with advances in German submarine technology, came to an end with the development of Soviet rocketry. While most language people were unable to trace a clear cause-and-effect relationship between rocket thrust and foreign languages, they were happy that foreign languages had regained a place in the sun. In a few years, when the full implications of the new prosperity became apparent, many began to wonder if the enrollment gains had not been bought too dearly.

Bibliography

The books and articles listed below are suggested as a minimal bibliography for anyone with a serious interest in the history of foreign language education in America. The items are listed in the order in which they might most profitably be read.

GENERAL

Parker, William R., *The National Interest and Foreign Languages,* 3rd ed., Department of State Publication 7324, Washington, D.C., U.S. Government Printing Office, September, 1961, 159 pp., $1.00.

BY LANGUAGE

The following reports of surveys and studies in the teaching of modern foreign languages are available from the Materials Center, Modern Language Association, 62 Fifth Ave., New York 10011.

Leavitt, Sturgis E., H37 *The Teaching of Spanish in the United States*— A historical survey, 1961, 18 pp., 50¢.

Watts, George B., H38 *The Teaching of French in the United States*— A historical survey, 1963, 165 pp., $1.00.

Zeydel, Edwin H., H36 *The Teaching of German in the United States*— A historical survey, 1961, 23 pp., 50¢.

The historical roots of foreign language teaching in America

If English was good enough for the Lord, it's good enough for me.
TWENTIETH-CENTURY AMERICAN EDUCATOR

He who knows no foreign language has never really learned his own.
GOETHE

Why should Americans study a foreign language?

A discussion of foreign language teaching methods can make little sense if it is not accompanied by a clear statement of what the methods hope to accomplish. And the objectives of foreign language study, in turn are closely related to the reasons for including the subject in the curriculum in the first place. The present-day proponents of foreign languages give reasons ranging from national survival to getting a better job. Entire books have been written listing in great detail the many advantages, both educational and practical, which come to him who has studied a foreign language (see Bibliography). While such lists provide valuable information regarding the current uses to which foreign languages are put, they do have several limitations. One of these is the tendency to give equal treatment to highly unequal items. For example, the need that Ph.D. candidates have for a reading knowledge in a foreign language is given equal status with foreign language study for the general education of *all* children who are attending school, despite the fact that few persons out of every thousand in a given age group ever earn the doctorate.

In the interest of reorganizing the mountains of disproportionate facts into some meaningful pattern, this writer has attempted to identify the main reasons currently given for foreign language study in contrast with attitudes that have existed from the early beginnings of foreign language study in America, some of which are evident even today.

Mental discipline and great books

From the more conservative classicists the modern language profession inherited a tradition which might be summarized by the term "grim humanism." The word "grim" is used in reference to an attitude which characterizes the learning process as consisting necessarily of hard, unpleasant work. In many foreign language teachers this attitude is associated with a fierce devotion to literary and philosophical monuments of the past, especially those which have a high obscurity quotient. Naturally, the inclination toward literary content can exist separately from the predilection for subjecting students to hard labor. For example, there are those who believe in the laborious study of grammar for grammar's sake and there are others who believe in presenting literary masterpieces through pleasurable methods of instruction. The advocates of rigorous learning activity believe that mental dexterity is developed by such traditional language exercises as the memorization of rules, verb conjugations, and noun declensions and by other activities such as reconstructing sentences in the foreign language from English and translating sentences into English from the foreign language. In the pursuit of such exercises the mental-discipline advocate may look upon works of literature merely as convenient sources of material for parsing, decoding, and other forms of mental gymnastics. In this view, literature becomes merely a part of a long obstacle course through which the raw homo sapien must be run in order to convert him into a cultivated human being. Thomas Huxley, in an essay on science and education, points up the absurdity of using difficulty for its own sake by applying the grim school master's language-teaching method to scientific content.

It is wonderful how close a parallel to classical training could be made out of that palaeontology to which I refer. In the first place I could get up an osteological primer so arid, so pedantic in its terminology, so altogether distasteful to the youthful mind, as to beat the recent famous

Why should Americans study a foreign language?

production of the headmasters out of the field in all these excellences. Next, I could exercise my boys upon easy fossils, and bring out all their powers of memory and all their ingenuity in the application of my osteogrammatical rules to the interpretation, or construing, of these fragments. To those who had reached the higher classes, I might supply odd bones to be built up into animals, giving great honor and reward to him who succeeded in fabricating monsters most entirely in accordance with the rules. That would answer to verse-making and essay-writing in the dead languages.[1]

The great-books advocates from the older humanistic school will tend to focus more upon the literature and its content than upon the process of learning. This group tends to see the literary monuments as sources of truth and beauty; the foreign language itself must be learned only insofar as that learning is necessary to make these transcendent sources available to the student. As a rule, the emphasis is upon the "universal ideas," and this tends to place the language itself in a position of secondary importance. More often than not the student's exposure to the spoken language is passive, and the bulk of this active participation involves speaking or writing in English. All this gives rise to a seemingly logical question: If the chief activity of the student is to discuss the pan-humanistic ideas in English, then would it not be better to by-pass the foreign language entirely? An enormous amount of time is lost in having the students laboriously produce their own inept translations from original texts. Why not have them instead read expertly translated versions of the classics, thereby enabling the students to cover more ground and leaving more time free for discussion?

Modern humanism and anthropology

The writings of Sapir and Whorf and the investigations of various cultural anthropologists have produced a new humanistic rationale for the study of languages. In essence, the Sapir-Whorf hypothesis asserts (1) that the native language determines how a person views the world and (2) that he is unaware of his mental entrapment if

[1] Edward A. Krug, *The Secondary School Curriculum,* New York, Harper & Row, 1960, p. 92.

he remains monolingual. Thus the American who grows up speaking only English is never conscious of how thoroughly his ability to think is circumscribed by the way his language compels him to structure his thoughts. Just as a deep-sea creature would be unaware of the nature of water because he has never experienced non-water, a monolingual American is unaware of the nature of English because he has had no significant contact with non-English. His ethnocentric mind set traps him into believing that English is the only reasonable way to express reality. Actually, English, like all languages, causes distortions by the way it structures expression. For example, the language of the Hopi Indians is more accurate than English in expressing certain natural processes. In English we say,

John is dying.

The Hopi language, by contrast, would say something like,

Dying is taking place in John.

The Hopi more accurately expresses the fact that John is really not doing anything, whereas the Anglo-American, by the very nature of how his language symbolizes actions in the "real" world, is forced to attribute agent power to John even though John is passively, and perhaps unwillingly, in the process of dying.

From the Sapir-Whorf hypothesis it follows that the study of a second language is essential to understanding what language is all about. The American student can develop a clearer understanding of his native English by comparing it with a non-English communication system. But this understanding can come only by means of a thorough immersion in the language of a non-Anglo-Saxon culture. A sampling of "General Language" will not suffice—language is far too complex to be profitably sampled. The American student must be taught to communicate through direct immersion in a totally new system of oral and written symbols. He must to some degree become conversant in the mother tongue of some non-Anglo-American culture.

Just how powerful this attachment to the mother tongue is was demonstrated by the riots in India during the winter of 1965 when Prime Minister Shastri signed a parliamentary decree making Hindi the sole official language. According to newspaper reports at the time, Tamil-Bengali-speaking citizens reacted with such violence that more than seventy people were killed in the rioting and over two million dollars worth of property was destroyed. In an effort to calm the angry mobs, Shastri proposed elevating English to the status of an associate language. This only served to infuriate the one group which had theretofore remained calm. The 40 percent of India which speaks Hindi was incensed at the prospect of elevating an alien tongue to such a position of recognition. They began rioting, burning English books, and effacing signs written in English. Similar incidents have occurred in Europe, Africa, and the Middle East over the imposing of a non-native language upon a large segment of a country's population. It would seem from all this that the hope to establish any one language as a universal tongue is highly visionary.

Among those who cite the anthropological value of language study are people from a variety of disciplines. William R. Parker, whose background is English, comments as follows: "Learning a foreign language is an educational experience. By acquiring even a limited skill, which may or may not be retained, the individual finds himself personally breaking the barriers of a single speech and a single culture—experiencing another culture at first-hand in the symbols through which it expresses its realities."[2]

Marshall J. Walker, a professor of physics, says: "The main value to education of the study of a foreign language lies in its unique contribution to an understanding of the principles of the communication of thought. A basic aim of all serious education is a comprehension of the distinction between a concept and the words, or symbols, used to describe the concept. The person with only one language is at a hopeless disadvantage in such a task."[3]

The author, G. H. Fisher, puts it more strongly: "The American will never really penetrate the thinking of people in a new country until he has first penetrated the language which carries, reflects, and molds the thoughts and ideas of that people."[4]

[2] William R. Parker, *The National Interest and Foreign Languages*, 3rd ed., 1961, p. 8.
[3] *Ibid.*
[4] *Ibid.*

While the anthropological value of languages provided a new impetus for foreign language study, it also placed heavy demands upon the profession to change its ways. The exclusive focus upon belles lettres was no longer defensible, particularly in the beginning courses. Neither could the preoccupation with the written word be defended nor the heavy emphasis upon the disinterment of the dear dead past. The foreign language profession was called upon to relate itself to the present; to teach the language as spoken by people now living and within a contemporary cultural context. Moliere, Cervantes, and Goethe must share the stage with classified newspaper ads, motion pictures of the market place, and taped discussions about the everyday life of ordinary people. And, since all of this was to be done in the target language, the profession was given a powerful reason for existing.

The change to a modern humanistic outlook did not come overnight. In fact, the old-line humanists are still entrenched in all levels of instruction. However, the new, or modern, humanism spread rapidly, and by the mid-sixties had come to dominate the secondary-school curriculum.[5]

The word "modern" as it is used here refers to a willingness to change, to experiment, and to accept contemporary material along with the "tried and true" documents of the past. In fact, the modern humanist does not limit foreign language content to written documents alone; material reproduced on films, tapes, and records

[5] Compare this attitude with the following ideas expressed in Germany in the 1950s which Friedrich Schubel refers to in his widely read book *Methodik des Englisch-unterrichts,* Verlag Moritz Diesterweg, 1960, pp. xi ff. "Es liegt sogar im Sinne des von A. Bohlen kürzlich dargestellten 'modernen Humanismus,' bei der notwendigen Vorbereitung 'auf das Leben der Gegenwart' auch die 'Vermittlung von Kenntnissen und Fertigkeiten, ohne die der gebildete Mensch das Dasein unserer Zeit nicht zu meistern vermag,' zu pflegen." And also, "Will man an den echten Geist eines fremden Volkes herangelangen, so kann das nur durch dessen unmittelbarsten Ausdruck—die Sprache—geschehen." (Schubel here alludes to A. Bohlen's "Modern Humanism" which asserts that in preparing students to live in the present, certain skills and areas of knowledge must be mastered. Without these the educated man will not be able to cope with the contemporary world. The second quotation states that, if one wishes to make contact with the genuine nature of a foreign people, such contact can only be made through the most direct expression of that nature; that is, through the language.)

Why should Americans study a foreign language?

can also serve. But the insistence upon the fullest possible cultivation of human abilities—particularly the intellectual—remains an end in itself. Foreign language study is seen as an indispensable link in the chain of human intellectual development. In an article entitled "Foreign Languages and the Humanities," one writer states that the humanist's task is:

. . . to break down [students'] narrow horizons and make them partake of the existence of the world. It is their task, also, to struggle against the invasion of technology and machines, by reminding them that man's ideal does not consist solely in enslaving matter for his needs but also to multiply his powers of life, through the acquisition of a better nourished thought, a more delicate sensibility, and a more fraternal soul. . . . It is their task to make others understand that humanity is not limited to a single moment—the present—nor to a single nation—however powerful it might be; rather, it is while preserving both the memory and the cult of the desperate shouts, songs of love, hymns of hope, epics, comedies, dramas, which the most divine of the sons of men, geniuses, have scattered in space and time.[6]

Foreign language teachers and professors have historically belonged to one humanist camp or the other. The more forward-looking humanist has no objection to his students using their command of language to discuss business, ballet, films, or philosophy but he would be aghast at a university course called "ballet French," "cinema German," or "business Spanish." A properly taught language course will have equipped the student with two things: (1) A fundamental control of the language and (2) a flexibility of mind that will enable him to expand and apply his knowledge to meet the demands of any situation that might arise.

Utilitarian objectives

Anyone who views education *primarily* as a way to get a better job or to improve his social standing or to solve economic or social problems has a nonhumanistic outlook. The same might be said of

[6] Georges J. Joyaux, "Foreign Languages and the Humanities," *Modern Language Journal*, XLIX (February 1965), 105.

politicians who see education as a cure-all for unemployment; admirals who see its purpose in terms of producing better crews for atomic submarines; government officials who relate foreign language learning to the improvement of international understanding; or anyone who cites some utilitarian goal or national need, however noble, as the reason for learning something. Through most of its history, the foreign language community kept the nonhumanists on the outside. A story is told about a businessman who questioned a classical scholar regarding the practical value of Latin. "Thank God it has no value," the professor replied.

The time arrived, however, when the language people themselves—perhaps out of self defense—took up the habit of ascribing utilitarian values to the learning of a language. By the middle of the twentieth century—when language study had reached a all-time low—the modern language community showed itself willing to compromise with those who hold the nonhumanistic viewpoint. The new orientation is indicated by the title of a bulletin prepared by William Riley Parker called *The National Interest and Foreign Languages*. Mr. Parker explains that "What really happened was this. Beginning in 1952 the profession of modern foreign language teachers in the United States organized itself to discover and to meet its new responsibilities to American Society, and this constructive move coincided, providentially, with a growing public awereness that language study was being tragically neglected in American Education."[7] Mr. Parker, himself a Milton scholar, is able to reconcile the humanistic tradition with the national interest. "What is now most needed," he writes, "is an American Objective in language study; a goal or goals clearly seen, and the costs seen just as clearly, with the national interest put firmly above the vested interests of either foreign language teachers or their competition in our thousands of schools and colleges."[8]

The Modern Language Association, whose membership consists largely of college and university professors of English and modern foreign languages, also exhibited a wide tolerance for nonhumanistic objectives when it pushed for the inclusion of foreign

[7] Parker, *op. cit.*
[8] *Ibid.*, p. 9.

Why should Americans study a foreign language?

languages in the National Defense Education Act of 1958. The first Russian Sputniks had been launched in October and November of the previous year. This event led to widespread criticism of America's schools and focused public attention upon education in Russia and America. Comparisons were drawn in such a way as to show that schools in the United States were far behind in the teaching of mathematics, science, and modern foreign languages. Almost at once, Congress began working on a law which would provide federal funds to stimulate the improvement of these areas.

On September 2, 1958, President Eisenhower signed the National Defense Education Act into law. With full approval of the leaders of the foreign language community, America launched a foreign language improvement program backed by tens of millions of dollars. There was nothing new in the principle of having the federal government supply money in support of schools, colleges, or individuals. The government in Washington has been a major influence in shaping local education from the very beginning.

Most of the states were first organized as territories in all of which Congress provided for public school systems. Thus the majority of our state school systems were initiated by the federal government. Starting in 1785 with grants of federal land for public education in the Northwest Territory, the land grant program has since then aided all levels of education in the states and Alaska by federal grants.[9]

The first aid was in the form of land grants for the general support of education. Subsequent aids were usually earmarked for special purposes or for special subject areas. The Morrill Act (1862) was directed largely at state agricultural and mechanical colleges. Later Acts reveal a similar concern for practical education: Agricultural experiment stations (1887); resident instruction in land grant colleges (1890); agricultural extension service (1917); vocational rehabilitation (1920); school lunch program (1946). In addition, billions of dollars have been expended to individuals and educational research. The best-known personal aid program was Public Law 346, popularly referred to as the "GI Bill of Rights."

[9] Hollis P. Allen, *The Federal Government and Education*, New York, McGraw-Hill, 1950, p. 3.

Yet there was something novel about the National Defense Education Act (NDEA). Previous school aids had been largely directed at utilitarian subjects or at practical matters such as school lunch. First came foreign languages, mathematics, and science; later, English, reading, history, civics, economics, and geography were added. The implication behind the Act is that improvement of instruction in the eight areas is in the national interest. Thus, by legislative action, a new reason why Americans should study foreign languages was created. The new "American objective" which (as Parker expressed it) puts "the national interest . . . firmly above" other considerations was widely publicized in language gatherings and in post-Sputnik publications. Within a few years, entirely new sets of objectives in foreign language learning had found their way into curriculum guides across the nation. And, if we were to have a new American objective, clearly a new American method was called for to fit the objective. A brief survey of the chief reasons currently given for studying a foreign language will help to illustrate the new attitudes which have shaped the new American Method.

National defense

At the opposite end of a value scale from the humanistic ideal of developing the intellect, lies the very specific goal of physically destroying the human body. Yet, to a certain extent, this was one of the purposes of the much-publicized Army Specialized Training Program (ASTP) during World War II. Specialists were needed to monitor enemy broadcasts, interrogate prisoners, and otherwise obtain information which could be used to shoot down aircraft, sink submarines, and drop bombs and artillery shells upon infantrymen with maximum accuracy. Present-day Americans engaged in espionage and "brush-fire" wars still have need of such skills, although the number of such specialists needed is relatively small. The modern concept of foreign languages for national defense has been broadened to include all contacts which Americans might have with any foreigner either in his country or ours. The late Secretary of State, John Foster Dulles, expressed it as follows:

Why should Americans study a foreign language?

Each of you has a task in foreign policy. Foreign policy isn't just something that is conducted by secretaries of state and by ambassadors in different parts of the world; every one of you has got a part in making a successful foreign policy for the United States, because whether or not we peacefully succeed will largely depend upon the demonstration you make as to the value and productivity of liberty. . . . The heart of a successful foreign policy is our national conduct and example, and that is a matter for every individual and not just the diplomats.[10]

Others relate foreign language and national defense to the poor impression made by monolingual employees of the federal government particularly in critical positions such as the Diplomatic Corps and Foreign Service Offices. A best-selling novel, *The Ugly American,* emphasized this theme throughout. To document their case, the authors included a "Factual Epilogue" in which they cited examples of American linguistic ineptitude. They summarize the case with the statement, "Think for a moment what it costs us whenever an American representative demands that the native speak English or not be heard. The Russians make no such mistake. . . ." The authors also quote John Foster Dulles: "Interpreters are no substitute. It is not possible to understand what is in the minds of other people without understanding their language, and without understanding their language it is impossible to be sure that they understand what is on our minds." The enormous danger of failing to communicate in the modern world is dramatically illustrated by the circumstances surrounding the bombing of Hiroshima. There is evidence that the first atom bomb might never have been dropped if a Japanese translator had not erred in the translation of one word. The word *mokusatsu,* used by the Japanese cabinet in their reply to the Potsdam surrender ultimatum, was rendered "ignore" rather than correctly, "withholding comment pending decision." Thinking the Japanese had rejected the ultimatum, the Allies went ahead with the nuclear bombardment.[11]

Foreign language courses aimed at fulfilling the "national needs" outlined above have a very large task to accomplish. For

[10] Parker, *op. cit.,* Introduction.

[11] Lincoln Barnett, *The Treasure of Our Tongue,* New York, Knopf, 1964, p. 292.

they imply the ability to comprehend rapid native speech even under adverse listening conditions, to speak the language skillfully without committing social or cultural blunders, to write the language, and to read it. Further, all this must be done with full awareness of the fine nuances of meaning carried by utterances, gestures, tone of voice, or selection of vocabulary. Clearly, all this will not be accomplished in the typical high-school course, but under satisfactory conditions, a good start can be made. As an absolute minimum, the early work in foreign languages should not tend to inhibit learning of the language at a later date if national defense is the primary objective of language study. Such "later date" foreign language courses for federal employees is a large-scale enterprise.

More than 40 languages, including those generally offered in the Nation's schools, are being taught intensively in Government training programs. An interagency committee of language and area specialists, . . . listed 106 different languages needed in Government over a 5-year period by people with competence in other fields. That committee's personnel estimates have been found to be much lower than the actual needs. For example, the Army annually requires 3,000 specialists in various languages; the Air Force 1,500.[12]

International understanding

There are many who object to the identification of foreign language learning with making (or preventing) war. Harold Taylor, former President of Sarah Lawrence College, objects to a policy "which deliberately assumes that education is an instrument of national policy." He recommends instead:

. . . a return to the concern for communication with other people in the use of foreign languages in order to break through to other cultures, to penetrate the consciousness of humanity at large, and to bring the world closer together rather than to devise educational means through which one can add language study to the list of techniques of defense. In place

[12] Marjorie Johnston, "Language Needs in Government," *School Life*, Official Journal of the Office of Education, April, 1957.

Why should Americans study a foreign language?

of the ideals of military security I suggest the ideal of the Peace Corps, in which the study of foreign languages has a social and moral purpose.[13]

The purpose given here is nobler, but it is still essentially utilitarian. If the goal of language learning is to understand a man from another culture, who speaks a different language, the skills needed are essentially the same whether you are trying to destroy him or get along with him.

Foreign language and business

Inasmuch as the dollar value of American exports is greater than the total value of imports, a case could probably be made for maintaining the economic well-being of the nation through better foreign language programs. The usual approach here, however, is to appeal to personal vocational interests rather than the national economic interest. In a book called *Foreign Language Careers*, Theodore Huebner discusses the many hundreds of job opportunities for those with language skill. The $35 billion export-import business is only one of the many fields of opportunity mentioned. Another section of the book contains an alphabetical listing and discussion of twenty-two vocations in which a knowledge of foreign language is useful. Included in the list are airlines, advertising, hotel service, librarians, missionaries, scientific research, travel, and tourism.[14]

Dr. Roeming, Editor of the *Modern Language Journal*, summarizes the vocational application of foreign language study as follows:

. . . to be a member of an export department of an industry a girl must at least be a good secretary, with skills in typing and shorthand; as for a man, he must be trained in business administration unless he wants to be an ordinary clerk. An airline stewardess must first have the qualities to make her one, with or without language; at one time it was a require-

[13] *Modern Language Abstracts*, no. 15 (November 1964), abstract 801.
[14] Theodore Huebner, *Opportunities in Foreign Language Careers*, New York, Universal Publishing and Distributing Corp., 1964.

ment that she have nurses' training. A foreign sales representative must be a salesman, that is quite simple and obvious. Everywhere one turns the answer is consistently the same. A primary vocational skill may be enhanced by competence in a foreign language, but the latter is never the primary skill sought by the employer.[15]

The humanists have traditionally regarded foreign language training for specific practical purposes as appropriate only for vocational schools, or else they have held that such training should be paid for by the individual or his employer. The secondary schools, following the example of higher education, have also avoided vocational foreign language courses. The resulting vacuum has been filled by governmental institutes and private enterprises of various sorts. A multimillion dollar business has grown up around the latter type of activity. The Berlitz Schools alone are said to gross $8,000,000 yearly.[16] There is some indication, however, that certain elements within the business community want a larger percentage of their employees to come equipped with at least minimal language skill. A subcommittee report at the September, 1963 White House Conference on Export Expansion made this the first of its five recommendations: "The Committee recommends that teaching of foreign languages in the public schools be started at the earliest practical age and that schools of business encourage proficiency in at least one foreign language."[17]

Summary

In conclusion, it seems advisable to summarize the reasons given for foreign language study, while at the same time putting into perspective the relative importance of each reason as reflected in the textbooks and classroom applications.

[15] Robert F. Roeming, "Traditional," *Modern Language Journal, XLVIII* (February 1964).
[16] Edwin H. Zeydel, "The Teaching of German in the United States from Colonial Times to the Present," *The German Quarterly,* 37 (September 1964), 359.
[17] Donald Walsh, "Foreign Language Program Notes," *Newsletter of the Modern Foreign Language Association,* Summer, 1964.

Why should Americans study a foreign language?

Diversity of language is a fact of human existence—seven-eighths of the world's people do not speak English natively. Even if they have learned English as a second language, they still cherish their mother tongue as an essential means of communication. Therefore, a person who has failed to acquire minimal proficiency in at least one foreign language has missed an experience which is essential to understanding the world he lives in. Being a monolingual, he cannot grasp the nature, function, and social importance of languages both English and foreign. In his ignorance, he tends to assume that all languages convey meaning in much the same way as does English. This fundamental error leads to gross misunderstandings regarding the actions, customs, and beliefs of other peoples, an ignorance the modern world can ill afford. Also, many of the great monuments of human thought have been expressed in a foreign language. Some writings have not been translated, and, in any case, much is lost when foreign writings are translated into English. In this view, foreign language study is essential to the full development of an individual's latent potentialities as a civilized human being.

THE UTILITARIAN REASON

The student may or may not find a direct practical application for the knowledge and skill he has acquired in learning a foreign language, just as he may never use the skills gained in the chemistry laboratory or apply the insights resulting from the study of algebra or geometry. Almost never does education produce a set of skills or a body of knowledge which is applied directly in toto to some real-life situation. Yet in some way the broadly educated person has developed a knack of understanding new situations and of communicating his ideas to others, which he would not have had without benefit of schooling. Indeed, the multibillion dollar investment in education is based upon the belief that what is learned in school will transfer to situations which the student will later face in life. In this sense, the study of languages is "practical" because it reinforces the development of verbal skills in English. (It would not be an adequate substitute for the study of English, however, as some enthusiasts have implied.) The most direct transfer, of course, would be to the learning of still another foreign language should the need arise later in life.

Many of the other reasons so often given might be considered more as fringe benefits or by-products of language study. The doctor or the pharmacist may find that his knowledge of Latin has been useful in the writing and filling of prescriptions. The businessman may suddenly find that his four years of high-school Spanish was the deciding factor in his being selected to manage a new branch factory in South America. The scientist may draw information from French, German, or Russian scientific journals and thus gain knowledge which would have required needless months of experimentation and study. Any American may find great satisfaction in communicating with a visitor from overseas or in speaking a foreign language during his vacation abroad. In the age of jets, internationalism, world trade, and communications satellites, the list of conceivable applications of foreign language skill is practically endless. In this regard, it is certainly better to have the skill and not need it than to need the skill and not have it.

Bibliography

Discussion guide prepared for the U.S. National Commission for UNESCO. Single copies available free from the Commission, Department of State, Washington, 20525. Multiple copies must be ordered from the U.S. Government Printing Office, Washington, 20402.

FL Discussion Pamphlets based on this book are available from the MLA Materials Center, 62 Fifth Ave., New York, 10011, $1.00.

Hall, Edward T., *The Silent Language*, New York, Fawcett World Library, 1961, paperbound, 60¢.

Huebner, Theodore, *Opportunities in Foreign Language Careers*, New York, Universal Publishing and Distributing Corp., paperbound, $1.45.

Huebner, Thedore, *Why Johnny Should Learn Foreign Languages*, Philadelphia, Chilton, 1961, 142 pp., $4.00.

Johnston, Marjorie C., and Elizabeth Keesee, *Modern Foreign Languages and Your Child*, U.S. Department of Health, Education and Welfare, Office of Education, Bulletin OE–27020, Washington, U.S. Government Printing Office, 1964, 43 pp., 25¢.

Joyaux, Georges J., "Foreign Languages and the Humanities," *Modern Language Journal, XLIX* (February 1965), 102–105.
Reprints available from MLA Materials Center, 4 Washington Pl., New York, 10003, 4 pp., 25¢.

Modern Foreign Languages in the Comprehensive Secondary School, National Association of Secondary School Principals Committee on Curriculum Planning and Development, Washington, 20036, NASSP-NEA, 1201 16th St., N.W., June, 1959, 16 pp. one copy free, additional copies, 25¢.

Parker, William R., "The Case for Latin," *PMLA, LXXIX*, no. 4, pt. 2 (September 1964), 3–10.
Reprints available from the American Classical League, Miami University, Oxford, Ohio, 45056, 12¢ each or 10¢ in quantities of 50 or more.

Parker, William R., *The National Interest and Foreign Languages*, 3rd ed., Department of State Publication 7324, Washington, D.C., U.S. Government Printing Office, 1961, 159 pp., $1.00.

Reiff, Del. J., "Latin and the Guidance Counselor," *The Classical Journal, LX* no. 7 (April 1965), 307–909.

Remer, Ilo, *Handbook for Guiding Students in Modern Languages*, Bulletin OE–27018, U.S. Department of Health, Education and Welfare, Office of Education, Washington, D.C., U.S. Government Printing Office, 1963, 105 pp., 45¢.

"Report of the Commission on the Humanities," ACLS (American Council of Learned Societies) *Newsletter, XV*, no. 5 (May 1964), 7–16.

Report on a Conference on the Meaning and Role of Culture in Foreign Language Teaching, Held March 10–11, 1961 at the Publications Department, Georgetown University, Washington, 1961, 93 pp., $2.00.

Should My Child Study a Foreign Language? DFL-NEA pamphlet, NEA Publications, 1201 16th Street, N.W., Washington, D.C., 20036, no charge.

> "When I use a word," Humpty Dumpty said, in a rather scornful tone,
> "it means just what I choose it to mean—neither more nor less."
> "The question is," said Alice, "whether you can make words
> mean so many different things."
> "The question is," said Humpty Dumpty, "which is
> to be master—that's all."
>
> LEWIS CARROLL

What is language? The new linguistics

3   The long reign of the Latin language over the intellectual world did more than influence the content and method of teaching languages. According to many structural linguists the Latin grammar books of past centuries have tended to create and perpetuate a series of myths about language in general and grammar in particular. The cornerstone of this myth—say the linguists—is the belief that Latin was a universal and perfect form of language. Therefore, once grammar books had been written for Latin, it was considered a simple matter to apply the rules and terminology to English or any other lesser language. Once the basic fallacy was established, hundreds of subfallacies were built around it. The modern linguists look upon some of these misconceptions as mere annoyances; others, they feel, have had a disastrous effect upon the teaching of both native and foreign languages. A few samples of those which are considered to have been the most damaging are:

1. The fallacy that language is logical.
2. The fallacy that language is based on writing.
3. The fallacy that language is good or bad or that some language is right while other language is wrong.

4. The fallacy that language should be studied by learning rules of correctness.
5. The fallacy that present-day vernacular speech is a deterioration of an earlier more perfect language.
6. The fallacy that the language of one region is somehow better than the language of another.

These attitudes are by no means the exclusive property of Americans. During a study tour of German schools and universities, the author and four other educators from the United States were somewhat chagrined to learn that the language of educated Americans was considered "substandard" by many Germans. In one German high school, the head of the University system from a western state of the U.S. was asked to read a story about Buffalo Bill to an English class. He had hardly begun to read when the students broke out laughing. The German youngsters had been indoctrinated to believe that British "received English" (similar to Oxfordian English) was the only "good" English. The sudden shock of hearing an important, scholarly man "mispronouncing" his *As* startled and amused the German teenagers. Charles Dickens ran into a similar reaction from American audiences in the nineteenth century when he toured the United States giving oral readings from his better-known books; many people were disappointed to hear their favorite stories read with a "foreign accent."

As a scientist of languages, the modern linguist rejects such insular and moralistic attitudes toward the way people speak a language. The purpose of linguistic science is to *describe;* not to *prescribe* one type of language and *proscribe* another. For example, if someone is out of money in America, a second person might comment on that fact in any one of several ways:

> He don't have no money.
> He ain't got no money.
> He's broke.
> He doesn't have any money.

Since all of the above expressions do, in fact, occur and since all of them convey *with equal certainty* that the man has no money, the linguistic scientist has no choice but to record each. Furthermore, because he has no evidence that anyone has ever used "two negatives to make a positive" in this sort of situation, he rejects that rule as an example of school-teacherish folklore. It should be quite evident from these examples that the new linguistic science reflects a greatly changed attitude toward the analysis and application of grammar. When a recent edition of Webster's unabridged dictionary also applied this philosophy to its treatment of words, many highly literate people were incensed. To them, the scientific approach to language appears blatantly permissive and anarchistic. To others who are a bit more knowledgeable, it represents little more than a superimposition of new terminology upon facts which have long been obvious. However, to the modern language community in the second half of the twentieth century this approach has supplied the main rationale for sweeping changes in the manner of analyzing and teaching foreign languages. What, then, are the main features of the new linguistics, and how have they influenced language teaching?

Is language logical?

Language, like mathematics, is man made. Both language and mathematics are used to represent things, concepts, relationships, and qualities. Mathematics, for the most part, transcends time, place, language, and culture. It has even been stated that mathematics "represents a universal language which could be recognized by rational beings wherever they may exist. It is for this reason that the radio astronomers who are making a conscientious attempt to contact life elsewhere in the universe send their contact messages out in mathematical code."[1]

Perhaps the ways of eating, the method of mating, even the manner of breathing might be different in other rational creatures. Despite this, the mathematician will insist that his language is so pure, so unencumbered with emotionalism and provincialism, and

[1] Harry L. Phillips and Marguerite Kluttz, *Modern Mathematics and Your Child,* Publication no. 29047, Washington, D.C., U.S. Office of Education, 1963, p. 1.

so universal in nature as to be comprehensible and applicable to any world which may exist anywhere. The proof that mathematics is a universal language in the broadest sense will have to await further space explorations. For our purposes it is sufficient to observe that the science of mathematics has developed a notation system which is clearly understandable to educated persons regardless of culture, language, politics, or religion. The symbols below will convey the identical message to the knowledgeable Japanese, American, East Indian, German, Italian, Arab or Russian.

$$.. + :: + \therefore \quad = 2 + 4 + 5$$
$$2 + 4 + 5 \quad = a + b + c$$
$$a + b + c \quad = \sqrt{4} + \sqrt{16} + \sqrt{25}$$

$$\sqrt{4} + \sqrt{16} + \sqrt{25} = .. + :: + \therefore$$

While the mathematician would have no trouble communicating across cultures with written symbols, his communication would break down the moment he began to vocalize the little black marks, for then he would be compelled to fall back upon language. And it is virtually impossible to find a consistent pattern in one language which recurs with equal consistency in a different language. Notice below that other languages can be made to look chaotic if systematic aspects of English are used as a basis for comparison:

English	French	German	Spanish
I am young.	Je suis jeune.	Ich bin jung.	Soy joven.
I am cold.	J'ai froid.	Mir ist kalt.	Tengo frio.
I am glad.	Je suis content.	Ich freue mich.	Estoy contento.
I am fond of him.	Je l'aime.	Ich habe ihn lieb.	Quiero a el.
I am sorry.	Je regrette.	Es tut mir leid.	Lo siento.
I am hungry.	J'ai faim.	Ich habe Hunger.	Tengo hambre.

From this it might be concluded that English is a more logical language than any of the other three. Such a conclusion, the linguist would say, is typical of the type of false logic which led previous grammarians into basing the study of other languages upon

Latin grammar. As a matter of fact, any language can be made to appear as the most logical if it is the one which is chosen as the base of comparison. The German verb pattern shown below is regular; the English erratic in form:

Es muß gehen.   It must go.
Es mußte gehen.   It had to go.

And both Spanish and German have a consistent pattern of comparing adjectives while English uses now one, now the other:

Spanish (adj. + más)	English	German (adj. + -er)
grande–más grande	big–bigger	groß–größer
inteligente— mas inteligente	intelligent more intelligent	intelligent— intelligenter

If we used Spanish as the logical basis for comparing things and people we would have to say in English:

He is more smart than I.
His car is more fast than mine.
I am more tall than you.

If German were considered the logical language, we would say "smarter," "faster," and "taller." However, we would also have to say "resourcefuller" and "reliabler." Similarly, if French were set up as the model of logic, we would have to use a different form of verb in the sentence "I allow my boy *to go*," than we use in the sentence "I want my boy *to go*." In French (and in Spanish) it seems logical to use a subjunctive verb form and a different sentence structure to express that you want another person to do something. English and German do not consider this to be logical.

What is writing?

Writing, linguists tell us, is a partial and highly incomplete representation of language. Language itself consists of highly complex arrangements of sounds, including pauses, stresses, rhythms and the like. Once a person has learned to make the appropriate noises, then he can learn to attach meaning to the little black marks which partially symbolize the sounds he has learned to produce. The native speaker of a language has acquired the sounds without conscious effort usually well before the first year of school. The writing system can be mastered in the first few years of school if the language provides graphic symbols which are used consistently to represent the same given sounds. Italian and Hungarian have this near one-to-one correspondence between writing and sound. As a result, Italian and Hungarian children are able to master their respective spelling systems while they are still in the early primary grades. Spanish- and German-speaking children take a bit longer. Many Americans never learn to spell at all. The forty sounds of English are represented not by forty written symbols but by a chaotically complex and irregular maze of letters and letter groupings. For example, English spelling permits one symbol to stand for five different sounds:

Same symbol	Sample word	Different sound
-ough	through	[oo]
-ough	though	[oh]
-ough	cough	[awf]
-ough	rough	[uff]
-ough	plough	[ow]

In other cases, eight graphic symbols are used to represent a single sound:

Different symbol	Sample word	Same sound
-o	go	[ō]
-ow	tow	[ō]
-oe	toe	[ō]
-ough	dough	[ō]
-eau	beau	[ō]
-ew	sew	[ō]
owe	owe	[ō]
oh	oh	[ō]

The purpose of this section is not merely to show that English spelling is frustratingly inconsistent and unpredictable (which it is), but rather to emphasize the fact that written symbols (or graphemes) are highly incomplete representations of language even in those languages which have a consistent orthography. To speak a language "exactly as it is written" would reduce the effectiveness of communication, the linguists tell us. The human mind actually depends upon the slurring of vowel sounds to provide clues to the meaning of the complete utterance. This is why some people who speak perfectly all right become nearly incomprehensible when they begin to read aloud. In their desire to articulate every sound clearly they give undue importance to the little black marks on the paper. Such readers have not learned that writing is a pale, incomplete, and highly imperfect representation of language. Those who read well, such as radio and TV commentators, have learned to treat the little black marks as "clues" from which they automatically reconstruct a more or less normal flow of speech sounds. They have—perhaps intuitively—grasped the idea that language is primarily sound; or, as the linguists express it, "language is an arbitrary system of vocal symbols." Writing is the shorthand for that complex system of sounds.

Stress, pause, and intonation

Suppose someone asked you to read aloud the following series of capital letters printed on a card:

J I N V U

If you are like most people you will pronounce each of the letters with equal emphasis, and will allow a very definite pause of approximately the same length between each letter. Also, in your mind, the letters will remain separated as isolated meaningless utterances. Now, however, let us take the series of sounds which these letters represent and indicate that you are talking to a very successful man named Jay. Let us suppose also that you are a close friend of his and that you are going to tell him that you are envious of him. You could take the same sounds represented by the letters of the alphabet above and utter them in the same sequence:

Jay, I envy you. [J I N V U]

This may seem like childish word play, but it helps to illustrate one of the favorite ideas of modern linguistics; namely, that language is much more than a series of vocabulary items strung together in a certain order. If you speak English natively, you would automatically modify your way of speaking when you conceive of the five sounds in terms of communication. For example, you add certain pauses and you stress certain syllables more than others. The result cannot be represented adequately in print, but it would come out something like this:

Jay— I ^{en}vy yo$_u$.

This pattern will be repeated unconsciously by the native speaker whenever he makes a simple statement directly to an acquaintance. The elements of this pattern are just as much a part of communication as are the segments of sound which make up the words themselves. For we have seen that sounds can be read mechanically with the same stress on each syllable and the same pause between each utterance without communicating any idea whatever. In simple terms, the main characteristics of the above pattern are: (1) use of pause, (2) placement of main stress, and (3) use of a falling intonation at the end of the sentence. The words may change, but the pattern will not.

John— we ex^{pect} you to come.
Mary— he ^{is} leav$_i$^{n}g n$_{ow}$.

It is usually not possible to change the stress and intonation pattern of a sentence without altering the meaning considerably. For example, our original sentence could be stressed on the first and last syllables:

I $_{envy}$ yo$^{u?}$ (For what possible reason?)

In this case the rising end-intonation and the stress on the first-person pronoun would convey doubt; perhaps even sarcasm. Similarly, the main stress could be placed on the first word:

I envy you.   (Even if no one else does.)

In some cases, misapplication of intonation can produce a comical effect:

What are we having for dinner, fat$^{he^{rr?}}$ (cannibalistic implications)

By slightly modifying the pause after the word "dinner" and by using a falling rather than a rising intonation, this sentence means what it was intended to mean. With similar modifications the following sentence can signify either that the husband is asking his wife about the entire morning menu or that he wants information about what is being served with his toast:

What are we having for breakfast, honey?

The key to the meaning centers around the intonation used with the final word and the pause which precedes it.

It is easy for many people to lose patience with such discussions particularly if they are still convinced that the written language is of predominant importance. To the native speaker of English the facts seem obvious and hardly worth belaboring. In any case, what does it all have to do with learning a foreign language? The comparative linguist, as usual, has an answer: Languages differ in their use of rhythm, intonation, stress, pause, and pitch just as they differ in their respective use of sounds, words, and word order. An extreme example of this would be Chinese compared to English. What would seem to be one word in English can have four different meanings in Chinese depending on the pitch of the speaker's voice. Some faint notion of how Chinese words sound can be conveyed by humming the scales. Although each "hum" is the same "word" the mind may be registering the meaning associated with the musical symbols "do," "re," "mi," "fa," etc. However, it is not necessary to go into Asiatic languages to find a reason for concentrating on such matters. Even the closely related European languages differ in

What is language? The new linguistics

their use of stress, rhythm, intonation, and the like. In one language, a level intonation may indicate boredom; in another it may register normal interest. At the other extreme, the placement of stress can indicate enthusiasm or excitement in one language while it is the normal pattern in another. The problem comes when the American student tries to put foreign language words together using the speech mannerisms which are characteristic of American English. The results can be insulting, ludicrous, or baffling; they may even be totally unintelligible. The novice student of Spanish will often place the accent on the first syllable in accordance with the predominant English pattern. As a result he may say,

¿Sra. Gomez, esta lista?" (Mrs. Gomez, this list?)

when he wants to say,

¿Sr. Gomez, está lista? (Mrs. Gomez, are you ready?)

Similarly, a Frenchman whose command of English is less than perfect may carry over an interrogative pattern from his own language; he may ask,

Is it za left ^{door} or za right ^{door?}

rather than,

Is it the ^{left} door or the ^{right} door?

The American listener who is trying to help the French visitor may be just as badly misled by the wrong intonation as by the mispronunciation of individual sounds. The same lack of communication results when the American applies his native intonation to the French language.

A German example can be drawn from lesson one of almost any textbook most of which contain a greeting such as:

Guten Tag, Herr Schumann.

The American student will invariably overstress the word *Tag* by applying the English pattern to German.

Hello Mr. Schumann.

If the German intonation pattern is used in English it seems to convey a tone of indifference and distinterest which the speaker did not intend.

According to the linguist, there are several implications as far as the language teacher is concerned:

1. He should be aware of the main points of conflicts between English and the target language.
2. He should concentrate oral drill work—preferably using native models—on these areas of differences.
3. He should see to it that the student develops an awareness of each trouble spot so that he will be able to detect and correct his errors when the teacher is no longer present.
4. He must provide drill work which involves complete utterances; for even if the student knows how to pronounce flawlessly many thousands of individual words, he will still not know how to combine them into complete, understandable units of thought unless he is taught specifically to do so. Without proper instruction he will be inclined to pronounce each syllable mechanically or, worse, he will apply the intonational and rhythmic patterns which characterize his native way of speaking. In either case, communication will be blurred.

Phonemes and morphemes—the grammar of sound

Highly literate speakers of English can be incredibly naive in their statements concerning the sound system of the language they manipulate so well. A much-published author writing a popularized version of the history of the English language commented that "A further stride in the direction of simplicity came with the adoption of the letter 's' to indicate the plural form of all nouns." In reality there are three main plurals in spoken English, only one of which is the letter s (as represented by the s in the word *hiss*). The plural forms of three animals will illustrate the point:

What is language? The new linguistics

cats   [s]

dogs   [z]

horses [iz]

It is very simple to prove that these two plurals have different end sounds; one only needs to add the sounds to the same stem:

hiss

his

The change of sound in these two one-syllable words completely alters the meaning. The spelling difference is of no relevance; small children who have not yet learned to read or write can tell the difference with perfect ease, even though they may never have heard of double versus single *s*. For when the normal 6-year old American enters school he has already spent many thousands of hours in hearing and speaking English. After he learns to read, he may even accept the fallacious statement that "Nearly all English plurals are formed by adding *s*." In any case, he will continue to use the three plurals as the situation requires (as in cork*s* [s], bottl*es* [z], and glass*es* [iz].) His ignorance is of little consequence in his use of English.

However, the same misconceived rule proves disastrous to a person who is learning English as a second language, particularly if his native tongue does not contain words which end with a voiced sibilant (that is, the final sound in the word *his*). For example, the nonnative will ask:

Where are the docks? [s]

when he means:

Where are the dogs? [z]

Or he will say:

I need some carts, [s]

when he means:

I need some cards [z]

The American student of French, German, or Spanish makes comparable blunders when his English speech habits interfere with his attempts to speak in the target language. One of the chief functions of the linguist is to identify such pitfalls or conflict points and to construct oral drills aimed at minimizing their effect upon the student's attempts to speak the target (or foreign) language.

In his analysis of the foreign language the linguist identifies the minimal significant sound contrasts which may or may not be characteristic of the student's native language.

Again, for economy of time and efficiency of learning, the emphasis must be upon the pitfalls of pronunciation. To do an adequate job, the teacher must have a thorough understanding of both the native and the target language. If he is teaching English to those whose native language is Spanish, he must be aware that the student will hear no difference between words such as:

hash	hatch
cash	catch
wash	watch
lash	latch

The consonant clusters *sh* and *tch* are two phonemes of English; however, in Spanish no such meaning contrast exists. As a result, to the Spanish-speaking student, these word pairs sound identical. If someone asks him,

Where is my watch? *or* Where is my wash?

he may not know in either case whether the speaker is asking about laundry or a timepiece. The same sort of thing happens to Americans when they encounter sound contrasts which do not exist in English but which are phonemes of the target language. A South American friend of the author heard a college instructor teaching his students a Spanish sentence which meant:

The Korean hasn't come yet,

when he wanted to say:

The mail hasn't come yet.

What is language? The new linguistics

The teacher had not mastered a basic sound contrast, namely, the single-trilled *r* versus the multiple-trilled *rr*. His students were inadvertently learning *Koreo* for *correo*. In French, a similar confusion can result if the student pronounces *ils viennent* with undue nasalization and is understood as saying *il vient*. In German, pairs such as *Stadt* and *Staat* are nearly impossible for the American to differentiate. Even *schön* and *schon* are troublesome for some students.

Once the difficult sounds have been singled out, drills must be devised which teach the student first, to identify them; second, to imitate them correctly; third, to apply them in sentences which make sense; and fourth, to use the sounds correctly and without hesitation whenever the speaking situation calls for them. In addition, the drills must account for any elisions or merging of words which take place in normal speech, as well as any of the matters of stress or intonation which were discussed earlier.

Just as the term "phoneme" is used to refer to each significant sound contrast, the term "morpheme" is used in reference to minimal units which carry meaning. For example, the word *dogs* has two morphemes:

dog is a "free" morpheme—it can stand alone.

s is a "bound" morpheme—it has meaning in that it shows plurality, but it cannot stand by itself.

As is the case with phonology, the morphology of each language shows great areas of difference. For example, English and German commonly use separate free morphemes to express person and number: e.g., I eat; *ich esse*. Spanish, on the other hand, will regularly combine the morpheme showing person with the morpheme referring to eating: e.g., *como*. The stem *com* carries the meaning "eat" and the ending *-o* indicates that the person is "I." However, the important thing about the new linguistic analysis is not in the jargon used, but in the attitude toward the target language. The linguist attempts to describe each language scientifically. He avoids such statements as "Spanish does it backwards" or "In Spanish the pronoun is part of the verb." Such statements tend toward the traditionalist fallacy of using one language as the model; the other as a quaint deviation from the norm.

Traditional grammar versus modern grammar

The linguist shies away from the normative approach to grammar which sets up rules of correctness based upon the speech of a certain period or of a certain geographical area. Even a well-educated person may use a variety of language forms depending upon the formality of the situation in which he finds himself. Thus, at a formal tea, he may say:

A cup of coffee, please.

while at a crowded corner snack bar he may say:

Hey, how 'bout a cuppa coffee?

Changes of this sort are not corruptions of "good" language, but are looked upon by the linguist as normal features of all languages. The importance of recognizing such changes is particularly relevant to the teaching of listening. Since normal native speech contains numerous contractions, omissions, and elisions, the language student must be trained to comprehend the language as it is, rather than expecting it to conform to some arbitrary standard of correctness.

Methods based upon traditional grammar were also ineffective for teaching students to *speak* a foreign language, say the linguists, because they tended to treat language as a list of words to be strung together according to cookbook-like formulas. Many teachers had the notion that the major difficulty in learning a foreign language was remembering the meaning of words. Yet linguists tell us that whereas we should aim at virtually 100 percent control of pronunciation (learning the phonemes), possibly 50 to 90 percent control of grammar (the morphemes) we might get by with only 1 percent of the vocabulary.

Small preschool children who have acquired a tiny fraction of their total potential vocabulary can carry on rather lucid conversations in their native language. By age 5 or 6, normal children

What is language? The new linguistics

will control most of the sounds, structures, and word-order arrangements which are characteristic of informal speech. By contrast, a nonnative adult may have acquired a far larger vocabulary but may find that, lacking control of pronunciation, structure, and word order, his vocabulary is more of a hindrance than a help.

The following note from a Chinese firm to a New York importer illustrates what can happen when the nonnative speaker attempts to put words together according to grammatical rules.

As an auspice of beatitude to the community, as an omnipotent daily utilized novelty, as a pioneer of the scientifical element, as a security to metal, as agent to economy of both time and money, is the newly discovered wonderful Polishing Powder that is to be heartily welcomed wheresoever. Despite the heavy sacrifice of capital and the consumption of brains, we have thereby succeeded in researching out the usage of this Polishing Powder. We lose not promptitude in taking this opportunity to recommend to the attention of the Community. This Polishing Powder is the conqueror.[2]

In summary, what the Chinese translator was trying to say was, "Your firm has produced a useful, effective polishing powder. We have just finished trying it out; it's great!" Instead, however, the Chinese translator came up with a classic example of the limits of the traditional grammatical method. He has carried over into the English, elements of Chinese style and misconceptions of English word order. Further, he is unable to distinguish between antiquated forms (wheresoever) and appropriate vocabulary items (conqueror) in reference to a polishing powder.

Summary

Traditional grammarians have looked upon the new linguistics as an invitation to anarchy; as a departure from those rules which delimit meaning and thus make clarity of communication possible. The linguist rejects this static view of language. Instead, he attempts

[2] Alfred Aarons, ed., *The Florida Foreign Language Reporter*, January, 1965, p. 14.

to describe how language works rather than prescribing rules of correctness for how it should be used. While patterns do exist in all languages, there is no underlying logic upon which they are based. That is, each national group uses certain arbitrarily selected auditory signals to represent its version of reality. Each culture selects only certain vocal symbols and arrangements of them, rejecting all other possibilities. However, the utterances are not fixed and stable; they are modified with time, place, social station, and even with regard to whether they are used in a formal or an informal situation. Any given word is either an accidental creation or else is the offspring of an earlier accident. For example, there is no logical reason why English "the spoon," German, "der Löffel," and Spanish "la cuchara" happen to stand for a certain type of eating utensil. Neither is there logical reason why "spoon" is masculine in German, feminine in French and Spanish, and neuter in English. The question, "Why do the French refer to a spoon as a 'she'?" makes no sense to the descriptive linguist. The only answer is that "many nouns which refer to inanimate objects use the same forms that are used for nouns which refer to female human beings. This is true simply because that is the way the French speak."

At this point one is tempted to ask the following questions, which lead us out of the realm of the linguistics scientist and into the fields of applied linguistics and foreign language education. The answers are those most frequently given since World War II. Earlier language educators had given different answers.

Which Frenchman do we use as models for imitation?	Educated speakers of the foreign language.
Of what historical period?	Of the twentieth century.
What topics of their conversation do we emphasize?	Any topics which they normally read about, write about, or talk about.

The three main implications which linguistic science has for the teaching of languages to English-speaking American youngsters are:

1. Language is a system of sound symbols. These sounds must be learned not only as individual entities but also as they function in the normal flow of speech.

What is language? The new linguistics

2. The process of learning to use the sound system must not be contaminated by improper introduction of the writing system. The two must be kept distinctly separate in the student's mind.
3. Intensive oral drill must be directed toward the conflict points. These are the sounds, structures, and word orders in the foreign language which differ greatly from those of English (or which are nonexistent in English) and which, therefore, present a major learning problem.

Bibliography

Agard, Frederick B., and Robert J. Di Pietro, *The Sounds of English and Italian*, 1965, 76 pp., $2.00.

Agard, Frederick B., *The Grammatical Structure of English and Italian*, 1965, 91 pp., $2.00.

Buchanan, Cynthia D., *A Programed Introduction to Linguistics*, Boston, Heath, 1963, 137 pp., $4.40.
This self-teaching text provides an excellent introduction to phonology and phonemic transcription. It is also a good review for anyone who wishes to up date his knowledge of phonetics and phonemics. An additional value of this text is that it can familiarize the reader with the techniques of Skinnerian programming, which have had considerable influence upon current methods of foreign language instruction.

Hall, Robert A., Jr., *Introductory Linguistics*, Philadelphia, Chilton, Educational Book Division, 1964, 508 pp., $7.50.
An up-to-date presentation of linguistic science for the beginning courses.

Hall, Robert A., Jr., *Linguistics and Your Language*, Garden City, N.Y., Anchor Books, Doubleday, 1960, 265 pp., paperbound, $1.45.

Hughes, John P., *Linguistics and Language Teaching*, New York, Random House, 1968, 143 pp., $1.95.

Kufner, Herbert L., *The Grammatical Structures of English and German*, 1962, 96 pp., $2.00.

Lado, Robert, *Linguistics Across Culture*, Ann Arbor, University of Michigan Press, 1957, 150 pp., $2.75.
Applied linguistics for language teachers.

Lado, Robert, "Linguistics and Foreign Language Teaching," *Language Learning*, X, no. 2, special issue (March 1961), 29–41.

Moulton, William G., *The Sounds of English and German,* 1962, 144 pp., $2.75.

Politzer, Robert L., *Foreign Language Learning: A Linguistic Introduction,* (prelim. ed.), Englewood Cliffs, N.J., Prentice-Hall, 1965, 155 pp., $1.75.

In his preface the author states: "I hope that this book will be of interest to language teachers, educators, and parents of language students, but I want to emphasize that this is not primarily a book on how to teach foreign languages, but rather a discussion of how to learn them. The book is thus addressed to students of foreign languages." The definitive edition will be published in 1967.

Politzer, Robert L., "The Impact of Linguistics on Language Teaching: Past, Present, Future," *Modern Language Journal,* XLVIII (March 1964), 145–151.

Politzer, Robert L., "Teaching French," *An Introduction to Applied Linguistics,* New York, Blaisdell, 1960, 140 pp. $3.00.

Explanation of linguistic teaching method with detailed information on teaching pronunciation, morphology, syntactical patterns, and vocabulary.

Politzer, Robert L., and Charles Staubach, *Teaching Spanish: A Linguistic Orientation,* New York, Blaisdell, 1961, 136 pp., $3.00.

A practical aid to teachers of Spanish, giving an analysis of the contrasts between the sound systems and syntactical patterns of English and Spanish.

Stockwell, Robert P., and John W. Martin, *The Grammatical Structures of English and Spanish,* 1965, 328 pp., $3.75.

Stockwell, Robert P., and J. Donald Bowen, *The Sounds of English and Spanish,* 1965, 168 pp., $2.75.

How well can Americans learn a second language?

4 There are many factors which limit the extent to which the student can expect to become bilingual. Chief among them are the following: (1) The student: his age, environment, and motivation; (2) the educational system: available contact hours, scheduling procedures, and financial structure; (3) the teacher: his preparation and pedagogical orientation.

It is understood here that we are dealing with foreign language instruction not in some theoretical, idealized situation, but within the framework of American educational institutions as they are now formed and are likely to be formed in the foreseeable future. These educational facts of life tend to limit the degree to which instructional goals can be attained. They are included here simply because no meaningful discussion of methods is possible if they are not taken into account.

The American student and his environment

The natural way to learn a language is to grow up in a culture where the language is spoken. In many cases, the highly proficient bilingual has spent his childhood in a region where two languages of somewhat comparable status were used for everyday communication.

Such individuals have not really learned a foreign language; they have learned two native languages to refer to a single cultural context. Their acquisition of sounds, structures, word-order arrangements, and basic vocabulary takes place without conscious effort. The bilingual child may later enter a bilingual school where he begins the formal study of the two languages he has already learned to understand and speak. In elementary school he begins to use graphic symbols to express his thoughts in writing and to expand his knowledge of the world through reading. However, before the formal study of graphic language symbols begins, the child has already become quite proficient in the active skill of speaking and the more passive skill of listening to others. In fact, these skills were acquired so automatically that the youngster tends to take the listening-speaking aspects of the language for granted.

Because his first conscious study of language dealt with written symbolization, he identifies language learning with learning to read and write. Thus, for example, a bilingual child in New Hampshire might spend part of the school day writing compositions and reading stories in French with a French-speaking teacher and another part of the day studying spelling and reading with an English-speaking instructor. In the first situation he would listen and recite in French; in the second he would hear and speak English. But in either case, if he is asked what he is doing, he is likely to reply that he is learning to read and write French or English. It would usually not occur to him to mention that he was also hearing and speaking these languages as part of the learning process.

Unfortunately, American bilingual communities are limited in number and usually, where they do exist, educators have failed to capitalize upon the language skills of the non-English-speaking segment of the local population. Too often, in fact, the ability to speak another language has been viewed as a mental disability. As a result, most Americans who learn a second language begin their study of it in the formalized atmosphere of the schoolroom. Also, the study of the second language is undertaken, in nearly every case, long after the pupil has learned to understand, speak, read, and write English. Accordingly, educators and parents should not expect pupils to achieve anything approaching full coordinate bilingualism

How well can Americans learn a second language?

59

even in school districts which offer foreign languages in the elementary school. According to contemporary learning theory, a number of factors make such expectations unrealistic. Chief among those that are often listed are the following.

AGE AND MONOLINGUALISM

The American's habitual manner of relating to the world about him is exclusively by means of the English language and the Anglo-American value system which this language reflects. The older he becomes the less flexible he will be in adjusting to the different sets of values reflected by non-English-speaking cultures. Also, he will tend to assign American cultural values to vocabulary items in the foreign language. The fact that Americans generally begin the study of a language relatively late in life tends to magnify the adverse effects of monolingualism.

FIRST-LANGUAGE LITERACY

The American student of language is literate or semiliterate in English when his study of the second language begins. Thus, like the bilingual student, he will expect to read and write in the second language within a short time after he is introduced to it. However, unlike the bilingual student, he has not spent thousands of hours conversing in the second tongue. He will consequently be reading and writing a language he does not control conversationally. As a result, his American-English habit system will cause considerable interference with his reading of the foreign language.

OPPORTUNITY FOR USING THE LANGUAGE

Unlike the bilingual student (or the student in some European countries), the American language learner has little opportunity to practice conversational skills in a natural manner. In this regard, a European educator visiting in America has observed:

In this country a student's contact with a foreign language is completely academic, divorced from any cultural feeling for it, cold. It is at best a necessary evil which somehow must be endured. In Europe, a child's approach to another language is an integral part of his life before he enters school. It is something he lives with daily and something he can continually read, due to the availability of foreign newspapers, films, even such an insignificant thing as a candy wrapper. To the European student, a foreign language never becomes a purely academic matter. It is a part of a culture different from his own which he respects and which he is eager to learn thoroughly. Language for him is alive.[1]

The educational environment—the system, the schedule, and the teacher

Some of the more significant achievements in foreign language instruction have involved radical departures from (1) traditional scheduling procedures, (2) the manner of utilizing staff, and (3) the age at which language learning was begun. Less is known about a fourth departure—the replacement of the teacher with self-instructional devices; but there is some evidence to show that a rather large portion of the foreign language teaching task can be performed by machines. (This is discussed further in the chapter on programmed learning.)

With regard to the question "How well can Americans learn a foreign language?", the factors of pupil age, schedule, staff, and instructional devices may be more significant than the instructional techniques per se. The stereotype of the ideal language teaching situation has twenty adolescent students meeting five one-hour periods weekly during four academic years (or more) with an instructor who has an academic degree in the target language. These matters are so firmly rooted in the established way of doing things that they are almost taken for granted. Yet there are many responsible language educators who feel that we do not attain our objectives in foreign language learning because we begin at the wrong age, make improper use of time, and employ the wrong type of teachers. Such factors apparently cannot be overlooked in a discussion of teaching techniques.

The age of the pupil

The profession is fond of assigning names to the different levels of foreign language study such as FLES (foreign language in the

[1] "Learning a Foreign Language in Europe and America," *Indiana Newsletter,* *12* (April 1966).

elementary school) and "Elementary College French." Someone has even suggested the term FLOP (foreign languages for older people). The designations "Conversational Spanish," or "Scientific German," are also in common use to differentiate course objectives. This sort of labeling misleads many people into believing that the schools are teaching many different varieties of the same language. The modern linguist deplores such clouding of the issues. To him, the French that a child needs to learn is essentially the same French that an adolescent or an adult should learn. The *way* he learns will perhaps be different, the amount of vocabulary he can acquire in a given period of time will be different, and the sophistication of content will necessarily reflect the age of the learner. But the French itself remains constant as a system of sounds which must be uttered in a certain unique way if communication is to take place. The same is true of any language. The learning process, regardless of the pupil's age, must be directed at the mastery of those sounds and word arrangements which are characteristic of the language being studied. The small child may learn better if the material is presented to him in songs, poems, games, and stories while the adult may require a more sophisticated analytical process; yet, in the end, both must learn to attach meaning directly to the "strange" sounds which flow from the native speaker's mouth, and to form utterances of their own at a rather rapid rate—utterances which are pronounced and arranged in such a way as to be comprehensible to the native listener. And ultimately, both must learn to derive meaning from the little black marks on paper known as writing—the shorthand representation of speech—and to produce their own little black marks in an acceptable manner.

There is ample evidence that a well-motivated adult can, in a relatively short time, gain a functional command of a foreign language. Drawing upon his greater knowledge, his ability to organize his thoughts and discipline himself, and, having a clearer sense of purpose, the adult can cover much more ground in a given period of time than can the small child. Why, then, do we have FLES programs at all?

One reason is the element of time. While it is true that the adult *can* learn certain aspects of language more rapidly, he is generally so involved in the specialized business of adult life that he simply cannot fit into his schedule the several hundred hours of concentrated drill work which are necessary to acquire even minimal command of a language. However, the longer sequence of study, though important, is not the main reason advanced by the FLES advocates; instead, the rationale for FLES is rooted in the belief that the ability to learn a foreign language declines with age. As one FLES teacher expresses it:

Childhood is the ideal period for acquiring a native or near-native pronunciation. Medical evidence, experimentation, and objective observation have proven conclusively that children learn foreign languages more quickly and more accurately (at least as far as pronunciation is concerned) than adolescents or adults because of the flexibility of their speech organs, their lack of inhibitions that are typical of older persons learning a language, and their apparent physiological and psychological need to communicate with other children. To children a new way of expressing themselves, particularly if it is associated with a normal class activity, presents no problem. Children make no attempt to analyze a language as adolescents or adults do. They do not immediately compare what they hear or say in the new language to English. They experience no conflict because of similar or completely dissimilar language items in English. They do not look for difficulties. They even use the dreaded subjunctives as normally and naturally as they would use the present tense of the verb "to have."[2]

The medical evidence mentioned here refers to studies relating to the treatment of brain damage in children and adults. Several studies have indicated that there is a physical basis for advocating FLES programs.[3] When brain tissue in the speech areas of the adult cortex is damaged, only partial recovery of speaking ability is possible in most instances. But with children, it is another story. Doctor Wilder Penfield, the noted Canadian neurosurgeon, comments on this phenomenon as follows:

I had seen children under the age of ten or twelve lose the power of speech when the speech convolutions in the left hemisphere of the brain had been destroyed by a head injury or a brain tumor. I had seen them

[2] Mary Finocchiaro, *Teaching Children Foreign Languages,* New York, McGraw-Hill, 1964, p. 4.
[3] Wilder Penfield, "The Uncommitted Cortex," *The Atlantic Monthly,* July, 1964, pp. 77–81.

How well can Americans learn a second language?

recover after a year of dumbness and aphasia. In time they spoke as well as ever, because the child's brain is functionally flexible for the start of a language. They began all over again and established a speech center located on the other side of the brain in what is called the nondominant hemisphere. (In a right-handed person, the left hemisphere is normally dominant—that is, it contains the specialized speech centers.)[4]

The adult's failure to recover full control of his speech after suffering brain damage is apparently "because he has by that time taken over the initially uncommitted convolutions of his brain for other uses. The uncommitted cortex is the part of the human brain that makes man teachable and thus lifts him above all other species."[5]

The implications of the neurological evidence are that only a child of 10 or younger can ordinarily acquire a full coordinate system. (See Chapter 5.) One who grows to adulthood as a monolingual is compelled to superimpose the second language upon speech areas already committed to his native tongue. He may become a skilled compound bilingual with a considerable vocabulary at his command, but his accent and intonation will forever betray him as one who began his study of language beyond the optimum age; that is, after the speech areas of the cortex had been committed to nonspeech functions. (Bilingualism is examined in Chapter 5.) If the validity of this evidence is accepted, then the goal of coordinate bilingualism becomes unequivocally linked with the objectives of elementary-school education. Failure to provide adequate exposure to native patterns of foreign speech in the primary grades is tantamount to crippling a section of the child's brain. Whether it is done with the blow of a hammer, the slice of a surgeon's knife, or the apathy and ignorance of those who control educational policy, crippling will result if the first ten years of a child's life are allowed to slip by without implanting a second language in the "uncommitted cortex." Dr. Penfield states at the end of his essay, "What the brain is allowed to record, how and when it is conditioned—these things prepare it for the great achievement, or limit

[4] *Ibid.*, p. 78.
[5] *Ibid.*

it to mediocrity. Boy and man are capable of so much more than is demanded of them! Adjust the time and the manner of learning, then you may double your demands and your expectations."[6]

Studies of FLES students' performance in high-school foreign language programs have tended to support Doctor Penfield's contentions. When the program is a continuous, well-articulated course of study from the beginning point in the grades through to the senior high school, students with a FLES background have shown significantly better achievement than youngsters with a non-FLES background.[7] Studies have also shown that foreign languages can be added to the elementary-school program without adversely affecting pupil achievement in other areas of the curriculum. A carefully controlled experiment at the University of Illinois showed that the "pupils in this study who engaged in learning a second language for twenty minutes each school day showed no significant loss in achievement in other subjects as measured by the Iowa-Every-Pupil Test of Basic Skills."[8] An earlier study had also indicated that "a strong FLES program is especially important to the slow learner, who finds it one of his areas of highest achievement."[9]

Despite the evidence to the effect that FLES programs can be effective, many such programs have not achieved satisfactory results. One obvious reason for the difficulties is the shortage of properly trained elementary-school foreign language specialists. Dr. George Scherer has commented on some of the other reasons for the failure of the FLES programs:

[6] *Ibid.*, p. 81.

[7] For example, a 1963 Title VI, NDEA report from the U.S. Office of Education showed the Somerville, N.J. FLES students achieving 67 points higher than average on the College Board Foreign Language Achievement Tests. Also, the FLES students were at least one year ahead of other high-school students and showed no loss of achievement in other subject areas. Moreover, a much larger than average number of low-ability FLES youngsters elected foreign languages at the high-school level.

[8] C. E. Johnson, J. S. Flores, and F. P. Ellison, "The Effect of Foreign Language Instruction on Basic Learning in Elementary Schools," *Modern Language Journal, XLVII* (January 1963), 8–11.

[9] Paul C. McRill, "FLES in District R–1," *Modern Language Journal, XLV* (December 1961), 370.

How well can Americans learn a second language?

The practice of having FLES graduates start all over again with seventh grade beginners must be vigorously condemned. There are several possible reasons for such a procedure, each implying lack of foresight. a) The outcomes of FLES are so minimal or so nebulous that there is no ongoing program in junior high with which the children can be adequately articulated. b) While the outcomes are entirely adequate, the FLES and junior high materials are not sequential. c) The school cannot afford a special track for the FLES graduates. d) The school is unable to arrange to join FLES graduates with junior high school beginners who have advanced to the second or third year of study. Any of these reasons, or any combination thereof, means that there has been a lack of planning for articulation. And without such planning, the program should never have been initiated. The failure to provide for progressive continuity can only mean serious educational waste.[10]

The schedule

In most of the writings on foreign language teaching below the college level, the schedule—if it is mentioned at all—is treated as a constant rather than as a variable. It is assumed that 20 to 30 students will meet with the same teacher each day, 5 days a week, for 50 to 60 minutes in a rather traditional-type classroom. In his book, *Language and Language Learning*, Nelson Brooks devotes one paragraph to a description of the traditional schedule. He concludes the paragraph by stating, "Whatever variants of this pattern may be found serve only to emphasize its basic sameness."[11]

Since the class period is viewed as a constant, improving the schedule is usually seen in quantitative terms: A year of language study consists of 36 5-day weeks (roughly 180 hours for the school year). To improve the schedule a school can, for example, set four such years of study as the minimum in place of the traditional two. Contact hours with the language are thereby doubled without changing the "basic sameness" of the schedule or of the classroom situation.

[10] George A. C. Scherer, "The Sine Qua Nons of FLES," *German Quarterly* (November 1964), vol 37, pp. 9–10.
[11] Nelson Brooks, *Language and Language Learning*, New York, Harcourt, Brace & World, 1964, p. 46.

The schedule remains highly resistant to change mostly for reasons which have little to do with the learning process. Administrative expedience appears to be the chief reason for having divided a day into the "egg-crate" pattern; allotting equal daily modules to each area of the instructional program is the simplest way of proceeding. And the "egg-crate" pattern is resistant to alteration because it has become built into the method of defining the quality of secondary-school education within various regions of the United States. The 5-hour school week (multiplied by 36 weeks) constitutes the school year for grades 9–12. Completion of a school year carries one unit of credit. According to accrediting agencies, a "good" school offers a certain pattern of such units in various subject areas. Thus a school might not be fully accredited if it fails to show 2 units of foreign language, 4 units of English, 4 units of mathematics and so forth. It is presumed that the units have meaning in terms of what a student has learned in these subject areas as a result of having spent a certain number of hours in the classroom.

Colleges and universities lend support to the practice of assigning quantitative value to units of credit. College language departments apparently presume that the instructional goals of the high school are identical with those of the college but that the pace of instruction is approximately half that of the college. Accordingly, it has long been the practice to equate two years of high-school foreign language with one year of college instruction. Students who have completed two or four years of high-school languages are thus credited with one and two years of college work. (One and three are often considered less desirable as units of credit since they are not readily divisible by two.) There have been sporadic attempts to modify the "egg-crate" schedule and the credit system during the first half of this century. Such efforts have not been fully satisfactory in the eyes of many educators. As a Minnesota administrator expresses it:

The schedule often has come to dominate the students, the teachers, the administrators, and the curriculum. We see around us a struggle which has been left at a stalemate. By employing makeshift devices such as dropping required courses, conducting early morning or late afternoon classes, teaching during the lunch periods, students are allowed to take

How well can Americans learn a second language?

"extra" electives such as foreign languages. These devices are hardly the answer.[12]

The answer, as viewed by some educators, is to change the method of organizing the curriculum so that the instructional goals become the constant factors and everything else becomes variable. That is, the staffing policies, time allotment, class size, and pace of instruction are all adjusted to conform to the needs of the instructional objectives. This method of reorganizing the curriculum is often referred to as "flexible scheduling." Those who advocate flexible scheduling assume that such basic changes in the approach to teaching can and should be made. The most basic tenet of flexible scheduling is that the student should be directed toward attaining certain clearly defined educational objectives rather than toward serving time in a rather inflexible pattern of courses. The problems resulting from having daily variations in class size, period length, and staff utilization can be solved—it appears—through use of the computer. In fact, dozens of schools throughout the nation have operated successfully on computer-generated schedules produced by the Stanford School Scheduling System.[13] Two of the Stanford advocates of this system comment as follows upon the possibilities and limitations of computer-generated schedules:

School schedules are the result of the simultaneous availability of three basic elements: (1) teachers, (2) students, and (3) rooms, within well-defined limits of time. The nearly infinite number of combinations of these factors far exceed the capacities of the most astute educator. A sophisticated computer, however, has a memory capacity that will investigate millions of possible combinations within a few seconds. Consequently, the availability of teachers, rooms, and student requests for each class can be determined at each stage of schedule development. Thus, a high percentage of student requests can be satisfied. There are, however, important things that a computer cannot do. A computer is an intricate box of switches that is controlled completely by a logically designed program. The computer and the programs of control are logical

[12] Almon Hoye, "Can Flexible Schedules Affect Foreign Language Enrollments," *Minnesota Foreign Language Bulletin, VI* (May 1966), 1–2.
[13] Dwight W. Allen and Donald DeLay, "Flexible Scheduling, a Reality," *Stanford University School of Education,* May, 1966, p. 3.

and systematic procedures; there is no mystique—no magic. The computer cannot create needed rooms, additional teachers, or expand time available for a program. The limits of reality have not been altered, but the ability to manipulate the factors within these limits has been greatly enhanced.[14]

There is, of course, much more to flexible scheduling than the specification of educational objectives and the use of the computer. Enthusiasts of this type of instructional reorganization make certain assumptions regarding (1) use of staff, (2) allotment of time, (3) size of class, and (4) pace of instruction. By itself, changing the schedule will have little positive impact on foreign language learning unless major changes are made in these four areas. The four basic assumptions, as they apply to foreign language learning, are outlined below:

Assumption Number One: Staff flexibility
A significant amount of student learning is possible without the professional teacher being physically present in the classroom or laboratory, even though some aspects of language learning require the presence of a highly skilled professional.

Corollary a. Certain types of drill can be performed as well or better with audiovisual devices and programmed materials.

Corollary b. Nonprofessional native speakers can direct small-group conversational practice sessions.

Corollary c. A nonprofessional librarian-technician can perform routine laboratory functions in such a way as to make foreign language drills available to the student on an open-hour basis as an alternative procedure. Remote-access equipment can provide drill in a similar fashion by means of a dial or push-button system.

Corollary d. A hierarchy of staff members is implied by all this. A professional teacher directs the instruction for each language, and assigns instructional tasks to native-speaking teacher aides, interns, clerks, and other members of the instructional team. The number of people

[14] *Ibid.,* p. 10.

How well can Americans learn a second language?

needed in each category will, of course, vary according to the size of the school.

Assumption Number Two: Time flexibility
The length of the class period should be varied in accordance with the nature of the learning task.

Corollary a. Certain learning activities may require a continuous period of time in excess of the traditional 60-minute class period.

Corollary b. Other activities may be more adequately performed in smaller modules of time.

Assumption Number Three: Class-size flexibility
The size of a class group should vary from day to day and from class to class according to its purposes.

Corollary a. Some learning activities can be carried on effectively with groups as large as 100 or more.

Corollary b. Other types of learning are better carried on in groups of 6–8 students.

Corollary c. On still other occasions, total individualization is desirable.

Assumption Number Four: Pacing flexibility
All students in a foreign language program need not be studying the same material at the same time.

Corollary a. Some students can reach the instructional goals at a much faster rate than permitted under the present scheduling system.

Corollary b. Other students who are now failing or doing poorly can reach the instructional goals if more time is allowed for them to do so.

Corollary c. Each step in the learning process should be scheduled in such a way as to permit students to go faster or slower in accordance with their ability with respect to the learning problem in question.

Corollary d. The proposed goal-oriented curriculum can be established in the existing time-oriented system. (This presumes that each student's level of achievement can be converted into credit units for graduation from high school and to semester hours of credit for college entrance.)

At this writing, several dozen schools throughout the nation had tried flexible scheduling with varying degrees of success. An evaluation of the more successful programs shows that the flexible schedule reduces the psychological pressures upon the student and allows him a wider choice of elective subjects. In one school, the introduction of flexible scheduling was accompanied by a three-fold increase in foreign language enrollments within a four-year period.[15] At worst, the introduction of flexible scheduling can produce virtual chaos. The most common causes for instructional breakdowns resulting from the schedule are:

1. Failure to feed workable scheduling data into the computer; result: an unworkable schedule.
2. Failure to provide adequate self-instructional materials.
3. Failure to provide adequate laboratory facilities so that the students can use the self-instructional materials without teacher supervision.
4. Failure to staff properly or to re-orient the staff to the instructional changes required by the flexible schedule.

The teacher

As is often the case, the key to the success or failure of schedules—flexible or otherwise—lies with the teacher and his skill—or lack of skill—as a trained professional. According to a nationwide study of teacher preparation in America, there is little cause for optimism in this direction. For, if thirty semester hours of study in a given foreign language are accepted as the equivalent of a major in that language, then less than half the foreign language teachers in the country are teaching in their major field of study.[16] Immediately

[15] Hoye, *ibid.*, p. 3.
[16] Donald D. Walsh, "The Preparation of Modern-Foreign-Language Teachers," *Modern Language Journal*, XLVIII (October 1964), 352ff. This article based on a nationwide survey shows 55.2 percent of all foreign language teachers with less than 30 semester hours; 15 percent with less than 17 hours.

How well can Americans learn a second language?

the question arises, "What does the term 'major' mean with regard to the person's effectiveness as a teacher?" For a partial answer we can turn to the findings of the Foreign Service Institute of the Department of State with respect to the average time required for adults to achieve functional mastery of a foreign language. In preparing federal employees for assignment overseas, 600 classroom contact hours were found to be the required time in the commonly taught languages.[17] Converting 30 semester hours into classroom contact hours produces a figure of 540; 60 hours fewer for the college major than for the federal employee. A narrow interpretation of these figures could lead one to conclude that over half the foreign language teachers in America have not even had the opportunity to become proficient in the language they are teaching because they lack even minimal contact with that language. However, there are other factors which may alter the picture somewhat. Many teachers have traveled in foreign countries and have engaged in special kinds of remedial work which may not appear as semester hours on the survey forms.[18] On the other hand, many of the nation's language teachers—including those with more than 30 semester hours—received their college training during the grammar-reading-translation era; the semester hours gained during that period can scarcely be equated with the hours spent in the intensive programs of the Foreign Service Institute. In view of the facts available, it appears safe to assume that a rather large proportion of the nation's foreign language teachers are not very proficient in the languages they are called upon to teach. If the majority of our teachers are in reality highly limited compound bilinguals, how realistic is the goal of coordinate bilingualism? In short, can the student achieve a higher degree of language proficiency than his teacher possesses? There are those who feel that, with proper use of audiovisual devices, he can. As Patricia O'Connor expresses it, "The notion that only a teacher with a wide range of conversational fluency can successfully conduct aural-oral practice in the classroom is a common error and reflects a mistaken impression of the function of a teacher

[17] Marjorie C. Johnston and Elizabeth Keesee, *Modern Foreign Languages and Your Child,* U.S. Government Printing Office, 1964, p. 29.
[18] Walsh, *op. cit.,* p. 356.

of a beginning foreign language."[19] The teacher, in Miss O'Connor's view, is needed to diagnose student problems, direct the amount and type of drill work needed to overcome such problems, to motivate, and to perform many other important teaching duties. However, the machine can make up for much of the teacher's linguistic deficiency, if good materials are available and if they are used intelligently.

In an effort to cope with the problems created by a shortage of well-prepared teachers, many schools have employed educated native speakers. However, even when they are fully bilingual, such persons do not always prove effective. Sometimes the failure is traceable to cultural differences; that is, the foreign speaker is simply unable to adjust to the American way of doing things. In other instances, the problem seems to be his inability to identify the problems confronting the English-speaking student. In short, the native speaker having learned his language the "natural way" cannot understand why anyone should have any trouble learning it. As a result, he fails to realize that even the simplest items can be major learning problems. (For example, the native teacher of English as a foreign language may fail to realize that those who speak Spanish cannot hear the difference between such word pairs as "hit" and "heat" or "watch" and "wash.") Therefore, the native speaker must receive thorough advance instruction in the linguistic, cultural, and psychological problems of teaching his own tongue to nonnatives. With suitable training, the native can become a highly competent instructor. The problems involved in such a training program are discussed in a letter to the Modern Language Association.[20]

No individual is inherently prepared to teach his own language—sometimes contrary to his own belief. In our some thirteen Peace Corps language programs we have dealt with close to forty language informants. Never have we been quite so successful as we have in this program for Afghanistan. Upon their arrival, they were plagued with the common adult misconceptions of language and how it is learned. Their concepts and attitudes toward their native language, Farsi, have changed. Their

[19] Patricia O'Connor, *Modern Foreign Languages in High School: Prereading Instruction,* U.S. Government Printing Office, 1960, p. 3.

How well can Americans learn a second language?

73

preconceived ideas of how to "tell" someone about their language and thus impart language skills have been obliterated. Their insistence that language is words no longer persists. Their recognition that language is pattern and must be thoroughly drilled is exemplified in the classroom by good classroom practices.

Summary

The fullest realization of the objectives of the American method is hindered by many factors. Chief among them are:

1. The difficulty of motivating students to become partial bilinguals when they live in a monolingual society.
2. The short sequence of study provided by an inflexible curriculum.
3. The tendency to delay language learning beyond the optimum age.
4. The lack of well-trained foreign language teachers at all levels.

Educators are experimenting with new instructional approaches which may provide partial solutions to such problems. Among those now being investigated are:

1. The team approach to language instruction which enables the school to draw upon the strong points of native speakers, American-born teachers, and language-laboratory drill sessions.
2. More flexible scheduling practices which provide longer sequences of study and which make language study available to more students.
3. Individualized pacing with self-instructional devices that can minimize continuity problems, thus enabling the high school to capitalize upon language skills acquired in the elementary and junior high school.
4. Electronically reproduced models of native speech presented in such a way as to allow the student to acquire a better accent than that of his nonnative instructor.

[20] David Burns, Language Coordinator, *Experiments in International Living,* 30 November, 1963, quoted in "Foreign Language Program Notes," Spring Issue, 1964, p. 2.

Bibliography

Agard, F. B., and H. B. Dunkel, *An Investigation of Second-Language Teaching*, Boston, Ginn, 1948.

Allen, Dwight W., "Individualized Instruction," *CTA Journal*, October, 1965, 28 f.

Allen, Dwight W., and Donald DeLay, "Flexible Scheduling, a Reality," *Stanford University School of Education*, May, 1966.

Allen, Dwight W., and Robert L. Politzer, "Flexible Scheduling and Foreign Language Instruction: A Conference Report," *Modern Language Journal, L* (May 1967), 275 ff.

Bush, Robert N., and Dwight W. Allen, *A New Design for High School Education: Assuming a Flexible Schedule*, New York, McGraw-Hill, 1964.

Frank, J. G., "Can One Really Learn a Foreign Language at School?" *Modern Language Journal, XLII* (May 1958), 379–381.

Hoye, Almon, "Can Flexible Schedules Affect Foreign Language Enrollments," *Minnesota Foreign Language Bulletin, VI* (May 1966), 1–5.

Kettelkamp, G. C., "Time Factor in Beginning Foreign Language Classes," *Modern Language Journal, XLIV* (February 1960), 68–70.

Penfield, Wilder, "The Uncommitted Cortex," *The Atlantic Monthly*, July, 1964, 77–81.

How well can Americans learn a second language?

> *"Would you tell me, please, which way I ought to go from here?"*
> *said Alice to the Cheshire-Puss.*
> *"That depends a great deal on where you want to get to," said the Cat.*
> *"I don't much care where—" said Alice.*
> *"Then it doesn't matter which way you go," said the Cat.*
> *"—so long as I get somewhere," Alice added as an explanation.*
> *"Oh, you're sure to do that," said the Cat, "if you only walk long enough."*
> LEWIS CARROLL

Goals of foreign language instruction: minimum essentials

5

In a world more rational than Wonderland, Alice would have known her destination and would then have requested precise directions as to how to arrive there. Similarly, in those real human enterprises which are subject to rational restraints, it is common practice to determine one's objectives and then to do whatever is necessary to reach them. An automobile manufacturer, for example, does not settle for an assembly line which turns out vehicles sans motor, sans fenders, sans steering wheel. The requirements of economic survival dictate that the production goals be achieved. Accordingly, the manufacturer hires staff and purchases equipment needed to arrive at those objectives with maximum efficiency. Failure to achieve the goals means economic loss and, ultimately, the dissolution of the enterprise.

But in the teaching of foreign languages in our schools and colleges, such restraints appear not to operate. Generations of Americans have enrolled in courses called French, German, and Spanish without having learned French, German, or Spanish. American language ineptitude continues to be a rich source of international humor. Apparently, we have not staffed and equipped our language teaching enterprise to accomplish results which native speakers consider adequate. What is more, the language teaching profession has failed even to agree upon what those results *ought* to be. There are those who would be satisfied with the reading-translation goals of the post-World War I era. On the other hand, a substantial segment of the profession advocates the teaching of all four language skills—listening, speaking, reading, and writing. Moreover, the advocates of the fundamental-skills objective generally insist that the foreign language be learned in such a way that the student is able to communicate directly in the target language. This implies at least a limited degree of bilingualism in the learner; a sharp contrast with the older reading-translation objective which required the student only to talk about the foreign language in English and to decode written material from the foreign language into English. Thus, in the relatively short post-Sputnik era, the expectations of many high-school language programs have changed drastically. Publications of the major American educational organizations state that ability to communicate in the foreign language should be a primary objective of the foreign language curriculum. California, New York, and other high-population states list similar objectives in their state curriculum guides.[1] And, as was noted in the second chapter, a rather high level of language proficiency is deemed necessary if foreign language study is to have significant educational value according to contemporary standards. All of this raises a very practical question regarding what degree of bilingualism is actually attainable within the framework of American education. This, in turn, calls for clarification of what bilingualism really is.

What is a bilingual?

A person who has some degree of facility in more than one language is a bilingual. That is obvious enough. However, researchers tell us that the method of acquiring the two languages and the conditions under which they are learned can be so different as to

[1] See foreign language bulletins from the Bureau of Secondary Education, State Department of Education, Sacramento, California; and from the Bureau of Secondary Curriculum Development, New York State Education Department, Albany, New York.

Goals of foreign language instruction: minimum essentials

produce significantly divergent types of dual-language behavior. The two extremes have been labeled *coordinate bilingualism* and *compound bilingualism*. To indicate what is implied by these terms it might be helpful to cite conditions of the sort that have produced various degrees and types of bilingualism. (Although these are hypothetical cases, they do have living counterparts which differ only in the specific details.)

In the case of the coordinate bilingual, imagine a person who had spent one half of his early childhood in Chicago; the other half in Paris, and that, as a result of this dual residence, he is able to function as a Frenchman in France and as an American in the Midwest without being distinguishable as a foreigner in either culture. Such a person is a coordinate bilingual in the fullest meaning of the term. His use of language, gesture, and other behavior patterns will reveal a perfect sensitivity to the cultural referents of either Paris or Chicago.

In contrast, imagine a man who has achieved bilingualism without ever having left the northeastern section of the United States. He is equally fluent in French and English, but he has learned his French within a Franco-American cultural context. After high school, he studied French at an Eastern University under the tutelage of a native Frenchman so that his accent is flawlessly Parisian. The resultant bilingual is identifiable in the East as a man who speaks American English; in Paris, he is identifiable as an American who speaks excellent French.

Both types described here are bilingual. Yet there is a basic difference. One uses two languages to communicate in two different cultures, while the other uses two languages to communicate in one culture. The dual-residence bilingual views such common phenomena as home, food, family, and school as being highly dissimilar in the two cultures. He will tend automatically to associate different images with the different words and expressions used to symbolize phenomena which are culturally divergent. However, the single-residence bilingual will be compelled to associate the same home, food, family, and school with the words which stand for these items in both languages. He can discuss everyday happenings with people who speak exclusively in one language or the other, but his cultural referents are largely the same in English as in French. Thus he has developed a *compound* system insofar as he ascribes the same meaning to words in the two languages, but he may be said to have a *coordinate* system to the degree that neither language dominates or interferes with his efforts to communicate in one language or the other. He is not confused by sounds, grammatical forms, or word arrangements as he shifts from one language to the other. But the shift, for example from the French word *famille* to the English *family* is an interchange of two words which refer to the same type of family organization rather than two words symbolizing two ethnically distinct social institutions. The single-residence bilingual may be consciously aware that differences exist, but his knowledge of divergence represents vicarious rather than direct experience. (See Figure 1 which illustrates three varieties of bilingualism.) The student who has learned his French exclusively by translation to and from English is an example of the totally compound bilingual. Since all meaning in French is defined through English equivalents, he perceives no meaning in the foreign language until all the words and expressions have been translated into English and interpreted through the Anglo-American value system. A three-way process is followed for both active and passive skills. The sequence for listening and reading is: *French expression* to *English* to *meaning*. Similarly, with speaking and writing, the compound bilingual can only express his thoughts in the foreign language by reversing the three-way process so that communication flows from *meaning* to *English* to *French expression*. Nelson Brooks describes the compound system as one in which "the mother tongue is not relinquished, but continues to accompany—and of course to dominate—the whole complex fabric of language behavior."[2] For the totally compound bilingual, all referents—whether linguistic or semantic—are through the mother tongue. Brooks goes on to discuss ways "to establish in the learners in our classrooms a dual system of verbal symbolism in which mother tongue and second language are coordinated but not compounded."[3] Like most pro-

[2] Nelson Brooks, *Language and Language Learning*, 2nd ed., New York, Harcourt, Brace & World, 1964, p. 49.
[3] *Ibid.*, p. 50.

Goals of foreign language instruction: minimum essentials

BILINGUAL WITH DUAL-RESIDENCE BACKGROUND

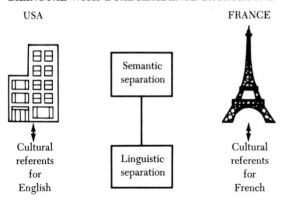

USA   FRANCE

Semantic separation

Linguistic separation

Cultural referents for English

Cultural referents for French

BILINGUAL WITH SINGLE-RESIDENCE BACKGROUND

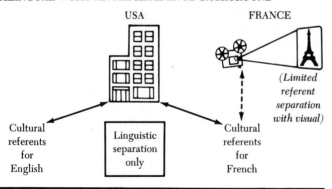

USA   FRANCE

(Limited referent separation with visual)

Cultural referents for English

Linguistic separation only

Cultural referents for French

BILINGUAL WITH TOTALLY COMPOUND SYSTEM
(All foreign language meaning filtered through English)

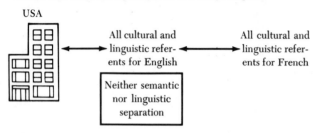

USA

All cultural and linguistic referents for English

All cultural and linguistic referents for French

Neither semantic nor linguistic separation

ponents of the new methodology, Brooks suggests that limited bilingualism of the coordinate type is feasible in American schools. Presumably this refers to the second type of coordinate system in which semantic referents to the target culture are either compound or vicarious. (That is, the language referents are either to the American culture or to a visualization of cultural phenomena in the target culture.)

Judging from past experience with dual-language learning in this country, it appears that few American students will ever become full coordinate bilinguals. In the areas of culture and vocabulary the American can, for example, gather knowledge about the Mexican home, the German school system, and the French family. But such knowledge, whether gained through reading, lecture, or visualization, provides only a pale, distorted, incomplete expression of reality as viewed by a native speaker who grew up in the culture. Vicarious experiences—valuable as they appear to be—cannot be expected to duplicate the experience which one gains, for example, by living as a child in a Mexican home, attending a German *Volksschule*, or growing up in a French family.

However, the Army Specialized Training Programs and certain post-Sputnik experiments have demonstrated that, under certain conditions, Americans can achieve a degree of fluency which resembles coordinate bilingualism of the single-residence variety. That is, the student can develop considerable skill in expressing his version of reality through the foreign system of auditory symbolization. But that symbolization, however skillfully it is manipulated, will be strongly influenced by the fact that the learner grew up in an American family and attended an American school. His essential outlook is likely to remain Anglo-American regardless of the degree of fluency and correctness which he acquires in the new language. In the final analysis, the serious student of language—whatever system is used—must approximate, to some degree, the language performance of a literate native.

Table 3 summarizes and categorizes the essential learning objectives that are applicable to any of the commonly taught European languages. Assuming that oral and written communication is the ultimate goal of instruction, it is evident that the student must

Goals of foreign language instruction: minimum essentials

Skills and concepts	*Phonology*	*Morphology*	*Syntax*
LISTENING: *the ability*	*to hear all the meaningful sound contrasts of the foreign language when it is spoken at a normal rate in complete utterances.*	*to hear all the changes of meaning caused by modifications of word forms when the language is spoken at a normal rate in complete utterances.*	*to hear the foreign language without being confused by syntactical arrangements.*
SPEAKING: *the ability*	*to produce all the significant sounds and intonation patterns of the foreign language in a manner acceptable to native speakers.*	*to express one's ideas orally using appropriate grammatical forms.*	*to express one's ideas orally using word order which is characteristic of the spoken language.*
READING: *the ability*	*to associate the appropriate graphic symbols with the sounds for which they stand.*	*to draw meaning directly from the printed page through recognition of changes in meaning caused by modifications in structure.*	*to read directly in the foreign language without being confused by syntactical arrangements.*
WRITING: *the ability*	*to spell the graphic symbols which stand for the sounds of the language.*	*to express one's ideas in writing using appropriate grammatical forms.*	*to express one's ideas in writing using the appropriate word order of the foreign language.*
CONCEPT: *the ability*	*to understand the relationship between sound symbols and written symbols (i.e., "phonemes" versus "graphemes").*	*to understand how the foreign language uses such devices as gender, number, case, agreement, verb endings, and other modifications of oral and written forms to express meaning.*	*to understand how the foreign language uses variations in word order to express meaning.*

Vocabulary	Culture	Ultimate goals
to hear and understand words in normal conversational contexts.	*to detect nuances of meaning relating to social position, family relationships, customs, national traditions, literary classics, etc.*	*to comprehend aurally new arrangements of familiar material when spoken at normal tempo and with normal intonation and rhythm.*
to acquire an active speaking vocabulary appropriate to the age, maturity level, and capacity of the student and one which is appropriate for communication in the modern world.	*to use culturally acceptable forms appropriate to the age, social standing, and occupation of the person addressed and to reveal some knowledge of the heritage of those who speak the foreign language.*	*to reorganize familiar vocabulary and grammatical forms and to apply them to new situations using pronunciation and intonation in a manner acceptable to a native speaker.*
to recognize in context a wide range of vocabulary items with sensitivity to the differences between spoken and written vocabulary and between contemporary and older literary forms, words, and expressions.	*to be able to read everything from newspapers to works of literature. This implies a basic knowledge of the history, literature, current world position, etc. of countries in which the language is spoken.*	*to read directly without constant recourse to a bilingual vocabulary list.*
to express one's ideas in writing using vocabulary which is appropriate to the occasion.	*to use the appropriate style according to the nature of what is being written.*	*to express one's ideas —idiomatically and freely—in writing.*
to understand that the semantic range of foreign words usually differs from that covered by the nearest English equivalents.	*to evaluate the foreign culture objectively and on its own merits rather than from the standpoint of Anglo-American culture.*	*to apply spontaneously everything one has learned to new situations.*

SOURCE: The preliminary edition of the *German Curriculum Guide*, Madison, Wis., Department of Public Instruction, 1968.

be able to produce all the sounds, grammatical structures, and word-order sequences of the new language and be able to recognize all auditory and graphic symbols as they are used in writing and in the normal flow of native speech. It is also clear that learning a considerable number of "content words" is a matter of high priority, perhaps second in importance only to the mastery of phonology, morphology, and syntax. Many would insist that the vocabulary be acquired with a clear understanding of the cultural implications carried by the foreign words. For example, peninsular Spanish has four patterns of pronouns and/or verb endings to express the idea of "you" while English uses one predominate pattern to express the second person. But the choice of the familiar forms (*tu—vosotros*) versus the polite forms (*usted—ustedes*) requires an understanding of Spanish attitudes toward age and social status. Certainly, more is involved here than the mere matching of vocabulary items from one language to the other. For this reason, Table 3 includes "Culture" in the horizontal headings. The column labeled "Ultimate Goals" refers to the synthesis of the five essentials which must take place in the student's mind if genuine communication is to take place. The vertical listing of the four skills is necessary because there are distinctly different objectives and learning problems for each skill. For example, the vocabulary which one uses for active speaking is vastly different in type and scope from the vocabulary which one recognizes in the more passive process of listening. A similar divergence exists between reading and writing. The instructional goals must reflect such differences. The final category entitled "Concept" is based on the belief that mastery of the four skills must be accompanied by a grasp of certain basic generalizations and concepts.

The content of the foreign language program

Each European language has a finite number of phonemes, morphemes, graphemes, and syntactical arrangements in the standard dialect. By one means or another, the student must gain functional mastery of these elements insofar as they apply to the skills of listening, speaking, reading, and writing. Most high-school programs attempt to "cover" all the principal aspects of phonology during the first year (180 classroom hours) of instruction. The basic aspects of morphology and syntax are frequently not presented in their entirety until the second or third years of instruction. The learning of vocabulary and culture is, of course, never completed. Attempts have been made to identify the basic vocabulary items for the commonly taught languages, but these efforts have never been fully, successful. As a result, most specification of vocabulary becomes a matter of arbitrary judgments based upon little more than common sense. In establishing priorities for learning, two categories of word types are often identified. First, there are a certain number of "function words" (i.e., articles, prepositions, conjunctions, auxiliary verbs, etc.), which are used constantly by all native speakers. Most of these basic items are relatively easy to identify. Secondly, there is an unlimited reservoir of "content words." Here we can only guess at certain categories of vocabulary which the language learner is most likely to need for daily communication. Basic lexical items pertaining to home, family, numeration systems, colors, and other everyday words will normally receive priority consideration along with the function words. Current practice in the European nations is to deemphasize vocabulary building as such until the student has a good control of phonology, morphology, and syntax. In Russia, for example, as few as 300 new words are introduced during the first year's instruction. American foreign language programs typically attempt to teach between 1000 and 2000 new items during the beginning levels. This could be an unrealistically high expectation in view of the concurrent emphasis upon phonology and grammar during the early years. In this regard, it appears that much research needs to be done in the direction of establishing reasonable content standards for the secondary-school program. The course content tables which appear in this chapter are intended to serve as *samples* of minimal goals for a full four-year program in each of the commonly taught languages (French, German, and Spanish). It is a well-established fact that a few students could master the content of this four-level course in two years or less while others would need five or six years to gain even limited control of the suggested items. To cite but one example of rapid individual learning, we can

Goals of foreign language instruction: minimum essentials

take the case of Robert Baker of Indiana University who is said to have learned Russian by himself when he was a junior in high school. While manning a fire watch tower for the U.S. Forest Service in South Dakota, he completed a year and a half of high school Russian in 75 days.[4] However, despite the pace, or the sequence, or the manner of learning, there are certain aspects of each language which must somehow be mastered if the student is to claim with justification that he has learned French, German, or Spanish. Tables 4, 5, and 6 attempt to summarize the most basic items and to suggest the optimum sequence of presentation for each year of a four-year sequence. The scope of this book obviously does not permit a comprehensive listing of all conceivable course content for each language. It is hoped, however, that the tables will prove useful as a guide for helping teachers and students to focus their attention away from peripheral textbook items and toward a more balanced approach to the acquisition of fundamental language skills and concepts. Ideally, each school would develop its own curricular goals and would carry out the program in somewhat the following manner:

1. Determine the ability of local students to master a desired course of study.
2. Establish a continuous sequence of language study with enough contact hours to enable youngsters to progress from their usual state of total monolingualism to one of partial bilingualism (perhaps of the single-residence variety).
3. Staff and equip the language program to whatever extent is necessary for the achievement of the stated instructional goals.
4. Test students regularly to determine whether the goals are being achieved.

To do less than this is to encourage aimless, unfocussed activity rather than systematic language learning. And, unlike Alice in Wonderland, a publicly financed educational enterprise cannot forever explain where it is going with some version of Alice's reply to the

---

[4] T. R. St. George (ed.), "Indiana's Russian Institute," *Education Age, 3* (September-October 1966), p. 9.

Cheshire Cat: "We don't much care where we are going, so long as we get somewhere." If it is to flourish, any educational enterprise must indicate its instructional goals in rather precise terms, and then must find the best way to achieve those goals. It is hoped that Tables 4, 5, and 6 will suggest ways to specify the content aspects of the language curriculum with greater clarity.[5]

4

I. FRENCH LEVEL I: Minimal Course Content

A. Phonology
  1. Listening and speaking skills
     a. all vowels, particularly u, eu; nasals in, on, an, un
     b. consonants and semiconsonants, especially l, r, gn, oui, ui, ail
     c. stress and absence of stress; 3 patterns of intonation, liaisons
     d. produce all of the above sounds accurately
     e. make obligatory liaisons
     f. reproduce short sentences with correct stress and intonation
  2. Reading and writing skills
     a. all vowels, nasals, consonants, and semiconsonants, particularly e and mute e
     b. liaisons (obligatory and impossible)
     c. syllable and word boundaries
     d. stress and intonation
     e. various orthographic representations
     f. all vowels, nasals, consonants, and semiconsonants, mute e
     g. silent consonants
     h. m for nasals before p and b
     i. liaisons
     j. understand that French and English differ considerably in sounds and stress, orthographic representations of sounds

[5] The items in Tables 4, 5, and 6 are selected excerpts from the French, German, Spanish Curriculum Guides published in preliminary form by the Department of Public Instruction, 146 North Capitol Building, Madison, Wisconsin. The native-born consultants were: Miss Gertrud Meyer of Wauwatosa Public Schools (German); Dr. Also Busot of Wisconsin State University, Whitewater (Spanish); and Mrs. M. D. Hage of Paris, France (French).

Goals of foreign language instruction: minimum essentials

I. FRENCH LEVEL I (Cont.)

B. *Morphology*
1. *Listening and speaking skills*
   a. *Determinatives (articles)*
      - (1) definite
      - (2) indefinite
      - (3) partitive
      - (4) possessive
      - (5) demonstrative
   b. *Nouns*
      - (1) singular
      - (2) plural
      - (3) masculine
      - (4) feminine
   c. *Adjectives*
      - (1) singular
      - (2) plural
      - (3) masculine
      - (4) feminine
      - (5) interrogative
   d. *Pronouns*
      - (1) demonstrative
      - (2) interrogative
      - (3) possessive
      - (4) reflexive
      - (5) personal (subjects and objects)
   e. *Verbs (3 regular groups)*
      - (1) être
      - (2) avoir
      - (3) faire, etc.
      - (4) infinitive
      - (5) present
      - (6) future
      - (7) imperative
      - (8) reflexive
2. *Reading and writing skills*
   Content as above plus an understanding that nouns, adjectives, determinatives agree with each other and with verb forms. There is generally one verb form to each person.

C. *Syntax*
1. *Listening and speaking skills*
   a. basic word order in statements (affirmative and negative)
   b. questions and commands (sp. qu'est-ce que c'est . . .)
   c. position of adjectives
   d. position of personal pronouns
2. *Reading and writing skills*
   Content as above plus an understanding that word order differs from English especially in questions (several interrogative patterns coexist) with adjectives and with pronouns.

D. *Vocabulary*
1. Listening skill   (approximately 1000 words and expressions)
2. Speaking skill   (approximately 500 words and expressions)
3. Reading skill   (approximately 1200 words and expressions)
4. Writing skill   (approximately 500 words and expressions)

I. FRENCH LEVEL I (Cont.)

    a. Content words
        (1) greetings
        (2) leave-taking
        (3) classroom, including conversational terms
        (4) numbers
        (5) colors
        (6) clothing
        (7) clock time
        (8) calendar time
        (9) school building
        (10) members of family, house parts, and functions of body
        (11) family life
        (12) meals
        (13) weather
        (14) Christmas
    b. Nouns, verbs, adjectives, adverbs pertaining to these subjects as well as function words such as et, ou, mais
    c. Emphasis should be placed on concrete descriptive vocabulary connected with reality familiar to the students.
    d. In spoken and written form, words make up a language. To communicate in that language, one must grasp the meaning, isolated or in context, without conscious reference to English.

E. Culture

    1. Introduction to French culture should be an integral and natural part of teaching French but should not take the place of teaching the language. The environment of the classroom, French books, magazines, tapes, films, records, pictures, should stimulate the students' interest in learning about the following cultural items:
    a. French names
    b. forms of address
    c. courtesy patterns
    d. French schoolday and schoolyear
    e. 24-hour clock
    f. French houses
    g. some typical foods and table manners
    h. French holidays—especially Christmas and Easter
    i. rhymes
    j. songs and music
    2. The units of vocabulary are obviously linked closely to the

Goals of foreign language instruction: minimum essentials

I. FRENCH LEVEL I (Cont.)

study of culture. As much of this as possible is done in French.

3. Cultural items are an integral part of a language. In listening to or reading the language, one must be aware of the nuances of cultural forms. To speak or write the language correctly also means to use culturally acceptable forms.

II. FRENCH LEVEL II: Minimal Course Content

A. Phonology
   1. Listening and speaking skills
      a. further work towards the mastery of sounds, especially those that differ most from English, r, u, etc.
      b. rhythm and melody of sentences
      c. French pronunciation requires clearer enunciation, more articulation (tension is more sustained with lips but breath has less force).
   2. Reading and writing skills
      a. association of all French sounds with the right orthographic representations
      b. cognates
      c. homonyms (real and deceptive)
      d. technique in word attack
      e. accent and syllabication
      f. rhythm and melody of sentences
      g. writing emphasis on mute letters and groups of letters
      h. homonyms
      i. adjectives denoting nationality or city are capitalized.

B. Morphology
   1. Listening and speaking skills
      a. prepositions and adverbs
      b. personal pronouns (indirect object) + en, y, on, and stressed forms
      c. verbs, passé composé
         (1) imperfect
         (2) pluperfect
         (3) future perfect
         (4) irregular imperative
         (5) past infinitive
         (6) immediate future
         (7) recent past
      d. irregular verbs
      e. relative pronouns qui, que
   2. Reading and writing skills
      a. the same as above plus passé simple (used mostly in writing)

  b. *tense functions almost always differ in French and English. There are many more verb endings in French than in English, also more irregular verbs.*

  c. *range of meaning of prepositions differs in French and in English*

C. *Syntax*
 1. *Listening and speaking skills*
  a. *position of adverbs*
  b. *position of personal pronouns*
  c. *position of negative particles* (ne . . . pas, rien, plus, personne) *with auxiliary verb*
  d. *verb construction (direct or indirect objects or with infinitive verb with or without preposition)*
  e. *causative* faire
  f. *various ways of expressing possession*
  g. *pattern,* c'est . . . qui, c'est . . . que
 2. *Reading and writing skills*
  Content as above plus an understanding that the position of direct and indirect objects will be different according to whether they are nouns or pronouns; note also, complex and rigid word order in negative patterns with various particles.

D. *Vocabulary*
 1. *Listening skill* (approximately 1000 words and expressions)
 2. *Speaking skill* (approximately 800 words and expressions)
 3. *Reading skill* (approximately 1200 words and expressions)
 4. *Writing skill* (approximately 800 words and expressions)
  a. *Content words*

(1) *daily routine*	(10) *transportation*
(2) *telephoning*	(11) *city*
(3) *shopping*	(12) *landscape*
(4) *money*	(13) *countryside, farming*
(5) *sizes*	(14) *travel, customs*
(6) *letters and post office*	(15) *animals*
(7) *restaurants*	(16) *holidays*
(8) *doctor, dentist*	(17) *sports*
(9) *community*	(18) *entertainments, arts*

  b. *Vocabulary should include functional words such as:*
   (1) que
   (2) aussi longtemps que
   (3) même se
   (4) alors que
   (5) *current idiomatic expressions*

Goals of foreign language instruction: minimum essentials

II. FRENCH LEVEL II (Cont.)

    c. Words and expressions in French are sometimes closely related to English but almost always differ in range and meaning; vocabulary is influenced by historical background, social customs, and other factors. Beware of cognates (false or true).

E. Culture
1. Visual and audio stimuli as well as the topics of vocabulary should suggest the following cultural items for study at the second level:
   a. forms of letters
   b. types of urban life
   c. type of rural life
   d. relationships (family, friends)
   e. France:
      (1) landscape in regions
      (2) main rivers and cities
      (3) highlights of economy, industry, and present political situation
      (4) holidays
      (5) entertainments
      (6) folklore
      (7) proverbs
      (8) music, popular and classical
      (9) current events
2. In listening and speaking, reading and writing, cultural patterns are obvious and must be observed by a native or non-native speaker of the language.

III. FRENCH LEVEL III: Minimal Course Content

A. Phonology
1. Listening and speaking skills
   a. introduction of regional differences
   b. increased length and speed of utterances
   c. nuances associated with different stresses and intonations
   d. perfecting pronunciation with increase in speed of utterance
   e. greater awareness of minute pronunciation differences
2. Reading and writing skills
   a. perfecting of reading skill with increase in fluency and expression
   b. perfecting of writing skill with attention to individual needs

c. not all French-speaking people pronounce sounds alike but French as it is spoken in the Loire Valley, considered the purest, is understood by all French-speaking people.

B. Morphology
   1. Listening and speaking skills
      a. comparisons (adjectives, adverbs)
      b. relative pronouns lequel, dont, ou
      c. conditional, present, perfect
      d. subordinating conjunctions with indicative
      e. more irregular verbs
   2. Reading and writing skills
      Content as above, plus the second form of the past conditional; also an understanding that various nuances of meaning result from tense variations of verbs in subordinate clauses.

C. Syntax
   1. Listening and speaking skills
      a. expressions of duration: e.g., il y a . . . que, cela fait . . . que
   2. Reading and writing skills
      Content as above plus an understanding that time and duration are expressed with different word order and word forms than is characteristic of English.

D. Vocabulary
   1. Increase in vocabulary cannot be stated in figures.
   2. Spoken and written vocabulary differ in volume and kind. The command of a large vocabulary can be achieved only through constant listening, speaking, reading, and writing practice.
   3. Passive vocabulary will be larger than active, but extent of both will depend on students' ability to speak and read French.
   4. A variety of graded readers may be used at this level. Much of the passive vocabulary will depend upon the selection of reading materials and textbooks.
   5. A vocabulary suitable for writing letters, outlines, reports, compositions should be developed.
   6. Topical vocabulary should include:
      a. current events
      b. education
      c. government

Goals of foreign language instruction: minimum essentials

III. FRENCH LEVEL III *(Cont.)*

      d. history

      e. biography

    7. Emphasis should be placed on:

      a. more abstract vocabulary connected with intellectual activity, criticism, judgment

      b. vocabulary designed to express emotions and feelings

E. Culture

    1. Cultural items studied at the third level should include:

      a. France

        (1) government

        (2) educational system

        (3) recreation

        (4) highlights of history

      b. Other French-speaking Countries

        (1) Belgium

        (2) Switzerland

        (3) French Canada

      c. French Influence In:

        (1) Africa

        (2) America

    2. The cultural study is done mainly in French with some supplementary reading in English. It takes in:

      a. the listening to recordings and viewing of films, filmstrips, and slides

      b. the discussing of what has been heard or read

      c. the reading of graded readers, periodicals, poetry, and literary prose

      d. the writing of letters, reports, compositions—revealing an understanding of the French culture

IV. FRENCH LEVEL IV: Minimal Course Content

A. Phonology

    1. Listening and speaking skills

      a. poetic variations in the language, in phrasing, rhythm, intonation

      b. perfecting pronunciation with attention to individual need

    2. Reading and writing skills

      a. perfecting reading skill with increase in speed

      b. perfecting writing skill

        (1) punctuation

        (2) apostrophes

        (3) syllabication

      c. poetic forms of the language may differ from everyday French. In turn, spoken French differs from written French. French requires strict punctuation.

B. Morphology
  1. Listening and speaking skills
    a. special uses of conditional
    b. subjunctive (present, imperfect)
    c. passive voice
    d. subordinating conjunctions and verbs with subjunctive
    e. direct and indirect discourse
    f. tense correspondence between main clause and subordinate clauses
    g. knowledge of the fact that the passive voice is used much less in French than in English and that on-forms or reflexive forms will often be used instead of the passive
  2. Reading and writing skills
    Content as above plus the past and pluperfect forms of the subjunctive; also, students gain an understanding of the importance of the subjunctive in French along with the tendency to avoid forms other than the present.

C. Syntax
  1. Listening and speaking skills
    a. word order in passive
    b. inversion of subject and verb in sentences other than questions
    c. word order with series of objects
    d. there are many patterns but each of them is specific
    e. emphasis is often conveyed by use of specific pattern (as well as by use of different intonation, as is mostly the case in English)
  2. Reading and writing skills
    Content would be essentially the same as for listening and speaking skills.

D. Vocabulary
  1. Amount of active and passive vocabulary is a matter of student's individual progress.
  2. A high rate of active vocabulary should be aimed for through a wide range of conversational topics, giving the student the ability to communicate in the modern world. Choice of literary works is up to the teacher, but should be based on the ability, interest, and maturity of the students, developing in them a sensitivity to the differences between spoken and

Goals of foreign language instruction: minimum essentials

written vocabulary and between contemporary and older literary forms, words, and expressions. Consideration may also be given to the grouping of college-bound and terminal students for selective reading.
3. A writing vocabulary appropriate to the occasion should be be mastered.

E. Culture
1. The increased ability of the students to communicate in French, to read everything from newspapers to works of literature, makes it possible for them to gain an appreciation and understanding of French contributions to:
   a. literature
   b. painting
   c. sculpture
   d. architecture
   e. dramatic arts
   f. music
   g. sciences
2. Current events are listened to, viewed, discussed, read, and written about. Books, periodicals, tapes, films, slides, records, and pictures are resource materials directly used by the students. The choice of these materials is up to the teacher who should take into consideration the age, maturity, ability, and interest of the student
3. A knowledge of cultural forms and of the French heritage is a part of learning the French language. Works of literature can be appreciated best in the language in which they were written.

5

I. GERMAN LEVEL I: Minimal Course Content

A. Phonology
1. Listening and speaking skills
   a. short and long vowels
   b. pure and umlauted vowels
   c. difference between certain consonants in German and English, especially l, r, ch, (ich—ach sounds)
   d. word accent
   e. intonation and rhythm in statements, questions, commands

I. GERMAN LEVEL I (Cont.)

2. Reading and writing skills
   a. short and long vowels
   b. pure and umlauted vowels
   c. diphthongs au, ai, äu, eu, ei
   d. consonants ch, chs, ck, dt, j, l, r, s, sch, st, sp, ß, th, v, w, z; silent h; final b, d, g
   e. off-glide, er; final e, word accent
   f. intonation of sentences
   g. capitalization of nouns; ich is not capitalized

B. Morphology
1. Listening and speaking skills
   a. agreement of subject and verb (especially important in speaking)
   b. definite and indefinite articles in nominative, accusative, dative
   c. personal pronouns in nominative and accusative
   d. predicate adjectives
   e. possessive adjective in nominative, accusative, dative
   f. interrogative and reflexive pronouns
   g. present tense of regular and irregular verbs and haben, sein, werden and wollen, müßen können
   h. imperative of regular verbs
2. Reading and writing skills
   a. nouns with definite and indefinite articles in nominative, accusative (dative: reading only)
   b. personal pronouns in nominative and accusative
   c. predicate adjectives
   d. possessive adjectives in nominative, accusative, dative
   e. interrogative and reflexive pronouns
   f. present tense of regular and irregular verbs and haben, sein, werden and wollen, müßen können
   g. imperative of regular verbs
   h. nouns and pronouns in agreement with present tense of regular and irregular verbs and haben, sein, werden, and wollen, müßen, können
   i. predicate adjective
   j. possessive adjectives in nominative and accusative
   k. interrogative and reflexive pronouns

C. Syntax
1. Listening and speaking skills
   a. normal word other and inverted word order after dann, hier, etc.

Goals of foreign language instruction: minimum essentials

      b. word order in questions and commands and statements
      c. word order with modals
      d. position of reflexive pronouns
      e. position of nicht
    2. *Reading and writing skills*
      a. normal word order and inverted word order after dann, hier, *etc.*
      b. word order in questions, commands, and statements
      c. word order with modals
      d. position of reflexive pronouns
      e. position of nicht

  D. *Vocabulary*
    1. *Listening skill*   *(approximately 1000 lexical items)*
    2. *Speaking skill*   *(up to 800 words and expressions)*
    3. *Reading skill*   *(approximately 1200 lexical items)*
    4. *Writing skill*   *(up to 800 words and expressions)*
      a. Basic Items
        (1) definite and indefinite articles in nominative, accusative, dative
        (2) personal pronouns in nominative and accusative
        (3) possessive adjectives
        (4) interrogative and reflexive pronouns
        (5) wollen, müßen, können
        (6) und, oder, aber, hier
      In addition, appropriate nouns, verbs, and adjectives are needed as they pertain to the adjoining categories of content words.
      b. Content Words

(1) greetings	*(9) school building*
(2) leave-taking	*(10) house*
(3) classroom	*(11) members of family*
(4) numbers	*(12) parts of body*
(5) colors	*(13) common foods*
(6) clothing	*(14) weather*
(7) clock time	*(15) Christmas*
(8) calendar time	

  E. *Culture*
    1. *Introduction to German culture should be an integral and natural part of teaching German but should not take the place of teaching the language. The environment of the classroom, German books, magazines, tapes, films, records, pictures,*

I. GERMAN LEVEL I (Cont.)

should stimulate the student's interest in learning about the following cultural items:
a. German names
b. forms of address
c. courtesy patterns
d. German school day and school year
e. regional costumes
f. 24-hour clock
g. German houses
h. some typical foods
i. German holidays, especially Christmas, Advent
j. rhymes
k. songs and music
2. The units of vocabulary are obviously linked closely to the study of culture. As much of this as possible is done in German.

II. GERMAN LEVEL II: Minimal Course Content

A. Phonology
1. Listening and speaking skills
a. combination of sounds pf, qu, zw
b. glottal stop
c. foreign words with ch, tion, initial c, initial ps
d. rhythm and melody of sentences
e. production of all sounds in German words and in words adopted into German
f. rhythm and melody of sentences
g. accent in all types of words
2. Reading and writing skills
a. association of all German sounds with the right graphic symbols
b. cognates (real and deceptive)
c. foreign words
d. accent and syllabication
e. rhythm and melody of sentences
f. learning to spell
g. capitalization of polite "you" in all forms
h. adjectives denoting nationality are not capitalized

B. Morphology
1. Listening and speaking skills
a. personal pronouns in dative

Goals of foreign language instruction: minimum essentials

99

      b. *demonstrative adjectives in nominative, accusative, dative*
      c. *adjective and adverb prepositions with accusative, dative, dative-accusative*
      d. *verbs (including all modals, separable and inseparable verbs, and imperative of irregular verbs)*
        (1) past
        (2) present
        (3) perfect
        (4) future
    2. *Reading and writing skills*
      a. *personal pronouns in nominative, accusative, dative*
      b. *demonstrative adjectives in nominative, accusative, dative*
      c. *prepositions with accusative, dative, dative-accusative*
      d. *verbs in past, present, perfect, and future tense (including all modals, separable verbs, and imperative of irregular verbs)*

C. *Syntax*
    1. *Listening and speaking skills*
      a. *position of direct and indirect objects (nouns and pronouns)*
      b. *inverted word order after adverbial and prepositional phrases*
      c. *word order in present and perfect tense*
      d. *word order in future tense*
      e. *word order with separable verbs*
    2. *Reading and writing skills*
      a. *position of direct and indirect objects (nouns and pronouns)*
      b. *word order in present, perfect, and future tenses*
      c. *word order with separable verbs*
      d. *inverted word order after adverbial and prepositional phrases*

D. *Vocabulary*
    1. *Listening skill*   *(1200 lexical items above level I)*
    2. *Speaking skill*   *(1000 lexical items above level I)*
    3. *Reading skill*   *(1500 lexical items above level I)*
    4. *Writing skill*   *(1000 lexical items above level I)*
      a. *Content words*
        (1) daily routine   *(4) letters*
        (2) telephoning   *(5) post office*
        (3) shopping   *(6) restaurant*

II. GERMAN LEVEL II (Cont.)

(7) community
(8) transportation
(9) city (German, American)
(10) landscape
(11) travel

(12) animals
(13) holidays
(14) fairy tales
(15) legends

b. Vocabulary should also include:
   (1) personal pronoun in dative
   (2) demonstrative adjective
   (3) prepositions with dative, accusative, dative-accusative
       dürfen, mögen, sollen
   (4) separable verbs
   (5) some foreign words

E. Culture
   1. Visual and audio stimuli as well as the topics of vocabulary study should suggest the following cultural items for study at the second level:
      a. forms of letters
      b. German restaurants
      c. places in a German city
      d. Germany:
         (1) landscape in regions
         (2) 4–5 rivers
         (3) 10–12 cities
         (4) highlights of economy, industry, and present political situation
      e. holidays, festivals, fairs
      f. fairy tales
      g. legends
      h. folklore
      i. proverbs
      j. music—popular and classical
      k. current events

III. GERMAN LEVEL III: Minimal Course Content

A. Phonology
   1. Listening and speaking skills
      a. introduction to difference between standard German and dialects
      b. aural comprehension of longer and more rapidly spoken utterances

Goals of foreign language instruction: minimum essentials

       c. perfecting pronunciation with increase in speed of utterance

       d. greater awareness of minute pronunciation differences

   2. *Reading and writing skills*

       a. perfecting reading skill with increase in fluency and expression

       b. introduction to Fraktur

       c. perfecting writing skill with attention to individual needs

       d. adjectives made from city names are capitalized

B. *Morphology*

  1. *Listening and speaking skills*

       a. nouns with articles in all cases

       b. personal pronouns in all cases

       c. relative pronouns in nominative

       d. all types of adjectives in all cases

       e. prepositions with genitive

       f. comparative and superlative

       g. special nouns like Herr

       h. adjectives and verbs as nouns

       i. es as subject

       j. use of present and past participle

       k. adjectives from city names

       l. all tenses of verbs in indicative

       m. use of helfen, lassen, *etc., with verbs*

  2. *Reading and writing skills*

       a. nouns with articles in all cases

       b. personal pronouns in all cases

       c. all types of adjectives in all cases

       d. prepositions with all cases

       e. comparative and superlative

       f. special nouns like Herr

       g. adjectives and verbs as nouns

       h. es as subject

       i. relative pronoun in nominative

       j. use of present and past participles

       k. adjectives from city names

       l. all tenses of verbs in indicative

       m. use of helfen, lassen, *etc. with verbs*

C. *Syntax*

  1. *Listening and speaking skills*

       a. position of verbs in all tenses (including modals and double infinitives)

    b. word order in clauses with coordinating and subordinating conjunctions and relative pronouns

    c. position of genitive before and after noun

    d. position of adverbial expressions of time, manner, and place

    e. participial constructions (in listening only)

2. Reading and writing skills

    a. participial and extended adjective constructions (in reading only)

    b. position of verbs in all tenses (including double infinitive and modals)

    c. word order in clauses with coordinating and subordinating conjunctions and relative pronouns

    d. position of genitive before and after noun

    e. position of adverbial expressions of time, manner, and place

D. Vocabulary

1. Increase in vocabulary cannot be stated in figures.

2. Passive vocabulary will be larger than active, but extent of both will depend on student's ability and willingness to speak and read German.

3. "Basic (Spoken) German Word List," by J. Alan Pfeffer is suggested as guide for active vocabulary.

4. A variety of graded readers may be used at this level. Much of the passive vocabulary will depend upon the selection of reading materials and textbooks.

5. A vocabulary suitable for writing letters, outlines, reports, compositions, should be developed.

6. Topical vocabulary might include:

    a. current events

    b. sickness and doctor

    c. education

    d. government

    e. history

    f. biography

E. Culture

1. Cultural items studied at the third level might include:

    a. Germany

        (1) government

        (2) educational system

        (3) recreation

        (4) highlights of history

Goals of foreign language instruction: minimum essentials

III. GERMAN LEVEL III (Cont.)

    b. Other German-Speaking Countries
      (1) Austria
      (2) Switzerland
    c. German influence in America
      (1) famous German immigrants
      (2) Americans of German descent
      (3) German settlements
2. The cultural study is done mainly in German with some supplementary reading in English. Activities might include:
    a. listening to recordings and viewing films, filmstrips, and slides
    b. discussion of what has been heard or read
    c. reading graded readers, periodicals, poetry, and literary prose
    d. writing letters, reports, compositions—revealing an understanding of the German culture.

IV. GERMAN LEVEL IV: Minimal Course Content

A. Phonology
  1. Listening and speaking skills
    a. poetic variations in the language of phrasing, rhythm, intonation, and in word forms (i.e., contractions, and the dropping and adding of syllables)
    b. perfecting pronunciation with attention to individual problems
  2. Reading and writing skills
    a. perfecting reading skill with increase in speed
    b. perfecting writing skill
    c. punctuation
    d. apostrophe
    e. syllabication

B. Morphology
  1. Listening and speaking skills
    a. passive voice
    b. substitutes for passive
    c. subjunctives (I and II)
    d. conditionals
    e. infinitive with or without zu
    f. relative pronouns in all cases
    g. all forms of negation
    h. all ways of forming nouns

IV. GERMAN LEVEL IV (Cont.)

    i. plurals
    j. indirect discourse (in listening)
  2. *Reading and writing skills*
    a. passive voice
    b. substitutes for passive
    c. subjunctives (I and II)
    d. conditionals
    e. indirect questions and quotations
    f. infinitive with or without zu
    g. relative pronouns
    h. all forms of negation
    i. all ways of forming noun plurals

C. Syntax

  1. *Listening and speaking skills*
    a. wenn *clauses with subjunctive; and omission of* wenn *in such clauses*
    b. word order after all relative pronouns
    c. all infinitive constructions
  2. *Reading and writing skills*
    a. word order in indirect questions and quotations
    b. wenn *clauses with subjunctive; omissions of* wenn *in such clauses*
    c. word order after all relative pronouns
    d. all infinitive constructions

D. Vocabulary

  1. *Amount of active and passive vocabulary is a matter of student's individual progress. A high rate of active vocabulary should be aimed for through a wide range of conversational topics giving the student the ability to communicate in the modern world.*
  2. *Choice of literary works is up to the teacher but should be based on the ability, interest, and maturity of the students, developing in them a sensitivity to the differences between spoken and written vocabulary and between contemporary and older literary forms, words, and expressions. Consideration may also be given to the grouping of college-bound and terminal students for selective reading.*
  3. *A writing vocabulary appropriate to the occasion should be mastered.*

E. Culture

  1. *The increased ability of the students to communicate in German, to read everything from newspapers to works of litera-*

Goals of foreign language instruction: minimum essentials

ture, makes it possible to let them gain an appreciation and understanding of German contributions to:

a. literature
b. painting
c. sculpture
d. architecture
e. dramatic arts
f. music
g. sciences

2. Current events are listened to, viewed, discussed, read and written about. Books, periodicals, tapes, films, slides, records, pictures are resource materials directly used by the students. The choice of these materials is up to the teacher who should take into consideration the age, maturity, ability, and interest of the student.

6

I. SPANISH LEVEL I: Minimal Course Content

A. Phonology
1. Listening and speaking skills
   a. Spanish vowels: a, e, i, o, u
   b. all consonant sounds
   c. initial and intervocalic: d, g, b
   d. differentiate between systems of stress in Spanish and English
   e. intonation and rhythm in statements, questions, and commands
   f. dental and velar n
   g. develop auditory discrimination among verb tenses (present to preterite, future, etc.)
   h. diphthongs
   i. production and differentiation of the sounds listed above
   j. produce liaisons between like vowels and consonants
2. Reading and writing skills
   a. associations of the sounds of the language with written symbols, especially: l, ll; qui, que; ca, co, cu, ch; h; r, rr; n; ga, go, gu, gue, gui
   b. read aloud with proper pronunciation and intonation
   c. knowledge of proper syllabication and placement of accents
   d. spell vowel and consonant sounds correctly, especially: l, ll; qui, que; ca, co, cu, ch; h; ua, ue, ui, uo

  e. formulate meaningful sentences in Spanish
  f. write complete sentences correctly in Spanish
  g. basic principles of stress (hablo, habló, estas, estás)

B. Morphology
 1. Listening and speaking skills
  a. familiar and polite (pronoun, verb contractions al, del)
  b. regular present of ar, er, ir *verbs*
  c. present of ser, *and* estar
  d. possession with de
  e. imperatives
  f. personal a
  g. articles, nouns, and adjectives (gender, number)
  h. placement of no
  i. placement and agreement of adjectives
  j. present with future meaning
  k. cardinals and ordinals
  l. pronouns with prepositions
  m. stem-changing verbs
  n. object pronouns (form and position)
  o. possessive adjectives
  p. preterite
  q. imperfect
  r. demonstratives, adjectives, and pronouns
  s. present progressive
  t. comparison of adjectives and adverbs
  u. future and conditional
  v. relative pronouns: gustar, faltar
  w. indefinite pronouns
  x. interrogative pronouns: por *and* para
 2. Reading and writing skills
  a. use of and exposure to above in reading, especially: number and gender of nouns and adjectives, number and person of verbs and pronouns
  b. agreement of adjectives with nouns and verbs with their subjects
  c. use of preterite and imperfect
  d. comparison of adjectives and adverbs
  e. use of above in writing
  f. knowledge of gender and number of adjectives and nouns
  g. person and number of verbs and pronouns
  h. agreement of verbs with their subjects
  i. write answers to questions stressing correct spelling and agreement

Goals of foreign language instruction: minimum essentials

I. SPANISH LEVEL I (Cont.)

  j. write simple text from dictations and narratives
  k. capitalization

C. Syntax
  1. Listening and speaking skills
    a. statements, interrogatives, and imperatives
    b. position of adjectives
    c. word order to denote possession
    d. negative sentences (the concept of the double negative)
    e. position of pronoun, including affirmative commands, infinitives, and gerunds
    f. difference between positions of demonstrative pronouns and adjectives
  2. Reading and writing skills
    a. expose students to additional basic forms or word order by introducing them to additional short readings
    b. provide more complex sentences where students encounter basic word order in a more varied context
    c. rewrite statements in the form of questions and commands
    d. change affirmative statements into negative ones
    e. written exercises requiring an understanding of:

    (1) adjectives   (5) demonstrative pronouns
    (2) negatives   (6) indefinite pronouns
    (3) articles   (7) word order in comparisons
    (4) object pronouns

D. Vocabulary
  1. Listening skill   (approximately 1000 lexical items)
  2. Speaking skill   (up to 800 words and expressions)
  3. Reading skill   (approximately 1200 lexical items)
  4. Writing skill   (up to 800 words and expressions)
    a. Basic items
       Samples of all forms listed under Morphology: i.e., definite and indefinite articles, interrogatives, verbs ser and estar in present tense, suitable examples of regular verbs, etc.
    b. Content words

    (1) greetings   (8) dates (calendar)
    (2) leave-taking   (9) school building
    (3) classroom   (10) family
    (4) numbers   (11) parts of body
    (5) colors   (12) common foods
    (6) clothing   (13) weather
    (7) telling time (clock) (14) Christmas

I. SPANISH LEVEL I (*Cont.*)

E. *Culture*
1. *Patterns of behavior typical of the culture, characteristics of the people who speak Spanish such as:*
   a. *greeting*
   b. *showing respect* (tu and usted)
   c. *introducing friends*
   d. la piñata
   e. la siesta
   f. el patio
   g. *names of married women*
2. *Student participation in the activities mentioned above. Teachers should try to obtain student participation by asking questions in Spanish about the materials covered.*
3. *Selections from children's literature, singing, etc.*
4. *Units of cultural content clarifying special points which vary between English and Spanish-speaking cultures.*
5. *Meals, holidays, etc.*

II. SPANISH LEVEL II: Minimal Course Content

A. *Phonology*
1. *Listening and speaking skills*
   a. *vowel clusters, emphasizing diphthongs*
   b. *fusion of vowels* (dónde, estás)
   c. *linkage* (los, alumnos)
   d. *phrases emphasizing the production of vowel clusters, diphthongs, fusion of vowels, and linkage*
   e. *sounds involving the points listed above—always with practical materials in complete meaningful sentences*
2. *Reading and writing skills*
   a. *vowel clusters, diphthongs, fusion of vowels, and linkage in reading selections*
   b. *practice reading sounds represented by the following spellings:* ll, y; qui, que; ca, co, cu; b, v; j; ge, gi, ga, go, güe, güi, gue, gua, guo
   c. *observance of accents which break diphthongs:* caído, traído, Raúl
   d. *dictations and other written exercises emphasizing knowledge of written symbols for sounds listed above*

B. *Morphology*
1. *Listening and speaking skills*
   a. *imperfect vs. preterite*

Goals of foreign language instruction: minimum essentials

II. SPANISH LEVEL II (*Cont.*)

    b. *progressives and perfects*
    c. *reflexive verbs and pronouns*
    d. *nominalization of:*
        (1) *adjectives*
        (2) *possessives*
        (3) *indefinites*
        (4) *articles*
    e. por *vs.* para
    f. *passive voice*
    g. *present and imperfect subjunctive*
    h. *indicative vs. subjunctive*
    i. *sequence of tenses*
    j. hacer *with expressions of time*
    k. *change from present to imperfect subjunctive*
    l. *passive voice with* se *and* ser
    m. si *clauses in the subjunctive*

  2. *Reading and writing skills*
    a. *supplementary readings involving the subjunctive in as many forms as possible*
    b. *graded readers or other material incorporating the basic grammatical forms listed above*
    c. *give students contexts requiring them to choose between the: imperfect and preterite, indicative, and subjunctive, sequence of tenses,* por *and* para, *the correct use of the passive-voice construction.*
    d. *additional written exercises involving the use of the grammatical forms listed above*

C. Syntax
  1. *Listening and speaking skills*
    a. *position of reflexive pronouns*
    b. *word order with* gustar, faltar, parecer, *etc.*
    c. *word order with passive voice*
    d. *word order with* hacer *in expressions of time*
    e. *use of subjunctive in subordinate sentences*
    f. *position of indefinite pronouns*
    g. *word order in comparisons of adjectives and pronouns*
    h. *position of relative pronouns*

  2. *Reading and writing skills*
    a. *expose students to supplementary readers where basic word order is found in new context. Provide more complex reading in order that students encounter basic word order in varied contexts.*

II. SPANISH LEVEL II (Cont.)

    b. *write short sentences in which word order is stressed.*

    c. *give the infinitive of reflexive verbs or expressions requiring the subjunctive.*

    d. *change active to passive voice.*

    e. *cues requiring the use of* gustar, faltar, *etc.*

    f. *all material written by the students should be in complete and meaningful sentences.*

D. Vocabulary
1. Listening skill   *(1200 lexical items above level I)*
2. Speaking skill   *(800 lexical items above level I)*
3. Reading skill   *(1200 lexical items above level I)*
4. Writing skill   *(800 lexical items above level I)*

    a. Basic items

    Necessary vocabulary to understand simple statements incorporating the basic grammatical forms outlined for Levels I and II within contexts utilizing the most functional patterns and vocabulary: verb forms like gustar, faltar; *use of the imperfect and preterite, future and present progressive, use of object pronouns.*

    b. Content words

(1) *daily routine*	(8) *transportation*
(2) *telephoning*	(9) *city (Latin American*
(3) *shopping*	*vs. North American)*
(4) *letters*	(10) *travel*
(5) *post office*	(11) *animals*
(6) *restaurant*	(12) *holidays*
(7) *community*	

E. Culture
1. *Expose students to selected topics presented in short conversations and illustrated by films, slides, tapes, records, and guest speakers; use questions in Spanish about the materials covered. Topics suggested at this level include:*

    a. *songs*
    b. *music*
    c. *childhood literature*
    d. *games*
    e. *climate*
    f. *cultural heritage*

2. *Elementary supplementary readings emphasizing cultural content.*
3. *Written exercises requiring students to use the key words*

Goals of foreign language instruction: minimum essentials

II. SPANISH LEVEL II (Cont.)

illustrating their knowledge of patterns of behavior and culture.

4. *Develop an appreciation and understanding of the patterns of behavior and units of culture characteristic of Spanish-speaking peoples.*
5. *Create an atmosphere in the classroom which fosters an interest in furthering knowledge about Spanish-speaking countries.*

III. SPANISH LEVEL III: Minimal Course Content

A. *Phonology*
 1. *Listening and speaking skills*
   a. *reinforce intonation patterns in statement, questions, and commands*
   b. *reinforce auditory discrimination among verb tenses studied*
   c. *review dental and velar n, initial and intervocalic d, g, b*
   d. *review vowel clusters, liaison, and linkage*
   e. *production of intonation patterns in statements, questions, and commands*
   f. *dental and velar n, initial and intervocalic d, g, b*
   g. *oral discrimination among verb tenses*
   h. *production of r, rr; initial, intervocalic, and terminal r*
   i. *stressed and unstressed vowels*
 2. *Reading and writing skills*
   a. *recognition of stress patterns and accentuation*
   b. *review qui, que, ca, co, cu, ch, ga, gue, gui, go, gu, gua, guo, güi, gue, j, ge, gi (je, ji), h, initial r and rr*
   c. *read aloud with proper pronunciation and intonation*
   d. *spell correctly vowel and consonant sounds listed above*
   e. *take dictations in the foreign language emphasizing the representation of these sounds*
   f. *written exercises using material previously illustrated*
   g. *reinforce the knowledge of the relationship between sounds and written symbols in Spanish*
   h. *listen and speak with respect to breath groups and meaningful phrases*

B. *Morphology*
 1. *Listening and speaking skills*
   a. *Expansion of the knowledge of the following points:*
    (1) *all pronouns*

        (2) ser *and* estar

        (3) *imperatives*

        (4) *gender and number of articles, pronouns, and adjectives*

        (5) *most commonly used irregular verbs*

        (6) *cardinals and ordinals*

        (7) *negative words*

        (8) *form and use of the subjunctive (recognition)*

    b. *reinforce ability of student to change person and number of verbs and pronouns; change number and gender of nouns and adjectives*

    c. *use of the subjunctive*

    d. *use of negatives*

    e. *reinforce points listed above in conversation*

  2. *Reading and writing skills*

    a. *exposure to readings in which the above-mentioned structures are emphasized*

    b. *reinforce ability to write answers to questions requiring the use of gender and number of adjectives and nouns, person and number of verbs and pronouns*

    c. *write simple sentences and do other written exercises requiring knowledge of the basic grammatical forms listed in listening and speaking*

C. *Syntax*

  1. *Listening and speaking skills*

    a. *reinforce use of the form and position of personal pronouns, adjectives, and indefinite pronouns*

    b. *comparisons of adjectives and adverbs*

    c. *utilization of the above items in meaningful utterances related to daily situations*

    d. *auditory discrimination with respect to the above items*

    e. *expand ability to distinguish between basic word order in statements, questions, commands, and negatives*

  2. *Reading and writing skills*

    a. *expose students to additional forms and word order by the continued use of supplementary readings*

    b. *provide more complex sentences where students encounter word order in a more varied context*

    c. *reinforcement of the use of the items listed in listening and speaking with emphasis upon written exercises*

    d. *rewrite statements in the form of questions, commands, and negatives*

Goals of foreign language instruction: minimum essentials

III. SPANISH LEVEL III (Cont.)

D. Vocabulary
1. Increase in vocabulary cannot be stated in figures.
2. Passive vocabulary will be larger than active but extent of both will depend on student's ability and willingness to speak and read Spanish.
3. A variety of graded readers may be used at this level. Much of the passive vocabulary will depend upon the selection of reading materials and textbooks.
4. A vocabulary suitable for writing letters and compositions should be developed.
5. Topical vocabulary might include:
   a. current events
   b. sickness and doctor
   c. education
   d. government
   e. history

E. Culture
1. Cultural items at the third level might include:
   a. Spain
      (1) government
      (2) educational system
      (3) recreation
      (4) historical highlights (especially the conquest of South and Central America)
   b. South and Central American nations (topics similar to those for Spain)
   c. Spanish influence in North America
2. The cultural study is done mainly in Spanish with some supplementary reading in English. Activities might include:
   a. listening to recordings and viewing films, filmstrips, and slides
   b. discussing what has been heard or read
   c. reading of various kinds including graded readers, periodicals, poetry, literary prose
   d. writing letters, reports, or compositions

IV. SPANISH LEVEL IV: Minimal Course Content

A. Phonology
1. Listening and speaking skills
   a. reinforce the contrast involving unstressed vowels vs. stressed vowels
   b. reinforce auditory discrimination of all consonant sounds

IV. SPANISH LEVEL IV (Cont.)

    c. review and reinforce liaison and linkage

    d. develop proper liaison and linkage in speaking at near-native speed

  2. *Reading and writing skills*

    a. read materials aloud with proper pronunciation and intonation at normal speed

    b. concentrate upon words which exemplify the ways in which changes in phonology affect meaning

    c. reinforce ability to associate written symbols with sound

    d. have students paraphrase in writing what they hear (short dialogues or stories)

    e. give dictations incorporating the more difficult spelling: h, j, ge, ji, (je, ji), gue, gui, y, n, ll, rr, v, b, *diphthongs, silent vowels in linkage*

B. Morphology

  1. *Listening and speaking skills*

    a. review use of the subjunctive, imperfect vs. preterite, por *and* para, *the passive voice, stem-changing verbs*

    b. progressive and perfect tenses, comparisons of adjectives

    c. reflexive verbs

    d. reinforce understanding of verbs like gustar, faltar, parecer, *etc.*

    e. use of the above items in speaking at near-native speed and in contexts that are understandable to native speakers

  2. *Reading and writing skills*

    a. use of the above items in written exercises according to a specific grammar point, using the passive voice, por, *and* para

    b. imperfect and preterite, subjunctives, comparison of adjectives, progressive and perfect tenses, gustar, faltar, *etc.*

    c. Stem-changing verbs, reflexive verbs.

C. Syntax

  1. *Listening and speaking skills*

    a. reinforcement of knowledge with respect to the word order in sentences with gustar, faltar, parecer

    b. passive voice

    c. comparison of adjectives

    d. use of subjunctive in subordinate clauses

  2. *Reading and writing skills*

    a. provide supplementary readings stressing the importance of basic word order as outlined above

    b. have students write sentences and do other written exer-

Goals of foreign language instruction: minimum essentials

cises according to specific points of word order, position
of pronouns, passive voice, use of subjunctives in subordinate clauses
c. comparison of adjectives
d. gustar, faltar, parecer, *etc.*

D. Vocabulary
1. A student should be able to understand almost any word in
standard Spanish in normal conversational contexts.
2. A student should have an active speaking vocabulary appropriate to his age and capacity enabling him to communicate
in Spanish with considerable fluency.
3. A student should recognize in context a wide range of vocabulary items. If he is planning to continue Spanish in college,
he should do extensive outside reading to familiarize himself
with many literary forms, words, and expressions.
4. A student should have a writing vocabulary which is appropriate to the occasion.

E. Culture
1. A student should listen with understanding to audio stimuli
and detect nuances of meaning relating to common aspects
of Hispanic culture.
2. A student should speak and write in culturally acceptable
forms and in his speech and writing reveal some knowledge
of the heritage of the people who speak Spanish.
3. A student should read everything from newspapers to works
of literature with an understanding of its place within the
Spanish culture.
4. A student planning to continue his studies of Spanish in
college should familiarize himself with literature in his field
of interest.

Bibliography

Grittner, Frank M. (ed.), *French Curriculum Guide, German Curriculum Guide, Russian Curriculum Guide, Spanish Curriculum Guide,*
Madison, Wis., Dept. of Public Instruction, 1968.
*Separate bulletins for each of the above four languages contain
specific goals for 6-year and 4-year programs. Cost: $1.00.*

Psychology and language learning:
motivation and method

6 There are indications that a rather large segment of the language teaching profession has, for the most part, accepted the goals listed in Chapter 5. It is also fairly safe to state that linguists have identified the priority items for the commonly taught languages. In fact, even before the linguists of today were well known, many teachers of language had successfully identified the sounds and structures that had to be learned for the purpose of communication in the commonly taught languages. However, even where there is general accord on matters of instructional goals and course content, there still remain some definite areas of disagreement about the language learner and the process by which he learns. In this regard it might be helpful to refer to a continuum of theories on how languages are acquired and use the two extremes as a means of identifying the principal schools of thought. On such a continuum we would find the cognitive-code-learning advocate on one end, the operant-conditioning enthusiast on the other. The "cognition" school insists that the use of grammatical generalizations is an essential part of language learning. The "conditioning" school tends to minimize the importance of conceptualization and to insist upon developing correct language habits in the student through a long series of carefully planned stimuli designed to elicit only correct responses. There is also a middle-of-the-road or "eclectic" school consisting of those who believe that language learning involves some cognition and some conditioning depending upon which aspect of a language is being learned. In fact, a careful review of the professional journals and books on methodology will reveal that there are few purists in either of the first two schools mentioned above. Apparently there is a considerable reluctance among language teachers to abandon the cognitive process, particularly where morphology and syntax are concerned. Even the newest text books usually make some provision for the learning of grammatical generalizations. However, here again there are widely differing views on the *manner* of learning the generalizations.

To illustrate the problem more clearly we have selected a type of language pattern in French, German, and Spanish which presents essentially the same learning problem for those who speak English natively. The following sentences show the English pattern; the conflict point is underscored:

He is a professor.

He is a student.

He is a salesman.

(etc. for any occupation)

Notice that the comparable pattern in French, German, and Spanish omits the article:

French	*German*	*Spanish*
Il est professeur.	Er ist Professor.	(Él) es profesor.
Il est élève.	Er ist Student.	(Él) es alumno.
Il est commerçant.	Er ist Kaufmann.	(Él) es vendedor.

The psycholinguistic problem here is to teach American students to omit the article (*un, una, ein, eine,* etc.) when referring to any profession or occupation in any form of the pattern:

Il est _____.

Er ist _____.

(Él) es _____.

Further, we want the language student to be able to apply the pattern to any appropriate situation in the language that he is learning. In conversing, he must automatically leave a "blank" between the verb and the word referring to professions or occupations. Generalized, the pattern becomes:

SUBJECT + VERB *to be* + (   ) + OCCUPATION OR PROFESSION
(unmodified)

As he learns new words to refer to occupations and professions and as he gains control of new forms and tenses of the verb, the student should *not* have to relearn the concept of nonuse of the article. Thus, if he has learned the generalization properly, he will be able to generate any number of sentences in the target language which express ideas such as:

He was a farmer.
Pablo wants to be a bull fighter.
Heinrich will be an engineer when he grows up.
Madeleine would have been a teacher if she had not married.
Do you want to be a bum?

If the generalization has been properly mastered, the student will not be confused by new verb tenses or moods, more complex sentence structures, or other possible distractions. Instead he will perceive the basic pattern in any of the infinite variations of sentences which he may subsequently need for purposes of communication. Moreover, he will have eliminated the compulsion to use the French, German, or Spanish equivalent of the English articles (a, an) to refer to human occupations, but will use the articles freely where they are appropriate (i.e., in reference to objects, in reference to people where no occupation is involved, in reference to occupations which are preceded by an adjective, etc.).

If we apply this specific question to the entire area of language learning the question then becomes: How does the teacher induce the student to learn the basic problem sounds, structures, and word-order sequences so that he can apply them unhesitatingly to new situations while avoiding the pitfalls created by interference from his native English? This is a very large question, and it will probably never be answered to everyone's satisfaction. Yet each

Psychology and language learning: motivation and method

year, teachers are faced with decisions relating to the selection of texts, tapes, and visual materials and the utilization of these materials in the instructional process. It is therefore imperative for them to develop a definite point of view on the psychology of language learning. Without such orientation, textbook selection becomes a game of chance; and teaching procedures tend to become aimless, unfocussed activities. The following discussion attempts to identify a few of the key psychological premises underlying the more widely used texts and methods and to comment upon their soundness in the light of psychological theory.

Grammatical generalizations versus rote memorization

One of the most basic, practical problems faced by the language teacher relative to the question of language learning and cognition is contained in the following two questions: Should the student memorize a foreign language utterance without understanding how each element of that utterance functions? Or, on the other hand, should he only commit to memory those expressions for which a grammatical explanation is immediately supplied or learned? That is, how much language material will the pupil be required to learn by rote without knowing such things as, how a verb ending relates to the whole pattern of verb structure, why a familiar noun suddenly has a different ending, or why a newly acquired pronoun comes before the verb instead of after it? The difficulty arises when the language teacher's desire to teach many useful expressions in a short period of time comes into conflict with his belief that language must be presented in an orderly fashion. For example, during the first weeks of instruction the teacher, wishing to use French or Spanish for giving classroom instructions, may say to the class:

I want you to learn this for tomorrow.

Yet in most high-school texts more than a year will pass before the student sees a systematic presentation of the grammatical principles necessary to make that type of statement in French or Spanish. Similarly, in German it is common practice to begin the first day with dialog material such as the following:

Hello, Hans, How are you?   Guten Tag, Hans, Wie geht's?

Fine, thanks, and you?   Gut, Danke, und dir?

Even this simple exchange of greetings contains grammatical problems which will not be dealt with for several months in the typical high-school German course. The same might be said of a large part of the material commonly taught in French, German, and Spanish classes everywhere. In each of these languages during the first week, youngsters are often required to memorize such conversational exchanges as:

My name is Carlos
What is your name?
My father's name is John.

These seemingly simple structures are loaded with pitfalls for the student who has learned them only by rote memorization. This is because the verbs, the possessives, and other structural elements function differently in each language than they do in English. Therefore, while the student *can* say from memory:

What is your name? *or* My father's name is John,

he is often unable to ask such questions as:

What is your father's name? *or* Is your name John?

The student who has memorized only a few pat utterances pertaining to peoples' names does not know how to change them for application to new situations. To perform the latter task he must first learn to manipulate with great rapidity all relevant verb forms, possessives, and other peculiarities of the language as they relate to asking and telling what someone's name is.

In short, the student must ultimately master the *general system* used for naming people rather than learning, parrot-like, a few *specific examples* such as those given above. On this point, most knowledgeable language theorists agree. After all, the possible variations of the naming system above are nearly infinite in number if one thinks in terms of specific sentences for memorization. (For example: What's your name? What was her name before marriage? What would her name be if she had not married? I know his name.

Do you know their names? etc., ad infinitum.) The same is true of hundreds of other situational dialogs. It is quite obviously unrealistic, therefore, to use the tourist-phrase-book approach as the sole method of learning a language. First, it is mathematically not possible to identify and tabulate all the conceivable word combinations in a given language. And, secondly, it would not be psychologically reasonable to expect anyone to memorize them all if they were available. Yet second-language learning does demand a considerable amount of memory work simply because the learner must acquire a basic vocabulary. Thus it becomes a question of how much rote memorization is desirable throughout the language course, particularly at the beginning levels where problems of student motivation are often most acute. Another problem relates to the sequence of introducing the student to grammatical structures; that is, should the presentation be orderly or random?

Random presentation of language structures

There are a number of recently published texts which present the foreign language lessons as a series of situational dialogs which the student is expected to memorize by rote. Although, in some instances, these books are supplemented with attractive visual aids, they frequently do not lend themselves easily to a systematic attack upon grammatical structures. Frequently, the authors of such texts have chosen to concentrate upon presenting genuine idiomatic utterances that fit the conversational situation rather than upon an orderly presentation of grammatical structures. In extreme cases, complex structures will appear in the very first lesson, while elemental ones may be scattered throughout the text. Other such texts present their situational dialogs in a less capricious manner, making certain that the more basic structures are presented in their entirety in the first few lessons while withholding the more difficult ones until later. With this latter approach, the teacher can, at various points, stop and focus the students' attention upon critical structural elements after they have been memorized in dialog form. When this is done, grammatical generalizations serve to organize and integrate material which the students may have previously viewed merely as a series of specific sentences without pattern. On the other hand, the inexperienced teacher may plod through a text in which structures are presented in random order without ever stopping to determine whether or not the student has grasped the generalizations contained in the specific sentences. Success in such a course is almost entirely a matter of brute memory.

The seeded dialog approach

The manner of presenting structure which is most characteristic of the new American Method is to combine situational dialogs with structure drills. Seeded into each dialog are selected examples of fundamental grammatical structures. Each lesson begins with a "basic dialog" which, typically, involves the memorization of a supposedly appealing conversational exchange between two or more teenage youngsters from the target culture. The basic dialog is supposed to serve as follows:

1. In the process of hearing and saying the basic dialog sentences, the student learns to imitate the individual sounds and intonational patterns of the target language.
2. In learning the sentences he is, hopefully, also learning vocabulary items in a meaningful context; he is not asked to memorize isolated items from a word list.
3. Where possible, the dialogs contain situations which point out sharp contrasts between the target culture and American culture.

A disadvantage of the basic-dialog approach is that a number of "advanced" structures invariably appear in the early dialogs simply because the conversational situation demands them. The student is told to learn these as if they were unstructured idioms, and not to ask questions, "An explanation will be provided in a later chapter," he is told. Meanwhile, he is permitted to concentrate upon a few sentences from the basic dialog which contain selected structural elements. These serve as models for drill upon phonology, morphology, and syntax. And the drills, in turn, provide material upon which to base a systematic presentation of grammatical generalizations. However, as is the case with the random presentation of structure, the seeded dialog approach requires that a large part of the learning process be devoted to the learning of utterances without a full understanding of how those structures are organized in the target language. Opponents of the seeded-dialog approach contend that the motivational value of the situational dialogs wanes rapidly after the first few months. For students eventually discover that many sentences which they have memorized with great effort are useless to them for the purpose of communication. They simply do not know how to transform these specific sentences to meet the demands brought forth by an unanticipated conversational situation. Consequently, student begin to resist an approach which requires still more memorization of utterances of questionable utility.

Monostructural presentation of language structures

There are several prominent foreign language educators who completely reject either of the previously mentioned polystructural approaches to morphology and syntax. There are even some who insist that phonology must be presented one phoneme at a time. Through the mid-1960s such monostructuralists formed a small but highly vocal segment of the foreign language profession. However, as we shall see in a later chapter, the monostructural approach is highly adaptable to self-instructional methods of teaching. Therefore, it may well be expected to assume greater importance in the future if the present educational trends toward automated learning and individualized study continue. Then too, there are several new texts which adhere rather closely to a monostructural presentation of grammar. It is possible that these have been overlooked or misunderstood by the profession. In any case, it seems advisable to examine this approach from the standpoint of the psychology of second-language learning.

Monostructural courses, with a few exceptions, are not "mono" in the strictest sense of the word. Beginning lessons will usually contain several structures simply because they are needed in order to create sense-making utterances and to elicit seminatural responses from the student. However, the number of new elements introduced in each lesson is severely limited, and the sequence of introducing grammatical elements is carefully planned. Moreover, every effort is made to focus the student's attention on the structure to be learned and to keep him from being distracted or confused by extraneous material. Accordingly, the monostructural approach makes heavy initial use of simple, concrete vocabulary items and nondeceptive cognates. Thus, for example, the first lesson of a monostructural course in Spanish would aim at teaching the masculine and feminine singular. The students would learn selected sentences containing the four singular articles (*un, una, el, la*). The teacher could use items from the classroom environment to teach all the basic elements.

LESSON I. *Masculine and feminine singular*

Masculine indefinite articles
> Es un libro.   (It's a book.)
> Es un lapiz.   (It's a pencil.)
> Es un papel.   (It's a paper.)
>   etc.   etc.

Feminine indefinite articles
> Es una pluma.   (It's a pen.)
> Es una regla.   (It's a ruler.)
> Es una tiza.   (It's a piece of chalk.)
>   etc.   etc.

Masculine definite article
> Es el libro, lapiz, papel, etc.

Feminine indefinite article
> Es la pluma, regla, tiza, etc.

Interrogation
> ¿Es un libro?

Affirmative reply
> Si, es un libro.

Negative reply
> No, no es un libro; es una pluma.

Psychology and language learning: motivation and method

Students and teacher can hold up articles (or point to them) saying:
¿Qué es esto? (What's this?)
Es un libro, es una pluma, etc.

Each of the foregoing structures would be drilled thoroughly as isolated phenomena. Later, masculine and feminine forms would be intermixed in the same utterance; (i.e., *un libro y una pluma*). Subsequent lessons would build upon the earlier ones using as little new vocabulary as possible. Among the succeeding lessons would be:

LESSON II. *Learning the plurals*

el libro	los libros
el lápiz	los lápices
la pluma	las plumas

LESSON III. *Agreement and word order— noun with adjective*

el libro rojo (the red book)
los libros rojos (the red books)
la pluma amarilla (the yellow pen)
las plumas amarillas (the yellow pens)

The well-conceived monostructural approach has logic on its side. Each new lesson builds upon that which went before, and in this process of reentry, the retention of previously learned material is strengthened through constant reinforcement. From the very outset, the student is able to use the new language to relate to the world which most immediately surrounds him. However, much of the early application of language structure to the real world is necessarily oversimplified and unnatural. Students may spend many weeks discussing yellow pencils, new books, brown tables, and low chairs. The teacher, meanwhile, may feel convinced that she is introducing sounds and structures in the most logical sequence; but will the students see it this way? Too often, they do not, particularly with the inexperienced teacher. And, if the youngsters cannot be made to see how each lesson is moving them another step closer to controlling the new language, they will begin to resist the course and the teacher. The resistance may manifest itself overtly in the form of discipline problems or covertly in the form of lethargic student responses. But some form of resistance is very likely to appear during the first few months of a monostructural course unless the teacher is a skillful motivator.

Thus, a polystructural approach using high-interest situational dialogs may show initial high motivation followed by gradual student disillusionment. Conversely, the monostructural approach runs the risk of losing the learner's interest before he has reached the point where he can be intrinsically motivated by the thrill of learning to express himself in the target language. On the other hand, the monostructural approach can produce a progressive growth of student confidence if the teacher knows how to capitalize on the strengths of the system. For at each step the student knows what he is doing and why. Ideally, he also knows how to *apply* all the vocabulary and grammar he has learned. At each step the emphasis is upon application of generalizations rather than upon rote memorization. Moreover, learning is cumulative, and most new vocabulary can therefore be integrated into the prelearned system of structures. Theoretically, the association of new material with old should improve the retention of both.

Phonology and overlearning

In the native speaker, phonology might well be explained in terms of stimulus-response conditioning. The tongue, lips, and lungs appear to function automatically to produce those vibrations in the air which carry meaning to the ear of anyone who belongs to the same speech community. At the same time nonphonemic sounds are automatically avoided. The monolingual speaker does not have to decide, for example, between the trilled *r* of Spanish, the uvular *r* of French and German, or the retroflex *r* of English. The native speaker simply uses the sound system he was raised with. Pronunciation problems do arise by accident or occur when a speaker attempts to modify the language of his childhood to conform to what he believes is a higher-status dialect. Thus, in the forties, an announcer introduced a radio play on a national network by saying, "Tonight we bring you that popular musical, 'Noo Meeoon.'"

He had intended to pronounce the word "New" using the "elegant" vowel of an east-coast dialect, which would differentiate between the vowels in "new" and "moon." Instead, he inadvertently reversed the sounds using the pronunciation of "new" which was standard in his midwestern dialect and transforming "moon" into a caterwauling sound which belonged to no American dialect whatever. Accidentally garbled or misplaced phonemes can be amusing. For example, there is the story of a general who pompously announced to his troops that "We will deliver the enemy a *blushing crow*." (He meant to deliver, of course, a *"crushing blow."*) But while such phonemic and allaphonic misplacements, humorous or otherwise, occur rarely with native speakers, they are a constant plague to the person who has imperfect command of a second language. For, in addition to all the problems involved in selecting meaning, vocabulary, word order, word endings, and the like, the nonnative is constantly fighting the interference of his native sound system. This writer has observed that interference in the area of phonology becomes strongest when the nonnative speaker is fatigued or under emotional stress. Thus, when accuracy is most important (such as when meeting influential people or when addressing a large audience), mistakes in phonology are most apt to occur. For example, the author has heard South Americans use the words "bitch" and "bowels" when they meant to say "beach" and "vowels." The results were embarrassing both to the speaker and to the audience. What is worse, the speaker of Spanish does not know what he has done wrong and the American listener is often unable to explain it to him.

It would seem, therefore, that in the teaching of phonology a strong case can be made for overlearning correct responses to the extent that all *combinations* of conflict-point phonemes are made part of the second-language habit system. It must be emphasized that certain *combinations* of phonemes are more difficult than phonemes in isolation. For example, many students of Spanish learn the single-flap *r* in the word *toro* with relative ease, but are unable to pronounce the same *r*-sound in the high-frequency lexical item *tarde*. In some cases, simple explanations and devices help the student to contort his speech organs into the positions needed for correct articulation. Below are a few examples of commonly used devices.

1. Using approximate English points of articulation

Example A

PROBLEM: German initial [ts] as in *zehn*

SOLUTION: (1) Pronounce the phrase "cats and dogs."

(2) Omit *ca*, and pronounce the remnant *"ts and dogs"* until fluent.

(3) Transfer English utterance to meaningful German phrases:

zehn Männer

Zehn und eins ist elf.

Der Zug ist schon hier.

Example B

PROBLEM: Spanish word *tarde*

SOLUTION: (1) Pronounce the English word "totter" closely followed by the word "they" (i.e., "totter-they").

(2) Practice, noting, if necessary, the tongue positions behind upper teeth and then between teeth.

(3) Drill in meaningful contexts from simple to difficult expressions:

Es muy tarde.

por la tarde

Buenas tardes

todas las tardes

2. Using approximate target-language points of articulation

Example A

PROBLEM: German uvular [r]

SOLUTION: (1) Pronounce German word *Hau* with force of articulation directed far back against roof of mouth until uvular vibration is created.

(2) Say *Hau-Frau* repeatedly until *r*-sound is produced in the word *Frau*.

(3) Repeat the process with other words (e.g., *Heu-freu*, etc.)

Psychology and language learning: motivation and method

(4) Use in meaningful utterances:
Das ist <u>Frau</u> Schmidt.
Es <u>freut</u> mich.

Example B
PROBLEM: French uvular [r]
SOLUTION: The above procedure could be followed with *hâle-râle.*

3. Using charts and diagrams

Example A. Charts of speech organs
Some students find it helpful to see a cutaway view of the oral cavity so that they can locate the correct points of articulation for subsequent practice on the difficult sounds. (It is desirable for the teacher to have a fairly good knowledge of the phonetics and phonemics of the native and target languages before attempting such an approach.)

Example B. Intonation diagrams
Increasingly, the new texts indicate foreign language intonation patterns with lines, dots, or music-like scales. These diagrams can be helpful, especially in conjunction with taped native voices.

At this point a word of caution seems in order regarding the dangers of overexplaining phonology. Diagrams and mnemonic devices are valuable only insofar as they enable the student to *locate* the points of articulation for the problem phonemes. His skill in *manipulating* the phonemes automatically whenever he speaks is the final measure of his control of those phonemes. And the acquisition of this skill seems to call for a great deal of rote memorization and overlearning. However, this appears to be in conflict with other aspects of language learning. For there is some evidence to the effect that rote learning of stereotyped responses actually interferes with the process of free application of language structures.[1]

There are a number of ways to minimize the negative effects of overlearning. The following two are most common.

[1] Wilga M. Rivers, *The Psychologist and the Foreign Language Teacher,* Chicago, University of Chicago Press, 1964, p. 67.

Select expressions which contain the desired phoneme combinations, but which also are nonparadigmatic. These are expressions which function more or less as conditioned responses in the target language. For example, in American-English:

Sure enough!   See you later.
You bet!   That's for sure.
How do you do?   What's new?
Hello.   Okay.
Not yet.

Most of the above expressions either do not fit a pattern or else their essential meaning will change if they are placed in a pattern. For example, it is possible to set up a paradigm:

How do I do?   How do we do?
How does he do?   How do they do?
How does she do?

But none of these are semantic variants of the greeting "How do you do," used when one American is introduced to another. "How do you do" is a complete, self-contained, stereotyped response which may justifiably be taught to a foreign student of English simply because the phrase can be used repeatedly in precisely that form whenever the student is introduced to an American or Englishman. The expression can therefore be used, not only for its own value, but also to teach certain phonemes which it contains.

USE OF IRREGULAR FORMS

Similarly, an entire class of irregular forms can be used to teach phonology if there are not too many of them. Forms which deviate from a main pattern tend to require rote, memorization rather than extension of a pattern. Thus, in Spanish the familiar singular commands would serve:

Utterance	Examples of phonemes
Ten cuidado.	frontal [t], intervocalic [d]
Ven acá.	bilabial consonant

Psychology and language learning: motivation and method

Also in German, the *ich* and *ach* sounds could be taught in conjunction with an irregular familiar-singular command form:

Benimm dich gut.
Nimm dich in Acht.

Even a quotation from Goethe could be used to present a number of problem phonemes (e.g., *l, r, ch*).

"Edel sei der Mensch
Hilfreich und gut."

Other pat expressions containing irregular singular commands can serve the double purpose of learning high-frequency vocabulary along with essential sounds.

In French, the following irregular or stereotyped forms contain problem sounds such as the contrast between *ou* and *u*, the nasal *ent* liaison between *comment* and *allez*, syllabification, and intonation.

Comment_a llez-vous?
Viens ici.
Où vas-tu?

If a course of study is carefully planned, the more difficult phonemes will be introduced gradually lesson by lesson. It would seem as unwise to cluster all the conflict sounds in the first few lessons as it would to begin a diving class by expecting novice students to execute a jackknife from the highboard. Phonology is clearly the most difficult aspect of language learning for the adolescent and postadolescent learner. (Few late learners of a second language ever eliminate all traces of first-language phonemes even decades after having mastered the morphology and syntax of the adopted language.)

Phonology and FLES

It appears that small children in the school environment are able to learn phonology better than adults (see Chapter 4), but are less able in the areas of morphology and syntax. Thus, the elementary-school foreign language program would seem to be justifiable only if this aspect of language learning shows good results. Certainly a FLES program which produces substandard pronunciation is of questionable value. Therefore, although the small children may sing songs, play games, engage in folk dancing, and present playlets, the adults directing the enterprise must be aware that the underlying purpose of the FLES program, insofar as foreign language education is concerned, is to develop good habits of pronunciation. Parents and high-school language teachers should be quite satisfied with a FLES program if it accomplishes little more than good control of the "problem" phonemes, learned within a limited framework of vocabulary items and grammatical structures. (Also, see Chapter 4.)

Overlearning morphology and syntax

It appears that the muscular reactions of the speech organs must be trained by some process of conditioning to contort rapidly into those unaccustomed positions which are necessary to produce the sounds of the target language understandably and without hesitation. Long hours of student practice must be devoted to correct positioning of tongue and lips with regard to the problem sounds. Exhaustive drill work must then follow until all phoneme combinations can be produced without effort and without conscious thought. It seems that a relatively large number of language educators can accept noncognitive training where phonology is concerned. However, there are fewer who would agree that grammar as well as phonology should be learned "out of awareness." Yet a number of influential language educators look upon the learning of grammatical forms as a process of conditioning. For example, Robert Lado contends that the student's attention should actually be drawn *away* from the problem structure during certain kinds of drill work.

This may seem paradoxical, but it is in effect a highly important feature of pattern practice. When the student expects a change at the crucial point, his attention is upon it, and his habit system is not involved. By fixing the attention elsewhere, the teacher forces the student to focus his attention away from the crucial point, and to carry the pattern increasingly through habit responses.[2]

[2] Robert Lado, *Language Teaching: A Scientific Approach*, McGraw-Hill, 1964, p. 106.

Psychology and language learning: motivation and method

In direct opposition to Lado's opinion is a statement by Paul Glande: "Should we not adopt as a cardinal principle that the student be kept aware of each structural point throughout drill on this point?"[3] Both men are prominent foreign language educators, yet one appears to believe that awareness of structure interferes with the development of oral proficiency while the other indicates that awareness is essential to the development of such proficiency. Behavioristic psychological theories favor the first view on the grounds that human reaction time is not swift enough to allow a cognitive process to regulate the flow of rapid speech. However, proponents of the cognitive theory contend that speech is far too complex to be explained by a series of conditioned responses alone. Thought processes must precede the actual production of speech according to this hypothesis, with desired word order and grammatical structures being determined in advance, then stored momentarily in the brain's "memory banks," and finally being released as needed to sustain the rapid flow of conversation. This theory would perhaps account for what happens when a person is interrupted midway through a statement and then is unable later to pick up the thread of conversation. The chain of thought making way for subsequent articulation is broken and replaced by a different, unrelated sequence of ideas. The speaker cannot resume until he reestablishes the severed link in the chain of thoughts which had been directing his speech. The interruption of simple habitual activities does not ordinarily cause this type of confusion. The person who has been interrupted simply continues automatically with what he had been doing. The expert swimmer, for example, whose path is crossed by a moving row boat, simply stops and treads water for a moment and then swims on when the path is clear. The stroke-kick sequence which the swimmer resumes automatically can be plausibly accounted for as a series of conditioned reflexes. But spontaneous conversation is hardly in the same category. The swimmer does not invent new strokes as he goes along; his reaction pattern is fixed and recurrent. When two people are speaking freely on the same general topic (as opposed to reciting from memory as in a play) a

[3] Quoted from the introduction of the bulletin, *Curricular Change in the Foreign Languages,* College Entrance Examination Board, 1963, p. x.

much more complex and amazingly rapid process of decoding and encoding takes place. That is, each participant in a free conversation must receive an auditory message which he then reacts to by producing his own appropriate message orally. Among other things, this response involves:

1. Deciding upon meaning to be conveyed.
2. Selecting suitable vocabulary from a vast repertoire of items.
3. Determining word order, word endings, and word forms.
4. Articulating the sounds in such a manner as to produce an intelligible message.

In this regard, Lambert believes that a thought process runs several steps ahead of the actual production of the message. Taking his cue from the theory of brain-cell assemblies developed by Hebb, Lambert comments:

Apparently some word ordering and grammatical sequencing must first be decided on, then rapidly scanned and found appropriate, and finally set in motion while active thought moves on ahead to the next phase. This whole chain of processes is remarkably fast and "automatic" in the native speaker, making a sharp contrast with the novice in a language who slows the process way down and makes evident to listeners that his thought and speech are running nearly in parallel.[4]

Following the implications of such cognitive theories, one could conclude that the student should first understand the grammatical generalization before he aims at rapidity of response. That is, he should begin by mastering very short utterances in patterns whose functions he comprehends completely. The longer and more complex utterances would be developed through a similar grasp of the general principles upon which the structures are built. All drill work would involve a conscious understanding of the underlying generalizations. Also, drill exercises would require intellectual alertness; they would force the student to respond orally to unanticipated stimuli which require him to make basic structural changes almost instantly. To the cognitive theorist, language learning is problem solving. And conversation skill is achieved by speeding up the

[4] Wallace E. Lambert, "Psychological Approaches to the Study of Language," *Modern Language Journal*, XLVII (February 1963), 58–59.

problem-solving process, not by by-passing it. Thus the cognitive theorists tend to disagree with the practice of having students memorize entire blocks of basic-dialog material from the very beginning of the course; there are simply too many underlying generalizations for the student to grasp. And if he is articulating without thinking, little or no language learning is taking place above the level of phonological training. To support this contention, advocates of the cognitive-code learning theory point to recent studies of how small children learn their first language. These studies of infant language learning seem to indicate that a child does not acquire language by imitating complete utterances from adult speech. Instead he appears to draw selected lexical items from the language environment and to manipulate these items according to simple grammatical rules. Thus, according to this line of thought, the fractured language called "baby talk" is different from adult speech precisely because the child is following basic—if somewhat primitive—patterns in applying his limited repertoire of words. His ability to combine these items into all sorts of nonadult patterns indicates that he is applying rational principles rather than merely imitating adult speech. The fact that he can form hundreds of meaningful utterances from a few dozen words seems to attest to that fact.[5] A number of linguists suspect that children possess an innate capacity for producing the basic structures of language. For example, McNeill comments "that the general form taken by grammatical rules and the general distinction between rules of formation and rules of transformation are part of children's linguistic capacity. . . . Indeed, it is possible that all the linguistic universals are part of the general capacity to acquire language; at least, this has been argued by Chomsky (1965) and Katz ·(1965)."[6]

The traditionalist grammarian will often leap upon any shred of evidence to the effect that language learning is a rational process

[5] David McNeill, "Some Thoughts on First and Second Language Acquisition," from a paper presented to the Modern Foreign Language Title III NDEA Conference, Washington, D.C., May 24, 1965. Preparation of this report was supported in part by a grant from the National Institutes of Health, No. 5–TI–GM 1011–03 to Harvard University, Center for Cognitive Studies.
[6] *Ibid.*, p. 28.

and use this to justify the learning of prescriptive grammatical rules. Yet in effect what he is often advocating is the replacement of one kind of rote memorization with another. In terms of student boredom, the memorization of grammatical rules, conjugations, and word lists can be at least as deadly as the memorization of unrelated dialog sentences. And furthermore, the memorization of grammatical rules appears to have negligible influence upon actual communication. This has been a well-known fact among educators in the field of English for half a century. Generations of American youngsters have been subjected to long years of memorizing rules about the evils of double negation, misuse of *will* and *shall*, and the "wrong" use of *I* and *me*. Yet as virulent as ever are expressions such as:

I don't have no book.
I will be there later.
It's me; me and John.

At the other extreme from rule learning is an approach which calls for the learning of patterns without conscious analysis. In support of nonanalysis, it is often pointed out that small children can produce most of the structures of their native language but are unable to explain the underlying rule for the operation of those structures. Even more significant, they can creatively apply the rules to unanticipated situations. For example, any normal 5-year-old can demonstrate his control of grammar in test situations such as the following:

ADULT: Today I am glinging. I did the same thing yesterday; What did I do?
CHILD: You glinged. (Or, "You glung.")
ADULT: (Holding up picture of an imaginary creature.) This is a gick. Now I have two of them; what do I have?
CHILD: You have two gicks.

The first reply shows that the child has mastered the system for changing regular verbs to the past tense. The second example demonstrates an ability to form regular plurals. The fact that the student can perform these operations with nonsense words proves that he has not merely memorized the forms from the adult speech

Psychology and language learning: motivation and method

community. The child has never heard of a "gick" nor has he ever seen anyone "glinging." At age 5 he has also not been introduced to the grammatical folklore that nouns are "the name of a person, place or thing" and that verbs show "action or state of being." Yet he quite correctly and instantly treats "gick" as a noun and "gling" as a verb. Similarly, a German 5-year-old would have no trouble answering the first question in his language with,

Sie haben geglingt. *or* Sie haben geglungen.

A Mexican child could easily answer the second question with,

Vd. tiene dos guiques.

In both languages a child unhesitatingly will select the culturally acceptable pronouns (*Sie* instead of *du; Vd.* instead of *tu*) and will use word forms, word endings, and word order as the situation demands. In fact, it appears that all normal children develop this ability to integrate new (or imaginary) lexical items into the native language system which they have largely mastered audio-lingually during the first five years of life. This ability for instant analogy will sometimes lead them astray (e.g., "He brung it," or "I don't got any"), but in the great majority of cases, the preschool child has developed a listen-speak communications system which is infinitely expandable to all the tens of thousands of vocabulary items which exist in his language and those which will later be created during his lifetime.

In the early stages of second-language learning, a basic problem is that of getting the young adult or adolescent to acquire at least a rough approximation of the analogizing skill of a 5-year-old. Proponents of the American Method generally advocate an inductive approach to the learning of grammar as the best method for developing this automatic control of base structure. This approach requires the student first to manipulate basic structures, secondly to arrive at the underlying generalizations relative to how they function, and thirdly to apply the generalizations to create new sentences for expressing what he wants to say. The student is permitted to phrase the generalizations in his own words so long as his grasp of concepts is accurate and functional. In fact, he is not tested on his ability to conceptualize but rather upon his ability to produce acceptable word forms and word sequences. There are some modern methodologists who feel that the inductive approach to learning grammar is often slow and inefficient. They feel that it is sometimes better simply to give the student the rule or generalization, and let him get down to the business of drilling upon the structure in question. As a matter of plain fact, there is no body of research to prove which approach is more effective. In the next section, we have provided an opportunity for the reader to examine sample lessons illustrating both approaches and to learn several structures of a second language using both processes. The first lesson is one in which the learner helps to formulate his own rules; in the second lesson the rule is given to him in advance. The language used is a modified form of Esperanto which we will call ME for simplicity. The problem of providing foreign language examples is a complex one. If the reader already has learned the language which is used for illustrative purposes, he very often will be unable to appreciate the difficulties encountered by the novice learner of that language. The same applies to examples given in English where most of the readers are native Americans. To overcome such difficulties, foreign language methods teachers often employ a "shock" language which the students must learn (in part) so that they experience the psychological problem of coping with an entirely unfamiliar language. Quite often a seldom-taught modern language is used. For the purposes of this book it was felt that an invented language would be adequate.

Approaches to learning grammatical generalizations— two sample lessons

The sole purpose of the following lessons in Modified Esperanto is to give the reader an opportunity to experience the two most common ways of presenting grammatical principles. This invented language was chosen in the belief that few readers would be familiar with it. Therefore, the value of this section would be somewhat reduced for a person who has already studied Esperanto. Since this section is not intended to illustrate other aspects of methodology, a number of shortcuts have been taken for the sake of efficiency. First, it is assumed that the phonology of the target language (Modified Esperanto) is identical with the phonology of English; a situation which never actually occurs in second-language learning. (However, phonology has been treated earlier and its reentry at this point would have produced needless complications.) Secondly, translation is used to a degree which would be unacceptable to many methodologists. Thirdly, an artificial, overly regular language has been used as a model. And finally, since the classroom situation obviously cannot be recreated in a book, it was necessary to employ a somewhat limited programming device. Despite these limitations, it is possible for the reader to follow the main steps of the inductive process and to gain some indication of how a creative teacher might use this process to draw generalizations from students in a live classroom situation.

LESSON I. *Grammar learned inductively*

Step One: *Learning the pattern without analysis*

To approximate the learning of a structure drill and to acquire the necessary minimal vocabulary, the reader may wish to learn the seven sentences in Step One. The Modified Esperanto sentences (hereafter referred to as ME) can be studied first in association with the English, then with the ME sentences covered by a card or folded sheet of paper. The sentences can be considered learned when the reader is able to produce them orally in 35 seconds by referring only to the English. English pronunciation can be used with the ME words, but care must be taken to get all endings and word forms correct. There should be no special effort to analyze the sentences at this time. The method calls for learning a pattern without prior analysis.

1. The lady is sitting on the chair.
   _____ *(On each problem place a card on the dash line until after you have responded. Then check your answer.)*
   La sinyorino sidas sur la sajo.
2. The teacher is sitting on the chair.

   _____
   La instruisto sidas sur la sajo.

3. The student is sitting on the chair.

La lernanto sidas sur la sajo.

4. The boy is sitting on the chair.

La knabo sidas sur la sajo.

5. The salesman is sitting on the chair.

La vendisto sidas sur la sajo.

6. The secretary is sitting on the chair.

La secretarino sidas sur la sajo.

7. The girl is sitting on the chair.

La knabino sidas sur la sajo.

Step Two: Learning generalizations about nouns

1. In the seven sentences above there were eight nouns; say them (or write them) and then check your answers:
lady, chair, teacher, student, boy, salesman, secretary, girl.
---------------- *(Remember to place card at dash line.)*
sinyorino, sajo, instruisto, lernanto, knabo, vendisto, secretarino, knabino.

2. What do all these nouns have in common? Before responding, find *two* unique characteristics. Then check your answers below.

The eight nouns end with the vowel *o*.
The eight nouns are all preceded by the word *la*. (*La* is roughly equivalent to the English article *the*.)

Step Three: Application of generalizations about nouns

Complete the following sentences and check your answers.

1. ___ bird ___ sidas sur la sajo. (The bird is sitting on the chair.)

La birdo sidas sur la sajo.

2. ___ hund ___ sidas sur la sajo. (The dog is sitting on the chair.)

La hundo sidas sur la sajo.

Psychology and language learning: motivation and method

3. ___ kat ___ sidas sur la sajo. (The cat is sitting on the chair.)

La kato sidas sur la sajo.

4. ___ knabin ___ sidas sur la sajo. (The girl is sitting on the chair.)

La knabino sidas sur la sajo.

Note: If all answers were correct in step three, you have achieved excellent control of the definite article and the nominative case of ME nouns.

Step Four: Learning verbs without analysis.

Using the directions given in Step One, learn the sentences below.

1. The bird is flying. (flies, does fly)

La birdo flugas.

2. The dog is barking. (barks, does bark)

La hundo boyas.

3. The cat is mewing (mews, does mew)

La kato miowas.

4. The salesgirl is chattering. (chatters, does chatter)

La vendistino babilas.

5. The student is studying. (studies, does study)

La lernanto studas.

6. The fish is swimming. (swims, does swim)

La fisho najas.

Step Five: Learning generalizations about verbs.

1. In the six ME sentences above there were six verbs; say them or write them, and then check your answers:
   fly, bark, mew, chatter, study, swim.

----

flugas, boyas, miowas, babilas, studas, najas.

2. To what kind of actions do these verbs refer: to present actions? to past actions? or to future actions?

The verbs refer to present actions.

142

3. What do all these verbs have in common?

_____

The verbs all end in *as*.

4. In the ME language, the forms *flug-, boy-, miow-, babil-, stud-, naj-*, are called verb stems. What must be done to these stems to make them refer to actions taking place at the present time?

_____

To make verb stems refer to the present time, merely add *as*.

5. Complete the following sentence:
La lernanto stud ___. (The student is studying.)

_____

La lernanto studas.

6. Express the ME equivalent of the following English sentence:
The student studies.

_____

La lernanto studas.

7. Express the ME equivalent of the following English sentence:
The student does study.

_____

La lernanto studas.

8. In summary, it can be stated that the _____ language has three verb forms to refer to present actions while the _____ language has only one verb form for present action.

_____

The English language has three verb forms . . . while the ME language has only one form to refer to present actions.

9. The ME language expresses present actions by adding _____ to the verb _____.

_____

by adding *as* to the verb *stem*.

Step Six: Using generalizations to create new combinations

At this point, the reader who has mastered all the material in steps one through six will be able to form dozens of new sentences simply by applying the generalizations to the vocabulary items. Some of the combinations which are grammatically feasible would have to be rejected because they would be semantically unacceptable (e.g., *La fisho studas*). However, most of the nouns can be combined with most of the verbs, and many of the people and animals could be made to sit on one another instead of sitting only on the chair. In ME it is simply a matter of filling in the pattern: *La* _____ *sidas sur la* _____. Occasionally,

Psychology and language learning: motivation and method

absurdity can be employed to advantage. For example, if the teacher would say, *"La instruisto sidas sur la birdo,"* and the students responded by laughing, then it can be assumed that a number of students understood what was said. Ideally, however, the teaching process would not be restricted only to the passive listening-reading skills. For communication to take place, the student must also learn to make his own reapplications in the active speaking-writing skill areas. One device for eliciting free application of generalizations from the student is to show him a series of pictures which he can comment upon using only the vocabulary and knowledge of grammar at his disposal. This frees the student from dependence upon the native language and helps to minimize the effects of interference from English. Another technique is to use English to describe a situation which the student is asked to comment upon rather than to translate. The reader who has mastered the vocabulary in steps one and four can now test his ability to apply his knowledge about the ME language by supplying oral responses in ME to the situations described below. A reasonable oral fluency has been achieved if the five sentences can be completed correctly in 60 seconds.

Using a simple sentence tell what each person is doing in the pictures below. In number 4, the actor will be a fish.
(Remember to place a shield card at the dash line and to check each response for correctness.)

    1. Comment on what he is doing.

La knabo najas.

2. Describe what he is doing.

La vendisto babilas.

3. Comment.

La knabino sidas sur la hundo.

Psychology and language learning: motivation and method

4. Comment.

La fiŝo flugas.

5. Tell what she is doing.

La knabino studas.

6. Comment.

La vendistino sidas sur la sajo.

LESSON II. Grammar by application of rules

To simplify this section we have drawn mainly upon prelearned vocabulary. Also, the format will change to the more traditional presentation of word lists and rules for application to the vocabulary items. This procedure should enable the reader to understand the two approaches more clearly, and to begin to form opinions about the pedagogical value of each.

Step One: Presentation of grammatical generalization

Learn the following rules, from the teacher or the text, regarding nouns, verbs, and adjectives in ME.

Rule one: In the ME language, all nouns in the objective case add the ending *n*.

The dog bites the boy.	La hundo mordas la <u>knabon</u>.
The teacher helps the student.	La instruisto helpas la <u>lernanton</u>.

Rule two: In ME all nouns and adjectives form their plurals by adding *y*.

The train is full.	La vagonaro estas plena.
The trains are full.	La vagonaroy estas plenay.

Psychology and language learning: motivation and method

Rule three: Note that verbs do not change form in the plural.
Rule four: Singular adjectives end with *a*, plural adjectives with *ay*.
Rule five: All adjectives in the objective case add *n*.
Rule six: ME omits the use of the indefinite articles (a, an).

Step Two: Learning vocabulary

Memorize the following words, and review the vocabulary from previous lessons.

vagonaro–train
granda–big
plena–full
saga–wise
ni–we

estas–am, is, are
havas–have, has
helpas–help, helps
mordas–bite, bites

Step Three: Learning the paradigms

Memorize the following noun and adjective declensions.

	Nominative case	Objective case
Singular nouns	vagonaro	vagonaron
	hundo	hundon
	birdo	birdon
Plural nouns	vagonaroy	vagonarony
	hundoy	hundony
	birdoy	birdony

	Nominative case	Objective case
Singular adjectives	granda	grandan
	plena	plenan
	saga	sagan
Plural adjectives	granday	grandany
	plenay	plenany
	sagay	sagany

Step Four: Drill exercises involving the new grammatical forms

Fill in the blanks in the sentences on the left. Check your answers by progressively uncovering the correct responses given on the right.

(Place shield at dash line)

1. La knabo havas _____
   (a cat)

   katon

148

2. La vendistino havas _____

          (a dog)

hundon

3. La hundo mordas _____

          (the boy)

- - - - - - - - - -
la knabon

4. La kata mordas _____

          (the girl)

- - - - - - - - - -
la knabinon

5. La knabino helpas _____

          (the teacher)

- - - - - - - - - - -
la instruiston

6. Ni haves _____

          (trains)

- - - - - - - - - -
vagonarony

7. La kato mordas _____

          (the birds)

- - - - - - - - - -
la birdony

8. Ni helpas _____

          (the teachers)

- - - - - - - - - - -
la instruistony

9. La instruistoy helpas _____

          (the students)

- - - - - - - - - - -
la lernantony

10. La instruistoy estas _____

          (wise)

- - - - - - - - -
sagay

11. La vagonaroy estas _____

          (full)

- - - - - - - - -
plenay

12. La knaboy estas _____

          (big)

- - - - - - - - -
granday

13. Ni havas _____

          (wise teachers)

- - - - - - - - - - - - - - -
sagany instruistony

14. Ni havas _____

          (big trains)

- - - - - - - - - - - - - - - -
grandany vagonarony

15. Ni helpas _____

          (wise students)

- - - - - - - - - - - - - - -
sagany lernantony

16. La knabo estas _____

          (big)

- - - - - - - - -
granda

17. La sinyorino estas _____

          (wise)

- - - - - - - - -
saga

18. Ni havas _____

          (a wise teacher)

- - - - - - - - - - -
sagan instruiston

19. La kato mordas _____

          (a big dog)

- - - - - - - - - - -
grandan hundon

20. La vagonaro estas _____

          (big)

- - - - - - - - -
granda

Psychology and language learning: motivation and method

Step Five: Drilling all forms through translation

Translate the following sentences applying what you have learned in steps one, two, three, and four. Check your answers.

1. The boy has a train.

   La knabo havas vagonaron.

2. The boys have a train.

   La knaboy havas vagonaron.

3. The boys have the dogs.

   La knaboy havas la hundony.

4. We are big boys.

   Ni estas granday knaboy.

5. We help the big boys.

   Ni helpas la grandany knabony.

Step Six: Testing application of rules to vocabulary

Translate the following sentences into ME. Check your answers.

1. The dogs are biting the big boys.

   La hundoy mordas la grandany knabony.

2. The cat is biting the dog.

   La kato mordas la hundon.

3. The cats have the fish. (singular)

   La katoy havas la fishon.

4. The teacher is helping the girls.

   La instruisto helpas la knabinony.

5. The girls are wise.

   La knabinoy estas sagay.

6. We have a full train.

   Ni havas plenan vagonaron.

150

7. We have big trains.

   Ni havas grandany vagonarony.
8. The birds are sitting on the trains.

   La birdoy sidas sur la vagonaroy.
9. A wise student helps the teacher.
   Saga lernanto helpas la instruiston.
10. We have big fish. (plural)

    Ni havas grandany fishony.

Rule memorization versus learning by induction and analogy

Anyone who has spent an hour or more on the sample lessons should be able to read hundreds of simple ME sentences and be able to produce a few dozen simple written sentences. According to advocates of the American Method, the reader should have found the first approach clearer and intellectually more stimulating than the second. To the traditionalist, on the other hand, the second approach is superior because the student has the rules and vocabulary available from the outset. Therefore he knows what he is doing at all times and can cover a great deal more material if he is only willing to work hard and to concentrate upon applying the rules to the vocabulary. As a matter of fact, both approaches appear to work equally well in actual practice if nothing more than the acquisition of the four language skills is taken into account. We will subsequently discuss other aspects of inductive learning versus rule application. First, however, a few words must be said about a third approach, namely one in which the student's attention is never drawn to the underlying generalizations either by means of induction or by rule. This is an extremely important point, because many teachers have assumed that students will automatically grasp grammatical principles and see relationships without having them pointed out. In the two ME lessons, a generalization was "seeded" into the drill material, but no rule was supplied for it, and no pattern drill or paradigm was set up to illustrate it. Thus, if the reader has grasped this "hidden" rule as he went through the sample lessons, he will at this point be able to supply ME words for "gentleman," "bitch," and "female cat," among others. Further, if told that the word "frato" means "brother," the reader should now be able to produce the word "sister" by simple application of principles he has already been exposed to. Chances are, however, that the generalization was not grasped by most readers simply because it was not pointed out in the lesson. If the principle has not been grasped, it should become evident in the first four exercises given below. By drawing simple analogies, the reader should be able to fill in all twelve blanks in items 2–7 below.

1. knabo	(boy)	knabino	(girl)
2. _____	( )	sinyorino	(lady)
3. hundo	(male dog)	_____	( )
4. kato	(tom cat)	_____	( )
5. _____	( )	onklino	(aunt)
6. frato	(brother)	_____	( )
7. patro	(father)	_____	( )

The simple analogizing power, which appears to operate below the level of consciousness in small children, can also operate with adults, although it may require the support of conscious analysis. Many adults and adolescents seem to feel the need to verbalize what they are doing and why they are doing it. In any case, the process of analogy should have produced the following answers to the above exercises:

2. sinyoro (gentleman)
3. hundino (bitch)
4. katino (female cat)
5. onklo (uncle)
6. fratino (sister)
7. patrino (mother)

If the reader now knows how to take the word for "Frenchman" (*Franco* and change it to to mean "Frenchwoman" or transform the words "cow elephant" (*elefantino*) to mean "bull elephant," then the main lesson has been learned. Should a generalization regarding ME suffixes then be added as a means of consolidating what has been learned? Or should the rule about the masculine suffix -*o* and the feminine suffix -*ino* have been given in the first place, perhaps along with comparable English word pairs such as prince/princess, host/hostess, etc.? Or should the teacher merely proceed to the next lesson without making it clear to the student that all feminines are indicated by the *-ino* suffix and that all masculines and genderless nouns are indicated by the *-o* suffix? The weight of opinion in the field of educational psychology seems to favor the learning of generalizations rather than the mere learning of patterns. One psychologist quite emphatically states that "the teacher must . . . abandon outright that Herbartian variety of teaching, in which after the examination of a considerable number of concrete instances, the solution is assumed to roll out into clear sight . . . and to wait not for validation but only for 'application.' "[7] Thus, if it is generally agreed that generalizations must be learned, then the question becomes one of how best to learn them. A number of studies in foreign languages and other academic areas have attempted to answer the question as to whether better learning results are achieved by the application of memorized rules or by the application of generalizations which the student has learned to formulate by himself. Is it best for the teacher to give a clear initial statement of the generalization so that the student understands what the drill work is all about? Or should the student first learn some specific examples from which he formulates his own generalizations for application to the subsequent drill work? One of the most elaborate studies ever conducted in the field of foreign language learning focussed specifically upon this problem. The control group used the traditional rule-application approach. With the experimental group, however, the investigators report that grammar was taught after the fact, "and such generalization was never attempted before functional practice with new principles. However, nothing in our directives to the instructors barred them from helping students to organize grammar, so long as this organization was made in retrospect."[8] At the end of the four-semester experiment, the 101 control students were not significantly different from the

[7] R. R. Palmer, "Straight and Crooked Thinking," in L. D. and A. Crow, eds., *Readings in Human Learning*, New York, David McKay, 1963, p. 399.
[8] George Scherer and Michael Wertheimer, *A Psycholinguistic Experiment in Foreign-Language Teaching*, New York, McGraw-Hill, 1964, pp. 85–86.

128 experimental students in terms of overall proficiency in the four skills. The experimental audiolingual group did show better attitudes toward the foreign language and culture and were able to associate meaning more directly in the target language. However, all measures of the ability to read, write, speak, and understand the foreign language indicated no significant overall difference between the audiolingual and the traditional groups.[9] Other studies of the effectiveness of rule application versus inductive formulation of principles tend to follow the same pattern where the learning of skills is concerned. For example, in a study of different ways to learn to read Chinese characters, it was found that the symbols could be learned equally well and with equal rapidity by either approach.[10] One study in the field of science showed that better results were achieved if students were allowed to formulate their own concepts when compared to students who had learned the same material by rote memorization and verbalization of definitions.[11] However, other studies relating to the learning of skills in chemistry and arithmetic have indicated that students learned equally well by the rule-application method.[12] One investigator felt, however, that since both approaches worked equally well, it would be desirable for students to have the additional experience in learning generalizations. In the final analysis, it appears that the inclination toward the inductive process for learning generalizations is based more upon the belief that it is an important educational experience in itself rather than upon any proof that it is conducive to better learning of the language skills. The idea that the learner should discover by himself a large fraction of the material to be learned is at least as old as the "Socratic method." Lichtenberg, an eighteenth-century German physicist, endorsed the inductive approach

[9] *Ibid.*, p. 245.
[10] C. L. Hall, "The Evolution of Concepts," in L. D. and A. Crow., eds., *Readings in Human Learning*, New York, David McKay, 1963, pp. 119–133.
[11] W. R. Hatch and Ann Bennett, *New Dimensions in Higher Education, No. 2: Effectiveness in Teaching*, Washington, D.C., U.S. Government Printing Office, 1963, p. 22.
[12] Frances Colville, "The Learning of Motor Skills as Influenced by Knowledge of Mechanical Principles," in L. D. and A. Crow, eds., *Readings in Human Learning*, New York, David McKay, 1963, p. 376.

when he wrote: "What you have been obliged to discover by your-self leaves a path in your mind which you can use again when the need arises." Similarly, Immanuel Kant in his *Critique of Pure Reason* stated that "Learning begins with action and perception, proceeds from thence to words and concepts, and should end in desirable mental habits." And, more recently, there is John Dewey who is often unfairly associated with certain abuses of the learning-by-doing approach to education. In reality, Dewey was as opposed to meaningless physical activity as he was to sterile, disembodied mental activity. In his book, *Democracy and Education*, Dewey comments that "Mere activity does not constitute experience. . . . Experience as trying involves change, but change is meaningless transition unless it is consciously connected with the return wave of consequences which flow from it."[13] Thus, according to Dewey, the actual "doing" is a step which must take place prior to or in connection with learning, because "the discernment of relationships is the genuinely intellectual matter; hence the educative matter. The failure arises in supposing that relationships can become per-ceptible without experience. . . ."[14]

In the minds of many great thinkers of the western world it would not be a question of which approach developed the best control of language skills. Instead, the value of the entire language-learning process would be seriously questioned if it were to con-sist merely of applying rules for the purposes of developing skills and gaining knowledge. For, as Dewey expressed it, "Acquiring is always secondary and instrumental to the act of inquiring. . . . While all thinking results in knowledge, ultimately the value of knowledge is subordinate to its use in thinking. For we live not in a settled and finished world, but one which is going on . . ."[15]

Proving student mastery of generalizations

In the final analysis, the value of learning generalizations must be measured by the psychological impact which that learning has upon

[13] John Dewey, *Democracy and Education*, New York, Macmillan, 1961, p. 139.
[14] *Ibid.*, p. 144.
[15] *Ibid.*, p. 151.

the student's attempts to use the foreign language when he wishes to express himself freely either orally or in writing. As far as the student's ability to communicate in the language is concerned, this is a more relevant issue than the question of whether he learned the rule by himself or had it drawn to his attention by the teacher or the textbook. The author has seen students who are unable to perceive—much less apply—grammatical generalizations even after hundreds of repetitions of pattern drills. The ability to retrieve a series of grammatical forms only in response to specific prelearned stimuli is no proof that any genuine language learning has taken place at all. If the student is unable to rearrange his repertoire of language forms in response to an unanticipated stimulus, then the value of what he has learned is questionable as far as genuine communication is concerned. At the other extreme is the student whose knowledge of generalizations prevents him from communicating effectively in the language because of the way he learned them. An example of this is the student who finds it necessary to mentally run through four forms of the future before he can say "We will." (He may have learned the forms by chanting all eight persons beginning with the first person singular and ending with third plural.) However, this does not prove that the student should not have learned the conjugation, but rather that he should not have memorized it as a numerical sequence. If he has properly grasped the concept of verb endings, then the sixth verb form in the conjugation should be just as instantly retrievable as is the first. Similarly, it does the student no harm to know that the days of the week are listed in a certain order starting with Sunday. But his learning of vocabulary has been deficient if he is compelled to count to seven on his fingers before he can say "Saturday." Fluency is destroyed if the student must mentally run through a sequentially organized system of rules, paradigms, and mnemonic devices before he can express an original thought. Thus, a student of French or Spanish may have memorized the rules for the use of the present and past subjunctive, or he may have learned them by observation and induction; further, he may be able to produce all the present subjunctive endings in conjugated form. Yet all of this has little relevance if he is unable to automatically supply the right verb form when the flow of conversation calls for a response such as:

The teacher wants you <u>to come</u> in early tomorrow,

or

I would go if I <u>had</u> the money.

Thus, testing the student's grasp of generalizations about the subjunctive must relate to his speed and accuracy in supplying correct subjunctive forms in new and unanticipated combinations of familiar verbs. Knowing the rules is no guarantee that he will apply them; but applying them spontaneously is proof that he knows them.

Aids to memorization of vocabulary

A certain amount of memorization is essential in the learning of a foreign language. Clearly the student must not invent his own vocabulary, grammatical structures, sounds, and word order sequences. Instead, he must approximate to the best of his ability the language as it is used by educated native speakers. Some foreign language teachers have interpreted this fact to mean that all the basic language material must somehow be imposed upon the learner's mind by force of repetition before he is allowed to do anything creative. To make the process of repetition more palatable, modern textbook writers have presented vocabulary in the form of natural-sounding connected dialogs which students can learn and retain more easily than isolated words out of context which were so often taught in the older traditional courses. Another aid to memory is the visual which allows the student to associate meaning directly with a colorful cartoon or photograph which is projected on a screen or which appears in a book or on a large card. But, however dramatic and impressive dramatizations and visualizations may be, they still involve the imposition of material upon the mind of the learner. Yet, if anything has been learned by decades of research in the field of learning psychology, it is that the mind is much more than a *tabula rasa* upon which knowledge is systematically imprinted by the teacher. It is quite generally agreed that optimum learning is seldom possible without positive emotional involvement on the part of the student. And the student's attitude is not likely to remain positive if he is never allowed to express his individuality.

Psychology and language learning: motivation and method

One investigator found that children could memorize word pairs more effectively if they were allowed to create their own mediators. They were instructed to learn the words by fitting them into a sentence of their own creation. A second group was told to memorize the word pairs in isolation, and a third group was given for memorization the sentences created by the first group. Finally, all three groups were tested to see which method produced the best learning results. The group which was allowed to create its own memory mediators did significantly better than the two which had the material imposed upon them. In the words of the investigator, "The chief result is, . . . that children who provide their own mediators do best—indeed, one time through a set of thirty pairs, they recover up to 95 percent of the second words when presented with the first ones of the pairs, whereas the uninstructed children reach a maximum of less than 50 percent recovered."[16] It may be that material that is organized in terms of a person's own interests and manner of thinking is material which is most likely to be recalled. In applying this principle to foreign language learning the problem is to keep the student's urge for originality within those bounds which are rather arbitrarily set by his limited knowledge of grammar, phonology, and vocabulary. Yet, if the teacher makes the students wait until they have memorized "everything," she may find that the process of rote memorization has driven them into other electives which are more intellectually stimulating.

There are teachers who have devised ways to capitalize upon the desire for originality while at the same time overcoming most of the dangers of premature use of partially learned material. One technique involves the use of "formula sentences" which enable the student to use newly acquired structures to refer to people and places within his realm of experience.

The name of my _____ is _____.
I live on _____ Street in _____, Illinois.
That car belongs to my _____, who is here on a visit from _____.
I would like my _____ to give me _____ for Christmas.
If I had a million dollars, I would _____.

[16] J. S. Bruner, "The Act of Discovery," in L. D. and A. Crow, eds., *Readings in Human Learning*, New York, David McKay, 1963, pp. 423–435.

This approach allows the student to relate what he has learned to the world as he knows it. The teacher helps to minimize error by structuring the nonpersonal aspects for the student. Theoretically the student will be more willing to learn the material because it refers uniquely to him and because he has had a hand in producing it. However, before he commits the sentences to memory, the teacher (or a native-speaking teacher aide) must check into each blank to make certain that acceptable structures have been supplied. Also, before using formula sentences, the student must have reached the point where he can write with reasonable accuracy and can read aloud without undue distortion.

As the students progress in knowledge and experience, they can be required to create the entire dialog material for themselves using current and previous lessons for models. This technique seems to work best with small groups of two or three students who first create the dialog, then check it with the teacher for accuracy, and finally present it before the class. The only limitations are that the dialog must be in keeping with the materials currently being studied, and that each member of the team must learn each role in the dialog. The experience of one teacher who uses this technique tends to confirm Bruner's thesis that students learn best when they devise their own memory mediators. As he expressed it, "I have had some success with having students construct their own dialogues. These are then memorized and presented to the class in a rather competitive fashion. I have continued it because this is one thing my students thoroughly enjoy. . . . The learning takes place during the dialogue construction. The students seem to enjoy bits of conversation long after it has been presented."[17] A further advantage of the self-produced dialogs relates to the problem of utterance length. The length of utterance which a student can retain in the foreign language is far shorter than in his native tongue. During the first few months of instruction, eight to twelve syllables are as much as most youngsters can handle. Thus, students who produce their own dialogs for recitation in front of their classmates tend to be quite realistic about sentence length. The desire to sound

[17] Arnold Schaeffer, "Conversation-Promoting Techniques Used in Secondary Modern Foreign Language Classes," *Voice of the Wisconsin Foreign Language Teacher,* 7 (1967), 30.

Psychology and language learning: motivation and method

adult and sophisticated will lead them away from infantile discourse, while the fear of floundering will help to prevent the introduction of overly complex sentences.

Total exclusion of English from the foreign language classroom

Many people have confused the American Method with an approach to language teaching which is popular in Europe today and which had a considerable following in America during the latter part of the nineteenth century. We refer here to all those methods that call for the total exclusion of the mother tongue from the foreign language classroom, and which, for the sake of simplicity, we can lump together under the designation "direct method." This approach is based upon the belief that second-language learning must take place in total isolation from the native language. The student must draw meaning from the foreign language by direct exposure and never by reference to native-language equivalents, which, as we have seen, are seldom fully equivalent to words in the foreign language. The teacher may use a wide variety of techniques to convey meaning more efficiently. The following are among the more commonly used devices.

Visuals. The student sees a still picture or motion picture and hears the teacher, the soundtrack, or some other audio source comment upon the visual stimulus. Hopefully, the student makes the correct association between the picture which he sees and the sound which he hears. He learns first by imitating the model sounds, then by responding to the visual stimulus without the sound. He has learned a given lesson when he can produce all the utterances in response to all the visual materials.

Charades. The teacher performs in various ways to illustrate the meaning of new words and expressions. For example, the arms may be flapped vigorously while saying, "I'm a bird." Then, while moving across the room, arms still flapping, the teacher may say, "The bird is flying."

Question and answer. Interrogation usually occupies a large part of the direct-method teacher's time.

(Holding up a picture of a bird in flight)

TEACHER: What is this?

    PUPIL: It's a bird.

TEACHER: What is the bird doing?

    PUPIL: The bird is flying.

Paraphrase.

A house is a building in which the family lives.

Opposites.

Hot is the opposite of cold.

Gouin series. The teacher goes through a series of actions while describing what she is doing as she is doing it. Then each pupil must do likewise.

I stand up. I walk to the window. I open the window. I put my hand out the window. I close the window. I walk to the chair. I sit down again.

A skillful direct-method teacher, given plenty of time, can achieve excellent results. In fact, there are some situations in which the direct method may be the most effective. For example, if the members of the class have a dozen different language backgrounds (as is often the case with adult classes for immigrants), then the teacher is compelled to use some sort of direct approach. (Clearly, it is unlikely that a teacher would be sufficiently well versed in twelve languages to be able to supply mother-tongue equivalents for all students.) Also, when the students of a new language are located in the country where that language is spoken, the direct approach can be quite effective. For then, the students are able to step from the classroom into direct contact with native speakers "on location" in the target culture. In this situation, the need for direct communication is obvious to the student during a large part of every waking hour.

However, the student in the American comprehensive high school does not normally attend classes which demand the direct method, nor is the need for direct oral communication as apparent as with students who are studying abroad. Another problem is that the direct method requires a teacher who is highly skilled both in methodology and in the use of the foreign language, a combination of skills frequently unavailable to American education. And, unless conditions are ideal, the direct method can be highly inefficient. Often students will be unable to ascertain what the teacher is getting at despite the use of visuals, charades, and other devices. The result is either that they are confused about the meaning of an utterance or else they try to guess at the intended meaning. Since the teacher is forbidden to explain the meaning in English, a student may go for months without having his guesses confirmed or corrected. (The author knows a girl who went through an entire semester in a direct-method course thinking that the French word for "notebook" meant "candy bar" because the visualization of the word was ambiguous.) And even if the student is able to determine the general meaning of words, there is no guarantee that he will not draw false conclusions about their significance in the target culture. Thus, without recourse to English he may indeed learn words which refer to secondary education in France or Germany, but if he equates attendance in these institutions with the process of attending and graduating from an American high school, then he is very little wiser in the end than the student who has been told that *lycee* and *Gymnasium* mean "high school" and that the school-leaving certificates from these schools are "like high school diplomas." Apparently, where abstract, culturally loaded expressions are concerned, the direct method will often result in nothing more than a fluent mouthing of misconceptions. On the other hand, when referents are largely to the American culture or to generalized topics and vocabulary (e.g., swimming, walking, books, pencils, trees, etc.), the psychological impact of having to rely solely on the foreign language can be enormously positive. Through total exclusion of English, some language teachers have been able to develop an esprit de corps among their students which carries beyond the confines of the classroom and even beyond the school itself. There is perhaps no sweeter music to the language educator's ear than the sound of students on the way home from school discussing yesterday's party or tomorrow's date in the foreign language. Indeed, this direct, spontaneous communication in the target language is the ultimate goal of most modern programs. The improper use of English is the deadly enemy of that objective. For if the student knows he can always fall back upon the native language, he is unlikely to take the target language very seriously as a vehicle for direct communication of ideas.

Discriminate use of English in the foreign language classroom

Proponents of the American Method believe that the mother tongue has a very definite place in second-language learning, and that, under proper conditions, the use of English can greatly speed up the learning process for the American high-school student who is studying a foreign language. On the other hand, they are aware of the dangers of indiscriminate use of English. The rule of thumb for proper and improper use of English in the foreign language classroom is rather simple: Any use of English which leads to more efficient and intensive practice *in the foreign language* by the student is good use of English; any use of English which leads the student *away* from the target language or which tends to make him a passive listener is bad use of English. The advocates of discriminate use of English base their thinking upon the belief that young adults in America cannot possibly escape the influence of English as they undertake the learning of a second language. The English habit is so strongly ingrained that no amount of direct-method drill can override its influence. Therefore, according to this line of thought, it is better to capitalize upon the student's knowledge of English than to pretend that it is not there. Although not all modern methodologists would agree on all points, the following uses of English are widely accepted.

ENGLISH TO CONVEY MEANING OF DIALOG MATERIAL

The student passively refers to English approximations as he first hears and then repeats the dialog sentences of the target language. He reads the English, but is never asked to recite or translate actively. Once the meaning of an utterance is fully grasped, the English is abandoned and the student concentrates upon speed and accuracy in committing the foreign utterance to memory. The great danger here is that the student may become too dependent upon English and may resist being weaned into full reliance upon the target language. To counteract this tendency, visual material can be used as the main stimulus for memorizing and recalling the dialog utterances. In this case English is used only to explain (and thus avoid) the trouble spots.

ENGLISH TO EXPLAIN TESTS AND DRILLS

A student could know his lesson thoroughly and still score badly on a test or do poorly on a drill simply because he failed to understand the directions. The danger of this happening is greatly increased when the directions are given in the foreign language. Thus it seems best to explain the mechanics of a drill or the directions for a test in English. This is particularly true when a new type of drill is being introduced for the first time. Another technique often used with drill work is to give both the English and the foreign language at the beginning, and then gradually to phase out the English with those types of instructions which are recurrent. Throughout the course, new drill formats can first be introduced in both languages, then gradually replaced by exclusive use of the target language. It is felt that the time saved by using English so that the student will always know what he is doing more than compensates for any loss in psychological conditioning that may result from the brief use of English.

ENGLISH IN CUES FOR PATTERN DRILLS

In certain cases it seems advisable to put an English expression into sharp contrast with its foreign language counterpart. The English is then used as an auditory stimulus for evoking an oral student response. The purpose of such drills is to point up the fact that the target language uses a vastly different structure to convey a particular kind of meaning. Perhaps one example will serve to point out the difference between this use of English and the traditional translation exercise:

I forgot the book.
I forgot the novel.
I forgot the bread.

I forgot the newspaper.
I forgot the ice cream.

The purpose of this particular drill is to "reset" the student's mind so that he replaces the English subject-verb pattern for expressing the idea, "I forget . . .," with the structure, *Se me olvidó.* . . . The student might find it helpful to realize that the Spaniard shifts the verb form into the third person, thus removing some of the implication of responsibility from himself when he has forgotten something. But the main intent of such drill is to replace "I" with *Se me* plus the third person preterite. Hopefully, the drill will also prevent the student from ever drawing a false analogy based upon the logic of English which would lead him to the pitfall expression *Yo olvidé.* . . . It would seem unwise ever to lead a student into producing an expression which is not used by native speakers. (Also see the chapter on pattern drills.)

ENGLISH FOR CULTURAL NOTES AND GRAMMATICAL SUMMARIES

Some teachers provide brief explanations of culture and grammar as they appear necessary for the student to progress without wrong learning taking place. At the very early level, the student may lack the vocabulary he needs to grasp basic concepts about cultural and grammatical patterns if these are presented in the target language. For example, the familiar and polite forms of "you" carry cultural overtones which cannot be conveyed by pictures and gestures alone, (and certainly not by the English words "you" or "thou"). Similarly, the student may become confused when he hears that there are three common equivalents for "wife" in Spanish. A few lines in English can point out that a man will often use *esposa* or *mujer* to refer to his own wife, but would usually use the more formal word *señora* to refer to someone else's wife. The same would be true of grammar. An example of the need for an explanation in several European languages would be the use of the present tense where English uses the present perfect tense (e.g., *Ich bin zwei Wochen hier;* lit. "I am two weeks here"). To many teachers, the psychological loss resulting from brief English explanations is more than compensated for by the fact that such explanations tend to

Psychology and language learning: motivation and method

minimize the danger of implanting a serious cultural or grammatical error in the student's mind. In some of the most modern texts, these notes are written into each chapter so that no class time need be lost to the use of English. Thus, the student is able to spend maximum class and laboratory time productively manipulating the foreign language forms without being puzzled by seeming irregularities in the form or content of the material he is learning.

ENGLISH TO DISPEL STUDENTS' DOUBTS

While some teachers will allow the student to *read* English and to *hear* English in class (and on the introductory segments of taped lessons in the laboratory), they will never allow the student to *speak* or *write* English in these situations. The underlying rationale for this limitation is the belief that the student must use every possible moment of the language class for active practice *in* the foreign language. Other teachers will allow several minutes at the end of the period for student questions in English. This enables students to clear up uncertainties which may have arisen during the period.

The experience of the past few decades has shown that many Americans have, in fact, learned a foreign language despite the use of the mother tongue in the instructional process. On the other hand, it is also true that many Americans have been subjected to years of something called "foreign language study" without developing any semblance of bilingualism. The critical factor may be not the exclusion of English from the instructional process, but rather its discriminate exploitation in that process. In general, this means using English for *passive understanding* of the precise meaning carried by foreign language utterances, while spending the majority of classroom and laboratory time in *actively practicing* those utterances. Studies of verbal learning have shown that visuals and certain direct-method techniques (especially the Gouin series) can produce excellent results as far as direct association of meaning with actions and concrete objects is concerned. As for the misuse of English, millions of Americans can attest to the results achieved by language instruction in which the chief activity is talking *about* the foreign language in English. Predictably, this system produces students who are able to talk about the foreign language in English.

Learning vocabulary in context

In the past, many people have considered the learning of vocabulary to be a relatively simple matter of identifying the high-frequency words and then committing them to memory. Studies have shown that approximately 95 percent of all conversation in European languages is carried on with only a few thousand separate word forms. There are, for example, several hundred thousand lexical items in English—yet "language surveys indicate that—95 percent of the time—we chose words from a library of only 5,000 to 10,000 words. The vast number of other words are rarely used."[18] On the basis of such word counts some people concluded that a foreign language could be learned simply by teaching the foreign language equivalents of the high-frequency words. There is a certain degree of logic in this. After all, the student must eventually acquire a content vocabulary. For, while the learning of phonology and grammar may have top priority at the outset, any language program which attempted to deal only with sounds and forms would soon lose its audience. And surely, once the student has good control of the phonology, morphology, and syntax of the target language, it becomes essential for him to master the lexicon which is most often used by native speakers of that language. Why not, then, identify the high-frequency lexical items and commit them to memory in association with an English equivalent?

Linguists and methodologists give several reasons why words should not be learned in this manner. In the first place (as was noted earlier in the chapter on linguistics), each language has its characteristic rhythm, stress, and intonation patterns. Clearly, these aspects of language are lost or distorted if the student memorizes individual sounds or words rather than complete meaningful utterances. Then too, psychological studies have indicated that vocabulary items are learned and retained better in sense-making contexts than in isolation. But beyond the linguistic and psychological reasons is the question of semantics. This is perhaps the major flaw in the practice of learning vocabulary equivalents; for while there may be only 10,000 commonly used word items, each item may

[18] Peter B. Denes and Elliot N. Pinson, *The Speech Chain,* Waverly Press, 1963, p. 12.

have dozens of meanings depending upon the context in which the item is used. Thus, the 10,000 high-frequency words actually represent untold tens of thousands of separate units of *meaning*.[19] And, since these meanings have few, if any, perfect matching pairs from one language to another, they cannot convey meaning in any useful way until they are placed in a specific context. For example, one can imagine the difficulties encountered by a lexicographer in attempting to provide matching pairs in French, German, or Spanish equivalents for so apparently simple an English word as "hit." A few samples of the semantic range of that word will perhaps

Lexical item (verb or noun; singular or plural)	Sample contexts in which the item may be used	Varieties of meaning
hit, hits	Don't hit him.	blow with the hand or an object
	The stock market hit a new low.	reach or attain
	The bombers hit the assigned target.	successful attack
	This LP record contains the top hits.	popular songs
	The play was a hit.	great success, something or someone well received by public
	You hit it off well with him.	establish rapport
	I think you've hit upon something.	discover
	Hits, runs, and errors.	baseball term
	Hit the road, you bum.	command someone to leave
	Hit me again! (blackjack, card game)	request another card

illustrate the point. To a person learning English as a foreign language, such varieties in meaning can be highly perplexing, par-

19 An extreme example of how misleading a word count can be is the word "honey" in a famous Spanish word list. After the word had been included in a number of basic Spanish readers it was discovered that "honey" itself appeared seldom in literature. It was the expression *luna de miel* (honeymoon) which was in reality the high-frequency item.

ticularly if there are no equivalent terms in the native culture. Thus, the baseball term "hit" mentioned above presents few problems to the Japanese or Mexican student. Because baseball is a popular sport in their homelands, each will have an equivalent term in Japanese or Spanish. However, the German-speaking student, being unfamiliar with baseball, will not grasp the fine distinctions which differentiate the word "hit" from other baseball terms—such as, grounder, foul ball, fly-out, line drive, dribbler, bunt, and home run. On the other hand, the term "song hit" will be grasped quickly by the German teenager. This is because the German noun *Schlager* carries a comparable meaning, and the verb *schlagen* has other points of correspondence with the English verb "hit." However, merely because the German student of English might learn to pronounce and use the word in two of its contexts is no assurance that he will even recognize its meaning in any of the other eight contexts. In fact, there is even a question as to whether a nonnative should ever attempt to use the specialized or slang meanings of the more common words unless he is entirely familiar with the limits of acceptable usage within the target culture. For example, the term "Hit me again," is a fully appropriate way to request another card when playing blackjack in a barracks card game; it would be absurd in a ladies' bridge club. Yet the nonnative speaker may not be aware that the semantic range of "hit" covers only one card game.

Semantic difficulties arise even with the most common words. Every American child in grade school knows that it is possible

to start a car,   *or*   to begin a lesson.

Yet the foreign student of English who has failed to learn the semantic limits of words may think it proper

to begin a car,   *or*   to commence a motor.

The student who makes errors of this sort may pronounce well and may use acceptable grammatical forms; yet this is not enough. He must also be able to select words which convey meaning accurately within a given context. One of the reasons behind the use of dialogs in the American Method is to present vocabulary in a natural situation so that the meaning is unequivocal both from the standpoint of word usage within the dialog sentences and social appropriateness within the cultural context which the dialog attempts to dramatize. To give the student complete confidence in what he is learning, some teachers use native speakers on tape, record, or sound film for the initial dialog presentation. As the student memorizes the dialog utterances, the teacher may explain the general meaning each word would have if translated literally. (Naturally, the student would be given only those equivalents relevant to the meaning of the utterance being learned.) On the other hand, teachers who incline toward the direct method would not approve of this use of English. In any case, modern methodology holds that it is more efficient to memorize a dozen connected, meaningful sentences each of which contains a word to be learned than to learn the same words in isolation with their matching English equivalents. It is felt that English equivalents given in the form of dictionary items tend to mislead the student into believing that a given item in the foreign language has the same range of meaning as the supposedly equivalent English word. On the other hand, the student who learns a new word in a specific context is less likely to push the new word beyond its semantic limits. By way of illustration we might take the French, German, and Spanish words *heure*, *Uhr*, and *hora* which can all be matched with the English equivalent "time," in the expression, "What <u>time</u> is it?" However, none of these words would be appropriate equivalents if one wanted to express many other meanings carried by the English word "time." Note below that completely different words are needed in French, German, and Spanish to cover the full semantic range of the English word "time."

English	French	German	Spanish
What time is it?	Quelle heure est-il?	Wieviel Uhr ist es?	¿Qué hora es?
This time, I'll go.	Cette fois-ci, j'irai.	Dieses Mal gehe ich.	Yo voy esta vez.
I don't have time.	Je n'ai pas le temps.	Ich habe keine Zeit.	No tengo tiempo.
I had a good time.	Je me suis bien amusé.	Ich habe mich gut amüsiert.	He pasado un rato agradable.

Summary

In the final analysis the degree to which the students themselves actually use the foreign language in the school environment (i.e., classroom, laboratory, seminar rooms, etc.) is the best measure of the psychological soundness of the language program. In a sense, it actually determines whether or not a given school has a foreign language program in the modern sense of the word. In some schools and colleges, teachers admit to spending as high as 75 percent of class time discussing grammar and other matters in English while others report that students spend 60 percent of available time translating into English and discussing literature in English.[20] In the interests of honest representation it would seem that such offerings should be labeled as "survey courses in grammar" or "seminars relating to foreign literature," rather than as courses in French, German, or Spanish. The problem of justifying the "foreign language" course designation increases in direct proportion to the use of English in the classroom. In fact, if English is the predominant vehicle of classroom communication, the very existence of foreign language as a separate subject area can be seriously questioned. Grammatical discussions could, for example, be rather easily formalized into a course or unit called "comparative linguistics," and literary assignments done in English might quite profitably be dealt with in a course called "world literature." It would seem that both types of activity could be transferred to the English department with no great loss to the humanistic educational values, either linguistic or literary. (In fact, a great deal more ground could be covered in literature if the reading were done entirely in good English translation rather than the ludicrous, bumbling translations produced by novice students.) Similarly, the anthropological and cultural aspects of language would fit logically into a modern social studies program. (Direct communication in the language of the target culture is the unique anthropological experience which foreign language study has to offer; if this educational experience is

[20] Scarvia B. Anderson, Lynn K. Gaines, and Rosemary Russell, *A Survey of Modern Foreign Language Instruction in High Schools and Colleges*, Princeton, N.J., Educational Testing Service, 1963, pp. 1–4.

Psychology and language learning: motivation and method

lacking, then it is difficult to justify social studies content in the foreign language curriculum.)

Thus, however important grammatical generalizations may prove to be in the instructional process, and however useful English may be for certain instructional purposes, their ultimate validity must relate to those objectives which are basic and unique to foreign language study. (See Chapter 5 for detailed objectives.) Accordingly, the teacher who subscribes to modern objectives must accept or reject given classroom practices on the basis of whether or not they promote direct, spontaneous communication in the target language. Apparently this acceptance is quite widespread. A 1963 survey of 23,537 high schools and 1,987 colleges and universities in 50 states indicates that, on the average, foreign language classes "spend about half of their time in the foreign language without using English" and that "grammar discussions in English" average well under twenty percent of class time.[21] Thus, if this sampling of tens of thousands of high school and college language teachers (French, German, Spanish, Russian, and Italian) is valid, we can conclude that a large segment of the active language teaching profession presently assigns to grammar and English an important but subordinate role in the language classroom. Although the field of psycholinguistics is far from an exact science, there does exist a body of knowledge relating to verbal learning and to the acquisition of skills from which certain tentative conclusions can be drawn. Clearly, more research needs to be done, and the existing hypotheses need to be further tested. However, until more exact information is available, the language teaching profession can act on the basis of evidence which now exists. The six principles listed below are drawn from psychological studies conducted over the past few decades:

1. The more meaningful (and personal) the material, the more likely it is to be learned and retained. Fluency and automaticity are important in language learning, but these can be achieved parrot-fashion without the learner being fully cognizant of what he has learned. Genuine learning must include the ability to

---

[21] *Ibid.*, pp. 4–15.

apply the target language to the world of reality in a personal way.

2. Drill work involving conscious choices between critical and contrasting elements is more effective than the same amount of drill work done in a repetitive manner and involving no contrasts. (However, introducing an excessive number of contrasts in a given drill can bewilder and discourage the learner.)

3. Learning of basic language skills will be more efficient if the student is aware of the generalizations underlying the critical features upon which he is being drilled. These critical features may either be learned inductively or may be pointed out by the teacher or text; it cannot be assumed that the student will perceive the important critical features by himself.

4. The more kinds of associations that are made the better the learning will be. Thus, at the appropriate time, all possible sense modalities should be brought to bear on each item to be learned. Different ways of associating meaning in verbal learning include auditory (hearing), pictorial (visual conceptualization), motor performances (Gouin series), tactile (handling objects), and graphic (written symbolization).

5. The use of visuals in association with spoken and written symbols can greatly facilitate verbal learning. Approximately 80 percent of all human learning is done visually. Hence, sole reliance upon auditory stimuli at any stage of learning must be considered questionable for sighted learners.

6. In the learning of skills it is more efficient to distribute the drill into regular daily modules than to mass drill work into time segments several days apart from one another. Thus, in the beginning course (where drill work predominates) it is preferable to schedule classes in 30-minute daily modules for 5 consecutive days than to have 60-minute modules 3 times a week.

Bibliography

Carroll, John B., *Language and Thought*, Englewood Cliffs, N.J., Prentice-Hall, 1964.

Carroll, John B., "The Contributions of Psychological Theory and Educational Research to the Teaching of Foreign Languages," *Moderner Fremdsprachenunterricht*, Berlin, Pädagogisches Zentrum, 1965, pp. 365–381.

Chomsky, N., *Aspects of the Theory of Language*, Cambridge, Mass., MIT Press, 1965.

Lambert, Wallace E., "Psychological Approaches to the Study of Language," *Modern Language Journal*, XLVII (February 1963).

Pimsleur, Paul, *Psychological Experiments Related to Second Language Learning: Report of the NDEA Conference*, Los Angeles, University of California, 1959.

Rivers, Wilga M., *The Psychologist and the Foreign Language Teacher*, Chicago, University of Chicago Press, 1964.

Scherer, George, and Michael Wertheimer, *A Psycholinguistic Experiment in Foreign-Language Teaching*, New York, McGraw-Hill, 1964.

*There is no reason why the school room should be any less mechanized . . .
than, for example, the kitchen. A country which annually produces millions
of refrigerators, dishwashers, automatic washing-machines, automatic
clothes driers, and automatic garbage disposers can certainly afford the
equipment necessary to educate its citizens to high standards of competence
in the most effective way.*

. . .

*The simple fact is that, as a mere reinforcing mechanism, the teacher is
out of date . . . the teacher has a more important function than to say
right or wrong.*

. . .

*The whole process of becoming competent in any field must be
divided into a very large number of very small steps, and reinforcement must
be contingent upon the accomplishment of each step.*

B. F. SKINNER

Teaching machines, programmed learning, and self-instruction

7

Of all the areas of American society perhaps no segment is more resistant to change and innovation than education. In an age of jet travel, automated dairy farms, and color television the educational enterprise has remained largely satisfied with a system of instruction which traces its last major innovation back to the sixteenth century when the widespread use of movable-type printing made books widely available. Over the centuries, a two-fold view of what constitutes an acceptable educational situation has developed. One stereotype has the teacher personally imparting knowledge to one or more less-learned fellow human beings using nothing but his wit, intelligence, and perhaps a sheaf of lecture notes for instructional support. Socrates discoursing to his youthful followers on the streets of Athens is the personification of this educational ideal. The other stereotype is the student with his book. Tradition has made it acceptable to learn without direct person-to-person contact provided that the nonhuman source of information consists of ink marks printed upon paper. Abraham Lincoln, reading

Hamlet in the flickering light of the family fireplace, is a cherished image in the minds of many Americans. But the vision of a youngster sitting at an automated push-button device is not an acceptable human-to-nonhuman educational situation in the minds of many educators. The concept of discriminate use of machines to improve instruction has not become established. Thus it is possible for an educator to travel across the nation in a jet airplane, to arrive downtown by helicopter, to ascend to the conference hall by a push-button elevator, and to deliver a speech (neatly produced on an electric typewriter) upon the topic of "The Dehumanizing Effect of Machine Teaching." The advocates of teaching machines and programmed learning are quick to point out the inconsistency of the traditionalists who, by their very actions in purchasing and utilizing machines in everyday life, support the contention that machines produce more—not less—opportunity for genuine human activities. In most fields of endeavor it has become common practice to assign the more routine tasks to machines. Giant steps have been taken in such areas as transportation, communication, industrial production, and even in the household; meanwhile, education has remained centuries behind the mainstream of progress in the mechanized western world.

Perhaps the most concerted effort to break down this resistance to machines in education has come from the manufacturers of the machines. For many years this effort was carried on, almost exclusively, by local and regional sales personnel working with schools and colleges. By the mid-nineteen sixties, however, some of the larger corporations began to appeal directly to the public through mass media. One nationally televised ad, for example, showed youngsters eagerly and intently responding to lessons delivered by a complex computer-directed tutorial machine. Apparently the large companies have decided that innovation in public education comes not from within the subject areas of the teaching profession, but is imposed from without by administrators and lay boards. There is a very real danger that this type of promotion will result in the purchase by local schools of elaborate teaching machines before the actual instructional programs for these machines have been adequately evaluated. Experience has shown that the "hardware" (i.e., the machine) tends to be developed to a high level of sophistication before the "software" (i.e., the educational program).

Yet the program is the most basic aspect of any machine-taught course; the machine itself is merely a device for making the program of instruction available to the student. Therefore, it would seem imperative for language teachers to be fully aware of what the programmed courses purport to accomplish, what the basic rationale for such courses is, and how successful they have been during the early stages of their development. Also, much of the drill material presented on tape which is now available with foreign language texts is based upon principles of programmed learning. In some cases, these commercially produced tapes follow the format of programmed materials but lack many other qualities of genuine programmed materials. Thus, there is good reason for anyone presently involved in the teaching of languages or in the acquisition of texts and materials to be fully aware of the nature of programmed instruction.

The rationale for programmed learning

To a considerable degree advocates of programmed instruction base their thinking upon behavioristic psychological theory. And, inasmuch as language is a form of human behavior, the key to language instruction lies in inducing students to produce responses which lead to acceptable second-language behavior. To many foreign language programmers, the traditional classroom situation is deemed highly unsuited to this task. Among the chief shortcomings usually cited are the following:

1. In the development of proper language habits, it is essential that each response by a student be followed immediately by a correct response. In a classroom of 30 students it is clearly impossible to achieve reasonable efficiency in this sort of instruction. For either students are responding one at a time with each answer being confirmed singly after each response, or else all 30 students are responding in unison without having their responses confirmed at all. The first procedure is highly wasteful since all students but one are passive most of the time. The second course

is almost totally ineffective from the behavioristic standpoint because students are never aware of whether or not they have responded correctly. Equally ineffective is the practice of waiting until the next day to correct responses. A delay of more than a few seconds is considered nearly as useless as total nonconfirmation of responses.

2. The regular classroom still uses largely negative inducements. While the hickory stick is no longer in common use, some form of punishment is still the basic motivating force in the curriculum. It may be the displeasure of the teacher, a bad mark on a paper or report card, the ridicule of classmates, or various kinds of punishment administered by the parent after the school informs him of his child's substandard performance. The programmer would replace the fear of punishment (low grades, harsh words from the teacher, loss of privileges, etc.) with the anticipation of rewards. The most desirable type of reward is the immediate knowledge that a response was correctly given. The regular classroom either fails completely to reward correct learning or else those rewards are so infrequent as to be totally ineffective. Thus the student becomes so concerned with avoiding the punishments built into the school system that he loses interest in achieving the genuine course objectives.

3. Students learn at different rates. The regular classroom makes no allowance for this obvious fact. Thus the bright student is rewarded for loafing along, accomplishing about half as much as his capabilities would permit while the slow student may strive diligently to keep up. Yet the bright student is rewarded with an A for coasting while the slow student is punished with a D for all his hard work.

4. The course of instruction is not well organized. The busy secondary teacher who must contend with a hundred or more students daily has no time left for careful planning of the instructional program. This is particularly true in foreign language instruction where the typical teacher has two to four different preparations daily (e.g., French I, French II, French III, and French IV). As a result, the teacher simply does not have time to break the course of study into several thousand small, achiev-

able tasks which would lead inexorably to the stated course objectives. Consequently, the entire teaching process lurches along with the teacher at one time giving large, indigestible doses of material to be learned while subsequently devoting an excessive amount of time to some trivial matter which has little to do with the final goal of the course.

These are but a few of the ills which programmed instruction aims at correcting. There are many types of programs, not all of which can be described within the scope of this book. The following discussion will deal primarily with those programming techniques which have been most commonly used in the teaching of foreign languages.

The basics of programmed instruction

What is programmed instruction? To begin this discussion, it will be helpful to keep three names in mind. The first is Sydney L. Pressey. Pressey is generally credited with starting the programmed-learning movement when, in 1926, he observed that his multiple-choice testing machine also performed a teaching function. This discovery had little impact on psychology or education until teacher shortages led industry and the military to experiment with teaching machines.

A second name of importance among those who work in programmed learning is Norman Crowder. In fact, there is a type of programming known as "Crowder Programming." The essential characteristic of Crowder programs is that the student is "branched." That is, he is presented with a "frame" of material, usually in the form of an expository passage, and when he has finished the "frame," he must answer a series of multiple-choice questions. According to how well (or how poorly) he answers, he is branched into a short or long series of frames. The Crowder program assumes that the student will make errors, and this assumption is built into the program. The student who makes few mistakes can proceed more directly toward the ultimate objective of the course. The student who continues to err is contantly branched back to ever-simpler frames until he has mastered the basic knowledge which will enable him to proceed. In summary, then, Crowder advocates the so-called "intrinsic" type of program which allows the bright student to skip ahead while the slow student can backtrack. However, this type of programming has not caught on widely for very simple reasons: time and money. It is time consuming and expensive to program this way and the equipment required is even more expensive. Ideally, a computer would be used which could analyze every response and immediately prescribe the exact next step which the student should take. Costs can run as high as thousands of dollars per student per hour.

Thus, because the Crowder program is so costly, the main influence in language instruction has come from a man whose theories were not so expensive to implement. In recent years the name, Skinner, has come to be almost synonymous with "programmed learning." Skinner is an advocate of linear rather than branching programs. That is, every student goes through every frame in the program. There is no individualization of content as with Crowder's system. A second difference between Skinnerian and Crowderian programs lies in the attitude toward error. Skinner disciples consider errors dangerous because errors may become fixed while disciples of Crowder make deliberate use of error to determine branching. The Skinner program will tolerate only a 5 percent rate of error. If a given frame produces a higher rate, then it must be reprogrammed into a series of smaller ones. The reason for this is clear; since there is no branching and no teacher to correct errors, then error must be largely eliminated. To accomplish this, programs must be checked out by experimentation with many students to determine which frames are producing a high frequency of errors. These troublesome frames are then broken up into smaller frames until student errors are nearly eliminated.

At this point it might be well to summarize the seven most essential characteristics of a linear program so that there is no confusion regarding the various systems which have been discussed.

1. *In any programmed course, the program must be based upon a precise analysis of the behavior desired; that is, "terminal be-*

havior" must be clearly specified. In this regard the person who does the programming is *extremely* important. Some programs show a great deal of sensitivity to the precepts of modern linguistics while others reflect mainly traditional grammatical rules.

2. *The program must organize instruction in the best possible sequence and in increments of the best possible size to produce optimal efficiency in learning.* These steps should be based on a systematic analysis of pupil performance, not upon arbitrary guesses by the programmer. The program must be tested and the course reprogrammed in accordance with test results.

3. *At every step in the program, the student must have the opportunity to check what he has learned within moments after he has learned it.* This confirmation (known as "reward" or "reinforcement") is essential to proper student motivation.

4. *There is no teacher to interpret the program.* The program *is* the teacher.

5. *There is no failure.* Anyone who stays with the course to the end will "succeed," provided that the educational system allows flexibility of time, schedule, and grading.

6. *There is no classroom atmosphere.* Some programs make no allowance for interaction of students with the teacher and with one another or even with a computer-directed robot. The relationship is rather that of the student with a machine or with a very large stack of printed materials known as a programmed textbook. Naturally, if speaking and listening are course objectives, a tape recorder and a considerable number of tapes are needed.

7. The most basic principle of all is that *the student must be induced or coerced into a series of overt responses.* It does not matter that each response may seem idiotically simple to the student. As long as he keeps performing, the process of operant conditioning will lead him to the desired terminal behavior. In effect what the Skinnerian programmer is saying is: Any normal individual can master a foreign language to the level of achievement which is commonly designated as "A" or "B" performance. There need be no failures or "Cs" or "Ds." All that is required is a good program and some kind of motivation which keeps the

student actively responding until he finishes the whole series of frames.

Some students are motivated by pulling a handle or turning a crank that reveals the correct response—sometimes with tinkling bells and flashing lights. One Skinner machine even dispenses gumdrops for every five consecutive correct answers. (This device has been referred to as the "sticky-fingered Skinner machine.") However, research has shown that a programmed textbook is just as effective a device for presenting a program as is the more complex (and more expensive) mechanical gadget.

To further illustrate the characteristics of Skinnerian programming, it seems appropriate to present a few sample frames. For, unless the reader understands the format of a linear program, he will be unable to evaluate such programs with full objectivity. The following twenty frames illustrate several variations of the standard linear format. To appreciate it fully, the reader should proceed as follows:

(1) Place a shield at the dash line, (2) Give an overt response, oral or written, and (3) Check the response immediately by sliding the shield down to reveal the answer. Begin by covering the entire page below number one with a card or folded sheet of paper.

1. A good program is based upon a precise specification of desired t_____ b_____.
   _____ (Place shield here.)
   terminal behavior.

2. A description of desired terminal behavior is not arrived at arbitrarily; it is arrived at by ex_____ with many students.
   _____
   experimentation

3. This experimentation is also used to determine which frames are causing the largest number of student errors. The difficult frames are then: (made to be more amusing/ broken into smaller units).
   _____
   broken into smaller units.

4. On a linear program, every student does every f_____.
   _____
   frame.

5. If the linear program has been properly developed, errors will be: (used to determine branching/ reduced to 5 percent).

----

reduced to 5 percent.

6. Linear programming is based upon the principles of operant conditioning as defined by a man named (Crowder/ Pressey/ Skinner).

Skinner.

7. Skinnerian programmers insist that a student must make an overt response in each frame. To elicit a response, the programmer provides a st_____ in each frame.

----

stimulus.

8. The stimulus is supposed to elicit a _____ from the student.

----

response.

9. Out of every 100 responses, the student is expected to be correct (5 times/ 50 times/ 75 times/ 95 times).

----

95 times.

10. After each student response, the program provides a correct response. This is also referred to as a (stimulus/ reward).

----

reward.

11. This reward will correct the student if he is wrong. More important, it confirms the correct student responses. However, to be effective, the reward must be (delayed/ immediate).

----

immediate.

12. The practice of handing back a corrected assignment a week after it was submitted violates the principle of _____ reward.

----

immediate.

13. Skinnerian programmers believe that student errors are (dangerous/ useful).

----

dangerous.

14. To minimize error, each step in the program is of (minimal length/ maximum length).

----

minimal length.

Teaching machines, programmed learning, and self-instruction

15. Therefore, the student in a Skinnerian program moves toward terminal behavior through a series of _____ steps.

----
minimal.

16. To allow for differences in student ability (there are three different programs/ the student does the program at his own pace).

----
the student does the program at his own pace.

17. If a teacher were to require an entire class to go through this program in unison, she would be violating the principle of self-_____.

----
self-pacing.

18. The size of the frames in this program was determined arbitrarily rather than through _____ with many students.

----
experimentation.

19. Other programs of this sort have contained between 60 and 100 frames. It is very likely, therefore, that this program violates the principle of _____ steps.

----
minimal steps.

20. Assuming that desired terminal behavior had been adequately stated prior to the construction of this program, we should now provide a series of t_____ questions to determine whether or not the desired terminal behavior had been achieved.

----
test questions.

Programming a foreign language

The computer-directed Crowderian program has not been developed into a four-skills course of study for several reasons, not the least of which is cost. However, even if unlimited funds were available, one basic shortcoming would still exist. It is simply that the quality of a student's oral response cannot be evaluated by any machine now available. And, unless the computer can be fed the information regarding whether or not the student has responded correctly or incorrectly, there is no way for it to branch him back to more intensive drill work on phonology or to skip him ahead to more advanced frames. Consequently, most computer-directed foreign language instruction has dealt with the reading and writing aspects of language learning. It *is* possible to connect an electric typewriter to a computer in such a way as to present typed stimuli and elicit typed responses from the student. The computer can also analyze the correctness of the typewritten responses and direct the student's program accordingly. Stimuli which result in incorrect responses are retaught until errors become nonexistent. Stimuli which repeatedly elicit correct responses are phased out according to a prearranged schedule. However, the limited objectives which can be achieved with this type of program hardly seem to justify the enormous per-student cost.

The less costly linear program has the additional advantage of being able to provide instruction in the listening-speaking skills. Because the student is never branched and because he evaluates his own responses, there is no problem with regard to the mechanics of presenting phonology. And also, since the opportunity for error is almost eliminated (at least theoretically), the danger of phonological interference from the English habit system is also largely eliminated. Through a long series of frames presented on a good-quality tape recorder, the student can be taught first to discriminate between the problem sounds in the foreign language and the conflict sounds in English. Then, after a long series of error-free responses in distinguishing the target sound from the conflicting English sound, the student learns to produce the foreign language sound. The student begins with the tongue positioning used to produce the nearest English sound and is taught, step by step, to modify tongue (and sometimes lip) positions until the correct points of articulation are realized. Habituation drills follow until the target phoneme becomes part of the learner's habit system. The sound is learned first in isolation, then in a word, then a phrase, and finally in a complete utterance. In several of the more successful programmed courses the student learns to associate graphemes with the corresponding phonemes as each new sound is learned. Also, he learns to produce the appropriate phoneme in response to a graphic stimulus almost from the outset of the programmed course. The theory behind this procedure is that delayed presentation of written symbols may lead to mispronunciation; it is considered better to consolidate the learning of phonology by utilizing all applicable sense modalities at the time that the initial learning of phonology takes place. Thus, the graphemes and (where possible) a pictorial representation will follow the learning of each word, phrase, and sentence. For purposes of illustration this section includes a vastly condensed representation of some of the steps that are typically followed in teaching a few selected sounds and structures in a programmed Spanish course. An actual program would consist of hundreds of additional frames and would include considerably more in the way of detailed instructions for the student. However, with a bit of imagination, the reader can visualize a completed program (one which has been tested and revised on the basis of actual experience with a broad sampling of students). One should also conjure up the image of a youngster sitting at a tape recorder, wearing a headset with an attached microphone, and looking at a large text the pages of which are covered with a sliding plastic shield. A foot pedal starts and stops the tape recorder. Instructions for starting and stopping are contained in the text.

DISCRIMINATION SERIES

The student reads in the programmed text: You will hear two sounds; tell whether they are the same or different. The student presses a foot pedal which operates a tape recorder. He hears two sounds through his headset:
a [a] (Spanish vowel) and *a* [ā] (diphthongized English vowel).
The student gives his response of "same" or "different." Then he moves the shield on his programmed text and reads the English word "different." This is repeated many times to assure that the student achieves at least 95 percent accuracy.

> TEXT: You will again hear two sounds. One will be English, the other Spanish. White the number which corresponds to the Spanish sound.
>
> TAPE: One, *a* [a] (Spanish sound). Two, *a* [a] (English sound).

The student writes 1 on his work sheet and moves the shield downward in the programmed text to reveal the correct answer. Again 95 percent accurate responses determine the number of frames.

TEXT: You will hear again two sounds. Imitate the *Spanish* sound.

TAPE: [a], [a]

STUDENT: *a* (Hopefully, the Spanish sound.)

TAPE: [a]

The series continues to point of near-native production.

TEXT: You will hear a Spanish word repeated twice. Listen carefully.

TAPE: casa, casa

TEXT: You will hear this word pronounced again. This time, listen closely and repeat what you hear.

TAPE: casa

STUDENT: casa

TAPE: casa

TEXT: Note the picture contained in this frame. (A Spanish house is shown.) Look at this picture as your teacher pronounces the word which describes it.

TAPE: casa, casa

TEXT: Now, look at the picture again and repeat the word which your teacher will pronounce.

TAPE: casa

STUDENT: casa

TAPE: casa

TEXT: In the next frame you will see the Spanish spelling for the word which you have learned. Listen to your teacher and look at the word that is written under the picture. (*casa* is written beneath the picture of a Spanish house.)

TAPE: casa

Similar procedures are followed until nearly all students in the test group can understand, speak, read, and write flawlessly everything they have studied. A typical progression (learning first sounds, then fragments, and finally complete utterances) would be the following:

> casa
> la casa
> la casa es
> La casa es grande.   (The house is big.)

Then there would be another series aimed at a slightly different set of objectives:

Teaching machines, programmed learning, and self-instruction

oso
el oso
el oso es
El oso es grande.   (The bear is big.)

Vocabulary is extremely sparse in the program until all critical phonemes have been mastered. However, basic morphology is usually introduced as soon as the student has learned enough phonology and vocabulary to produce sense-making utterances. Often these sentences will be quite irrelevant because of the limited vocabulary. Thus, to teach agreement of adjectives and nouns, the programmer may be forced to resort to such sentences as:

El oso no es rojo.   (The bear is not red.)
La casa no es roja.   (The house is not red.)

However, to the programmer, it makes little difference whether or not the intermediate steps sound ridiculous or whether or not his techniques follow some methodological "party line." All stimuli and responses are judged solely by their effectiveness in moving the student closer to the desired terminal behavior. The problems attending an accurate specification of terminal behavior are enormous. One of the pioneers in this area, Fernand Marty, commented upon such difficulties when, after eight years of experimentation, he stated, "It is only now that we feel we have a balanced terminal behavior."[1] Marty's book provides an excellent outline of the steps which might be followed in providing a thorough but concise description of what a programmed course ought to accomplish. A few samples of desired behavior in French will illustrate some of the problems. Marty begins by specifying content in a French course under such categories as:

1. Structures which the student must learn to handle without difficulty;
2. Morphological items that he must learn to use;
3. Optional liaisons that will be taught;
4. 1200 vocabulary items which must be learned, etc.[2]

[1] Fernand Marty, *Programing a Basic Foreign Language Course: Prospects for Self-Instruction,* Roanoke, Virginia; Audio-Visual Publications, 1962, p. 3.
[2] *Ibid.,* pp. 1–3.

However, Marty does not settle for a mere list of content to be mastered. He further refines his definition of terminal behavior to include a description of how rapidly the student must perform. For example, he states that

1. The student must acquire an oral fluency of 150 syllables per minute.
2. His audio comprehension must be 200 syllables per minute.
3. His reaction time must be three seconds or less [a native reacts in less than one].[3]

In line with newer linguistic theory Marty insists that the description of spoken French must be performed independently of the description of written French, and that the activities of speaking and reading be kept sharply separate in the program. And this brings up a very important point relative to the selection of programmed materials in foreign languages; namely, that one must examine carefully the stated terminal behavior before considering the adoption of any such course. It is essential to draw a clear distinction between course content, on the one hand, and the method of programming, on the other. For some programs show no sensitivity whatever to contemporary goals of instruction or to the precepts of modern linguistics. Thus, programs can be modern in programming technique but pedagogically and linguistically archaic. The psychological process of operant conditioning can be applied to traditional as well as to modern instructional objectives.

The adaptation of programmed learning to the language classroom

By the late 1960s, the actual implementation of programmed instructional techniques in foreign language classes followed four basic patterns. In some cases a given institution might employ two or more of the basic patterns, but the first one considered below appears to be far more prevalent than the other three combined.

PROGRAMMED MATERIAL AS A SUPPLEMENT TO REGULAR CLASS WORK

A large number of language teachers use tapes which follow the programming format of: (1) stimulus, (2) space for student re-

[3] *Ibid.*, p. 3.

sponse, (3) reward in the form of correct response, and often (4) another space to repeat the correct response. In a minimally equipped language program the teacher will play the tape on a classroom tape recorder and require student responses either individually or en masse. Where there is a language laboratory, the teacher will play the tape from the console and require all students to respond simultaneously into their microphones while the teacher monitors each student's responses through an arrangement of electronic switches. These two approaches have the advantage of exposing the student to a variety of native voices on tape, but they lack many of the characteristics of programmed learning as advocated by the behaviorist psychologists. Actually, only the principle of immediate reinforcement is present. Individual pacing is not possible, and the principles of logical sequence and minimal increment presentation of content are often absent. Some teachers have found it possible to combine lockstep drill sessions with individualized instruction by using the monitor facility of the language laboratory to diagnose student difficulties. They then prescribe drill work according to student performance in the mass drill sessions. Thus, students who are not doing well are branched backward into drill work upon the basic sounds and structures they had failed to master during the regular sessions in the classroom and laboratory. Conversely, students who perform well in the current drill work are either branched ahead or are given high interest "enrichment" material which expands their knowledge but does not move them ahead in the basic course objectives. This type of supplemental drill appears to be most consistently successful in schools that have several readily available language laboratories and one or more nonprofessional aides to perform routine clerical and technical duties. (In a few cases, such duties have been performed adequately by specially trained high-school students.) A final requirement with this latter approach is the availability of a large supply of carefully programmed tapes which are correlated perfectly with the text and are constantly available for use in the tape library of the language laboratory. Under ideal conditions, the teacher then becomes a motivator, diagnostician, and prescriber—functions which no computer yet designed can perform. In the best of all possible courses, the bright student would never be allowed to suffer the boredom of waiting for the slow student to catch up, nor would the slow student be humiliated by his inability to keep pace. The teacher would have the time and the instrumentation to judge each pupil's *optimal* (not *minimal*) pace and would place at his disposal the taped and written materials which would keep him moving at that pace. Theoretically, a highly trained professional teacher would have the time to perform such duties because the routine aspects of language learning would be delegated to the machine, and the noninstructional duties would be delegated to lower-salaried aides. Unfortunately, it is only rarely that the combination of circumstances described above actually exist in the secondary school.

PROGRAMMED MATERIAL AS THE PRIMARY SOURCE OF INSTRUCTION WITH SUPPLEMENTATION BY A QUALIFIED TEACHER

A second approach to the use of programmed materials which comes closer to meeting the budgetary limitations of the typical secondary school, is a system which provides for up to 90 percent of all instruction by means of a linear program. Ten percent of the student's time is spent in contact with the teacher who works with small groups of students. Sections form naturally according to how far students have proceeded through the linear program. In this system the complexities and costs of the teacher-directed program are eliminated. All students use the identical tapes and text, thus obviating the need for a tape library and for the process of providing individually paced materials for each student. Most of the time the student is sitting at his tape recorder where he responds to stimuli supplied by the text and the accompanying tape. In the small group sessions the student is required to apply what he has learned during the programmed sessions. That is, he must engage in free expression so that he develops the ability to generate his own sentences rather than merely responding to prelearned stimuli. To a lesser degree, the small group sessions can be used for remedial pronunciation and for motivation and testing. The main role of the teacher, however, is to use his limited time to elicit authentic conversational exchanges from the small group of students. He must not waste this period

Teaching machines, programmed learning, and self-instruction

by using it to explain facts about grammar or even for drill work. These functions have been delegated to the programmed materials.

PROGRAMMED MATERIAL SUPPLEMENTED BY A NONPROFESSIONAL NATIVE-SPEAKING TUTOR

A third approach involves the total elimination of the professional teacher from the foreign language program. In most states this could not be done legally under the certification regulations of the state educational agency. However, there are often ways in which a native-speaking aide can perform under the direction of a certified teacher. At the college level, the effectiveness of this approach has already been established.[4] As Boyd-Bowman expressed it:

> The role of a native speaker in a self-instructional program is to review with the students, either as a group or individually, material they have already learned from the tapes (never new material), to monitor and correct their pronunciation and use of idiom, and generally to provide the kind of feedback the students cannot obtain from the tapes alone. He must be cautioned not to try to talk like a book, substituting the sometimes stilted literary standard for the normal colloquial which all educated speakers use and which the student hears on his tapes. The native speaker should not talk *about* the language nor introduce extraneous vocabulary or idioms nor attempt grammatical explanations of any kind. The course material has been carefully sequenced and all grammatical discussions will be presented wherever necessary in the text itself. Since the main object of the course is effortless control of usage rather than the theoretical understanding of it, little time should be wasted on grammatical speculation. The tutor's task is to drill the students rapidly and intensively in their active use of the language and to furnish a correct model for imitation by the students whenever their responses are faulty or even merely hesitant. In view of all this it is not necessary to the program that the tutor have a good command of English. Even if he does, both he and the students should pretend that he knows little or none.[5]

It should be noted here that the program investigated by Boyd-Bowman was not programmed in the full sense of the word. Yet the

[4] Peter Boyd-Bowman, *Self-Instruction in the Non-Western Languages: A Manual for Program Directors,* report on research performed pursuant to a contract with the U.S. Office of Education, Contract No. OE–5–14–023, 1965.
[5] *Ibid.,* pp. 6–7.

course of study was carefully planned so that students of superior ability could proceed largely on their own in the learning of basic skills and concepts. The results of this particular type of self-instruction were excellent as judged by conventional standards. Nearly all of the twenty-three students studying a neglected language (Japanese, Chinese, Hindi, Persian, Swahili, or Portuguese) were judged to be at the A or B level when compared with students at universities in Michigan and Wisconsin who were learning these languages in regular courses taught by live instructors.[6] There is, of course, nothing to prevent teacher aides from performing at least some of the duties described by Boyd-Bowman as a part of a team consisting of a master teacher, programmed materials, and native tutors. Programs described by Marty,[7] and Valdman[8] would seem to be adaptable to this approach. However, it may be that superior students can make better progress with a text containing adequate explanations of grammatical generalizations and liberally supplemented with taped drill material of the stimulus-response-reward type. Perhaps such students are able to take optimal rather than minimal steps toward the desired terminal behavior. More investigation seems needed regarding the superior student's ability to judge for himself both the size and pace of learning increments in self-instructional foreign language programs.

PROGRAMMED MATERIAL FOR TOTAL SELF-INSTRUCTION

Several studies which contrasted the effectiveness of programmed instruction with instruction carried on by live instructors have, by and large, tended to favor total self-instruction as the more effective method. For example, Ferster and Sapon found that in 47.5 hours 6 students learned an amount of German comparable to that pre-

---

[6] Peter Boyd-Bowman, *Experimentation with Taped Materials and Native Informants to Develop for Small Colleges Some Programs of Independent Study in the Neglected Languages*, report on research performed pursuant to a contract with the U.S. Office of Education, Contract No. OE–5–14–023, 1965, p. 22.

[7] *Op. cit.*, pp. 21 f.

[8] Albert Valdman, "Toward Self-Instruction in Foreign Language Learning," *International Review of Applied Linguistics in Language Teaching*, 1964, pp. 1–36.

Teaching machines, programmed learning, and self-instruction

sented in a first-semester college course.[9] Similar results were reported in the learning of Russian at the Albuquerque Naval Training Center.[10] In a carefully controlled study at the University of Rochester, Clark found that the conventionally taught control group did significantly better in reading than the experimental group using commercially available programmed materials. However, students in the programmed course did significantly better in speaking. There was no significant difference between the two groups in listening comprehension and writing. In overall skill, both groups compared favorably with norms furnished by Educational Testing Service.[11] A similar study conducted at the high-school level showed that "Highly motivated students of proven language aptitude and experience can instruct themselves in an additional language with programmed materials. Such students can join a level II class, adapt to class procedures, and pursue their study successfully."[12]

Arguments against programmed learning

Instrumentation has been widely accepted in nearly every other aspect of American life. There are strong indications that the educational world will soon be "tooling up" for automated teaching. Major textbook corporations have recently merged with major electronic corporations, and it is very unlikely that these industrial giants will fail to influence education in a major way. As one educator expresses it, "Too much has been committed by too many educational, industrial, scientific, and governmental leaders for this to

[9] Wilbur Schramm, ed., *The Research on Programmed Instruction, an Annotated Bibliography*, Bulletin No. 35, Washington, D.C., U.S. Office of Education, 1964, p. 44.
[10] *Ibid.*, p. 94.
[11] William H. Clark and Margaret G. Clark, "Achievement in Elementary German Under Programmed and Conventional Instruction: A Preliminary Study," *Modern Language Journal*, L (February 1966), 100.
[12] Robert Bell and Pearl McDonald, *Experimental Use of Self-Instructional Courses in Russian and Spanish by Secondary School Students*, report on research performed pursuant to a contract with the U.S. Office of Education, Contract No. OE–3–14–033, 1963, p. 18.

happen."[13] In the face of this apparently inevitable trend toward automated teaching, it seems essential that educators in each discipline take an honest look at the disadvantages and dangers inherent in mechanized programmed learning. A summary of the criticisms which have been directed toward programmed instruction during its early application to modern languages would therefore seem to be in order.

PROGRAMMED COURSES ARE EXPENSIVE

Estimates of costs for the development and production of existing programs range from $4.00 per frame (to teach reading-writing skills) to $25.00 per frame (to teach all four skills). Reasonably effective programmed courses aimed at total self-instruction in the four skills have contained nearly 10,000 frames.[14] Thus, $250,000 can easily be spent merely to develop and test a linear program in foreign language. Additional millions must then be expended for the publication and mass production of texts, tapes, and visual materials. Such costs must eventually be defrayed either through government subsidies or through mass sales. For unless the costs of programmed materials can be cut drastically below their 1967 levels, they are unlikely to interest many local school administrators. The initial cost of texts and binders is in the $25 per pupil range. Tapes, even with permission granted to copy a master set, are likely to cost $60 per pupil. Thus, the texts and materials alone represent an initial cost of $8,500 for instructing 100 pupils. And that is only the beginning. Each student also must have a tape recorder available in order to work with the listening-speaking aspects of language. This implies the need for a $15,000 language laboratory which will occupy $30,000 worth of classroom space. The

[13] Myron Lieberman, "Big Business, Technology, and Education," *Phi Delta Kappan*, 47 (January 1967), 186. Among the big-name mergers listed in this special issue of *Phi Delta Kappan* are D. C. Heath with Raytheon, CBS with Creative Playthings, Xerox with American Educational Publications, RCA with Random House, IBM with Science Research Associates, and General Electric with Silver Burdett.
[14] Alfred I. Fiks, "Foreign Language Programmed Materials: 1966," *Modern Language Journal*, LI (January 1967), 7–14.

Teaching machines, programmed learning, and self-instruction

local school district is, therefore, faced with an initial investment in excess of $50,000, even before the program is staffed. Continuing costs, including at least a half-time certified teacher, clerical and technical personnel, and costs for repair and maintenance of equipment are likely to run at the level of $10,000 yearly for 100 students. At present, it is not unusual to find one teacher providing language instruction for 150 students at an annual salary of less than $6,000. How willing will school boards be to make the additional outlay of money when they discover that the available evidence shows, at best, a slight advantage in programmed learning over the competent teacher. A widespread swing to programmed language instruction appears likely only if the lack of competent teachers reaches disaster proportions or if some form of subsidization is available to cover the high costs mentioned above. In the absence of one or both of these conditions (particularly the latter), programmed instruction is likely to remain in the experimental stages for a long time.

SELF-INSTRUCTIONAL PROGRAMS ARE NOT SELF-MOTIVATING

A large part of programmed learning theory is based upon experiments with pigeons in which correct behavior was rewarded with food pellets. It was found that the hungry birds could be taught to perform some rather complex acts by means of step-by-step rewards for all forms of behavior which led toward the instructional objectives. However, withholding food is not an acceptable motivation device in most human educational circles, and the student's appetite for knowledge is seldom strong enough to be piqued by a sustained intellectual diet consisting only of the confirmation of an answer which is 95 percent sure to be right. Thus, extrinsic rewards are usually needed to keep the student going. In the Arlington, Virginia experiment, for example, the high-school students were paid for completing the programmed course.[15] In other cases, students have been rewarded with special recognition or with promises of special advantages for completing the programmed courses. Also, the students who have thus far been exposed to programmed foreign language courses have been drawn largely from an intellectually

[15] Bell and McDonald, *op. cit.*

select group. There is no large body of evidence to show what would happen with the academically average or below-average student.

NOT ALL STUDENTS ARE CAPABLE OF SELF-PACING

It has sometimes been assumed that the pace determined by the student himself will necessarily be the optimum pace for him as an individual. However, studies conducted with eighth-grade science students in Pittsburgh indicate that the student is not always the best judge of his own learning rate.[16] Thus, for example, the bright student may pace himself too slowly while the slow student may race through the program with an unacceptably high error rate. Perhaps such students could be more profitably grouped and subjected to an externally paced program which would speed up the rate of presenting frames for the high-ability pupils and slow it down for the low-ability group. Only those students who demonstrate an ability for self-pacing would be allowed to engage in total self-instruction. Thus, research may eventually show that programming techniques can most profitably be applied to students who are grouped according to ability. The early successes of individualized instruction may be partly due to the voluntary nature of the experimentation. Perhaps the experiments tended to draw mostly students who were uniquely suited to learning by themselves. Thus, it might be as great a mistake to force all youngsters to choose their own rate of learning as it is to have that rate arbitrarily determined for them as is the case with the existing lock-step instruction.

PROGRAMS CANNOT PRODUCE FREE EXPRESSION IN THE FOREIGN LANGUAGE

In order to reward a student's efforts, each stimulus must lead to a preplanned response. In foreign language learning this is fine, up to a point. After all, the student must learn to produce these sounds, grammatical forms, and word-order sequences which a native will understand; he must not invent his own. Accordingly, for that

[16] Gerard Kress and George Gropper, *Studies in Televised Instruction,* research conducted under a grant from the U.S. Office of Education, Grant No. 7–48–0000–159, 1964.

Teaching machines, programmed learning, and self-instruction

substantial portion of the language learning process which calls for convergent thinking, programming techniques may be quite appropriate. However, the ultimate goal of foreign language instruction is spontaneous expression of one's own ideas by means of the target language. And programmed instruction does not lend itself well to this. For, according to Marty, "Divergent thinking (expressing all the ideas suggested to you by a single topic) cannot be indulged in since the programmer cannot foresee the student's response. Self-instruction does not permit creativity, flights of imagination, and the free interchange of ideas."[17]

PROGRAMMED LEARNING IS NOT COMPATIBLE WITH THE EXISTING ADMINISTRATIVE STRUCTURE OF THE SCHOOLS

However effective programmed instruction may eventually prove to be, the lock-step tradition is so thoroughly built into the high-school and university programs that it will tend to negate the positive aspects of programmed learning. A student's progress is generally measured by the credits he has gained. Professional myopia on this point is sometimes carried to incredible lengths. The author has seen immigrant teenagers receive low grades in high school courses in their native language largely because they were unable to match the correct grammatical rules with the language forms which they had correctly supplied on the final examination. Habituated accuracy would be no less of a problem if it were machine-learned. Also, what is to be done with a student who completes a full year of work in one semester? Does he receive a full unit of credit? If so, does this mean that he may earn as many as eight units for four years of work? And what happens to the slow student? At the university level, for example, would a student who is slow in language learning be allowed three semesters to master the basics of a language if it took that long? Would it be possible to prevent his being placed on probation (or perhaps failed) for not having completed the course on schedule? Unfortunately for programmed learning, the answers to such questions are usually negative. Mass instruction requires tight educational bookkeeping practices. Stu-

[17] Marty, *op. cit.*, p. 20.

dents must be assigned grades and grade-point averages. In most cases there is no way to indicate partial mastery of course work except by assigning a low grade. Conversely, there is usually no way to assign a double grade to the student who is inconveniently brilliant. Thus, one of the basic principles of self-instruction is in conflict with the academic establishment. And there is little to indicate that the methods of educational bookkeeping are about to change within that establishment.

Summary

For quite some time the main influence of programmed instruction will probably be in the form of an adjunct to more conventional teaching. However, there is some evidence to indicate that programming techniques can prove useful in the following aspects of foreign language instruction.

1. Programming can be used to accelerate students into liberated reading by teaching them the vocabulary in advance of reading a given selection. Several experiments have shown positive results in the programming of traditional reading-translation skills.[18] Computer-assisted instruction is feasible in this area because the student is dealing with written symbols.

2. In teaching phonology (especially the discrimination of critical phonemes), programmed learning may prove to be superior to the live teacher in the usual classroom situation. Also, the amount of oral drill that a program can make available is far greater. Thus, the student who is able to produce (as well as discriminate) the correct sounds is likely to develop superior speaking ability (as far as correctness of pronunciation is concerned) simply because the program allows him to practice constantly rather than having only occasional opportunity for active drill provided by a teacher in the classroom situation. However, the student who is unable to monitor (and thus to correct) his own errors is likely to engage in many hours of practicing nonacceptable language forms. Thus, much of the programmed oral drill

[18] Schramm, *op. cit.*, pp. 22–25.

Teaching machines, programmed learning, and self-instruction

work might still be best carried on under the close surveillance of the teacher.

3. Many teachers now accept programmed pattern drills as a standard part of their teaching procedures (see Chapter 8). Most commonly such drills are used for mass practice with an entire class. However, some teachers have found that the drills are excellent for remediation, where students are having difficulties with grammatical structures or word order. Such students are required to come into the language laboratory during free hours and to work with programmed tapes until each problem structure becomes a habituated response.

4. It would appear that most language departments at all levels could profit from some of the principles of programmed learning even if they do not accept the entire concept. For example, foreign language teachers have long been in need of "a more precise specification of terminal behavior" as is evidenced by the severe articulation problems which exist at all levels from junior high school to the university graduate school. It will never be possible to determine exactly how many potential language scholars have been sacrificed because the course objectives in foreign languages differ greatly from one level to the other. It is possible that the number of casualties is catastrophic.

One basic principle of programmed learning—the organization of instruction into the best possible sequence and into increments of optimum size—has apparently made an impact on the newer language texts and materials. One sees fewer of the maddeningly complex translation drills which characterized an earlier period. Drills tend to be simpler and more sharply focussed in the newer texts whether programmed or nonprogrammed.

Finally, the programmed learning advocates, by drawing attention to the fact that much of language learning is, after all, habit formation, have tended to discredit the practice of spending endless hours of precious class time talking about the foreign language in English. While it is true that the mere formation of habits does not assure that the student will learn to speak, it is also true that failure to form the proper language habits is a guarantee that the student will *not* be able to speak. Whether the habits are acquired by machine teaching or by human instruction is of little relevance. In either case, the teacher can fail in his responsibility, which is to teach the student how to apply what he has learned to the world of reality. In this task the live human teacher is not yet replaceable. If self-instructional materials are used as intended, the machine will make it possible for him to perform that task more efficiently.

Bibliography

Boyd-Bowman, Peter, "Self-Instruction in the 'neglected' languages: a progress report from Kalamazoo College," *Modern Language Journal*, L (January 1966), 21 f.

Bushnell, Donald D., *The Role of the Computer in Future Instructional Systems*, Monograph No. 2, *AV Communication Review*, Washington, D.C., Department of Audiovisual Instruction, National Education Association, 1963.

Carroll, John B., *A Primer of Programmed Instruction in Foreign Language Teaching*, Heidelberg, Julius Groos Verlag, 1962.
Also available from MLA Materials Center.

Fiks, Alfred I., "Foreign Language Programmed Materials: 1966," *Modern Language Journal*, LI (January 1967), 7–14.
This article contains a definitive list of commercially available foreign language courses along with information on content, costs, age for which the courses are intended, publisher, and a great deal of other pertinent information.

Hayes, Alfred S., *et al.*, "A New Look at Learning," Reports of the Working Committees, 1962 Northeast Conference on the Teaching of Foreign Languages.

Holland, James, and B. F. Skinner, *Analysis of Behavior, a Programmed Text*, New York, McGraw-Hill, 1961, $5.95.

Lane, Harlan, *Programmed Learning of a Second Language*, Heidelberg, Julius Groos Verlag, 1964.
Also available from MLA Materials Center.

Marty, Fernand, *Programing a Basic Foreign Language Course: Prospects for Self-Instruction*, Roanoke, Virginia, Audio-Visual Publications, 1962.

Morton, F. Rand, "The Teaching Machine and the Teaching of Languages: A Report on Tomorrow," *PMLA* (September 1960), LXXV, 1–6.

Sapon, Stanley, "Programmed Learning and the Teacher of Foreign Languages," in *Final Report of the Seminar in Language and Language Learning*, Department of Romance Languages and Literatures, University of Washington, Seattle, 1962.

Valdman, Albert, "The Application of Programmed Instruction to Foreign Language Teaching," *Moderner Fremdsprachenunterricht*, Berlin, Franz Cornelsen Verlag KG, 1965.

Christ, What are patterns for?
AMY LOWELL

*Pattern practice is a means to an end. The end to be achieved is the
ability to use the language freely, . . . Traditional exercises
. . . are usually a test of whether or not the patterns have been
learned, rather than a way of practicing the patterns.*
POLITZER AND STAUBACH

The pattern drill

8 Of all the elements which constitute the new American Method, the pattern drill appears to be the most widely misunderstood. In the hands of a knowledgeable teacher, such drills are capable of producing an exhilarating classroom atmosphere with students sitting on the edge of their chairs listening intently for their cues and responding instantly when called upon. However, when used by a teacher who is not aware of the function and purpose of this type of drill, the results can be as stultifying as the choral chanting of verb conjugations and noun declensions. Visits to hundreds of foreign language classrooms and discussions with colleagues in other states have convinced the author that only a small percentage of language teachers are fully aware of the uses and limitations of pattern practice. Lack of knowledge in this area can greatly limit a teacher's effectiveness since a major portion of most of the newer texts and tapes consists of pattern drills. Furthermore, a number of publishers have produced drills which—although described as pattern drills in the advertisements—actually meet very few of the criteria established by linguists and foreign language educators. The following discussion will attempt to explain what pattern drills are and to describe ways in which they have been successfully used by teachers of foreign language.

What pattern drills are not

It is not uncommon to have a teacher react to a new technique by saying, "Oh, I've been doing that for years." In this statement lies the basis of a problem. For, if pattern drills are to be effective, it is necessary for teachers to desist from certain practices which have been associated with the teaching of languages in the past. Pattern drills have highly specialized purposes not easily furthered by some of the more traditional techniques of years past. It is true that pattern drills can be adapted to traditional purposes in much the same way that a boxcar can be taken off the tracks and converted into a dwelling. However, the boxcar in being converted becomes a substandard residence while at the same time totally losing its value as a transport vehicle. Similarly, the misuse of a pattern drill usually results in the total negation of its value as a drill device. Thus, although the eight negative criteria listed below may—in their positive forms—have relevance for certain purposes, they are not compatible with the intent of the pattern drill. A teacher who fails on any of the eight criteria may, indeed, be engaged in a worthwhile teaching activity. That activity, however, will have very little in common with the intended application of pattern drills in the foreign language classroom.

Thus, in evaluating oral classroom drills, it can be stated that:

1. It is not pattern practice if the teacher takes the time to call on each student by name.
2. It is not pattern practice if the teacher allows students to reflect for 5 or more seconds prior to responding.
3. It is not pattern practice if the teacher engages in discussion midway through a drill.
4. It is not pattern practice if the students have their books open or if they in any way refer to printed words during the drill.
5. It is not pattern practice unless each successive response in a given drill is directed at a common structural problem.
6. It is not pattern practice if the drill material contains unfamiliar vocabulary.
7. It is not pattern practice unless nearly 100 percent of all student responses are complete, understandable, and fluent.

8. It is not pattern practice if more than 5 minutes are devoted to eliciting correct responses from 25 students using a 10-syllable pattern sentence.

It should be noted that the above criteria refer to a live teacher working with students in the usual classroom situation without a laboratory, electronic classroom, or tape recorder. Naturally, the criteria would be somewhat different in reference to using drills with electronic teaching aids.

Pattern practice does not involve the learning of new vocabulary. In fact, any groping for words on the part of the student tends to destroy the effect of the drill. Therefore, students should have learned all lexical items prior to beginning the drill. Quite often, this prelearning will be accomplished by mimic-memorization drills in which the student first listens to words and sentences modeled by the teacher or by an audiovisual device. The meaning of the individual words may be conveyed by pictures, by English equivalents, or by some of the other techniques discussed in Chapter 6. A commonly used technique during the acquisition of the basic vocabulary is to begin by having the entire class imitate the teacher and then progressively to work down to smaller and smaller group responses until each individual can produce the material with reasonable accuracy. Learning vocabulary in dialog form will often proceed as follows:

1. The entire class imitates the teacher.
2. Half the class recites one part of the dialog while the other half responds with the other part.
3. The roles are reversed and the dialog is recited again.
4. The same technique is used with one row of students designated by the teacher to recite to another row.
5. Finally, individual students recite across the room to one another or stand in front of the class to act out the dialog.

When all students can produce the basic sentences with an acceptable pronunciation, and when they understand the meaning of what they are saying, then the teacher proceeds with the pattern practice. Some teachers will launch directly into the drill without prior analysis of the structures which the students are to learn. Others

The pattern drill

205

will provide a grammatical explanation in advance so that the students know what it is they are learning. (See Chapter 6 for a more complete discussion of this matter.)

Phonology drills have been discussed at some length in Chapters 6 and 7. Although such drills often have the same format as the pattern drill, they lack several of the characteristics of pattern-drill exercises. In fact, under ideal conditions, the student would have been thoroughly drilled on all the phonological problems that occur in the pattern-drill sentences before he engages in pattern practice. For pattern practice is directed toward the mastery of morphological and syntactical patterns in the target language. It is assumed, however, that the student will be using acceptable pronunciation throughout the structure drills both with respect to segmental and suprasegmental phonemes. In actual practice, the prelearning of phonology is often neglected. There is perhaps no more agonizing a supervisory task than the observation of students who are being systematically drilled upon structural features while simultaneously fixing habits of pronunciation which are unintelligible to the ear of the native speaker. To grasp the significance of this problem, imagine a group of Spanish-speaking youngsters who have learned to sing a song entitled, "Da Gude Sheep Lowly Pope." Only the music provides a cue to the meaning of the lyrics of the popular children's song, "The Good Ship Lollipop." Similarly, pattern practice in French, German, or Spanish which permits total anglicizing of the critical phonemes is of questionable value. Therefore, some form of prior phonology drill is called for, either in classroom or laboratory. The Spanish-speaking children, for example, could have profited by drill work which taught them first to discriminate the differences between the various English vowel sounds, and then to produce these sounds (see p. 186).

To develop in students the ability to discriminate between basic phonemes, the teacher may say (or play a tape recording of) two sentences containing the problem phonemes. The drill might proceed as follows for the Spanish-speaking student of English:

TEACHER: You will now hear two sentences. If they are the same, say "same"; if they are different, say "different."
TAPE: Bring me the wash. Bring me the wash.
STUDENT: Same.

TAPE: Same.
TAPE: Wash the car while I'm gone. Watch the car while I'm gone.
STUDENT: Same.
TAPE: Different.

The student learning English as a foreign language would go through a long series of such drills until he could distinguish the difficult sounds without error. Drill tapes ordinarily provide the correct response immediately after the space allowing the student time to react and respond. Thus, with properly designed materials, the student can teach himself if he has a tape recorder at his disposal. Normally he has achieved reasonable mastery when he can produce all the correct answers in the space provided before the taped master voice supplies the correct answer.

The drill above is based upon the principle of matching sounds of minimal contrast which exist in the target language. In addition to this use of minimal pairs, drills can be so structured as to require the student to contrast his native language with the conflict sound in the target language.

TEACHER: You will now hear two words. Tell which is the French word. If neither word is French say "neither." If both words are French, say "both."
TAPE: Number One A. rue. B. roo.
STUDENT: A.
TAPE: A.
TAPE: Number Two. A. rue. B. rue.
STUDENT: Both.
TAPE: Both.

To do away with the necessity of having students give an overt response in English and, incidentally, to provide a running record of student progress, a printed sheet can be used for the student responses. Thus, instead of responding orally, the student would merely circle the one correct answer among the choices provided with each listening drill.

1. A. both.
   B. neither.

This would apply only for sound discrimination. The production of the correct sounds would, at the simplest level, involve the ability to imitate sounds which the student had learned to identify aurally. At a more advanced stage he would be required to produce the sounds in response to written stimuli.

In the early stages of learning the dialog utterances, something resembling pattern drill may take place. Most beginning students of foreign language are unable to retain even rather short utterances with sufficient accuracy to repeat them correctly after the teacher. Thus, the teacher will build upon small blocks of partial sentences until the student is able to retain and repeat the complete utterance. Often, the learning proceeds as follows, until good control is achieved:

TEACHER: Mr. Schmidt is a friend of mine. Now, repeat after me. Mr. Schmidt . . .
CLASS: Mr. Schmidt . . .
TEACHER: is a friend . . .
CLASS: is a friend . . .
TEACHER: Mr. Schmidt is a friend . . .
CLASS: Mr. Schmidt is a friend . . .
TEACHER: of mine.
CLASS: of mine.
TEACHER: Mr. Schmidt is a friend of mine.
CLASS: Mr. Schmidt is a friend of mine.

Some teachers prefer the so-called "backward buildup" on the theory that the correct intonation is more easily preserved that way. The same mimic-memorization techniques would be used, but the sequence would now be:

of mine.
a friend of mine.
Schmidt is a friend of mine.
Mr. Schmidt is a friend of mine.

These and other techniques may form an important part of the language learning process, but they do not constitute what is commonly understood as pattern drill.

What is a pattern drill?

The main function of the pattern drill is to make habituated responses out of those structures in the target language which present significant learning problems to the American student. Proponents of pattern practice see the technique as the link which had heretofore been missing in the chain of skill development which begins with dialog memorization and ends when the student is able to apply language patterns spontaneously to express what he wants to say in an unanticipated situation. To be fluent in a foreign language the student must have an immediate command of all the sounds, structures, and word-order sequences which are used commonly by native speakers. The drill is intended as a means of providing systematic practice on these elements so that the student has the *potential* for free conversation. Whether or not the students actually develop the ability to converse freely depends upon teacher and student followup (or lack of followup). The theoretical underpinnings of pattern practice are partly linguistic and partly psychological. The basic principles upon which this type of drill is based are:

1. Learning the conflict points in the target language is the priority task in second-language learning.
2. In the initial stages of second-language learning, the listening and speaking skills must be acquired directly rather than being learned from the printed page.
3. Phonology, morphology, and syntax must be learned before the student begins to build a large passive vocabulary.
4. Foreign language material is best learned in complete meaningful contexts.
5. Language learning should proceed in small increments from the simple to the complex and from the known to the unknown.
6. Each stimulus should lead to one—and only one—correct response.
7. The student should always receive immediate confirmation of the correctness or incorrectness of a response he has given.
8. Automaticity of response does not develop of its own accord; the teacher must supply the necessary drill work in classroom or laboratory as the basis of fluency.

In a monostructual course, the pattern drill may be the heart of the program. In this case, the first lesson will aim at mastery of certain basic phonemes. Subsequent drills will become increasingly complex as the student gains control of additional sounds, grammatical structures, and vocabulary. Pattern drills are also used with traditional courses, usually in the form of oral drill work as a followup to the study of vocabulary, grammar, and reading selections. Ideally, only those structures and lexical items which lend themselves well to conversational work will be selected for pattern practice. However, in the texts which emphasize antiquated words and idioms, this is often difficult. For the traditionally oriented text is designed to build a large recognitional vocabulary for the purpose of reading the "classics." As a result, the nonnative teacher may develop drill material which—to the ear of a native—sounds ridiculous. It is possible to have combinations in the foreign language as absurd as:

> Behold yond stripling who driveth a hotrod!
> Would'st care to indulge in a tankard of beer?

In the polystructural course the pattern sentences are drawn from the basic dialog which typically consists of present-day conversational material. These "overlearned" dialog sentences provide the student with an ever-expanding supply of memorized lexical items. These items are continually reused throughout the course as the pattern drills focus upon the mastery of increasingly complex structures. Some textbooks are liberally supplied with pattern drills which are available in the book and on tape. In other texts, pattern drills are unsuitable or are totally lacking. In any case, it is often necessary to supplement the commercially available drill material with exercises which meet the special demands of a given teaching situation. Thus, the language teacher may find it helpful to have some knowledge of the basic steps to be followed in constructing his own pattern drills.

Constructing pattern drills

The first step is to make a complete vocabulary inventory of all the words, phrases, and expressions contained in each chapter. These items should be listed by parts of speech for easy reference. Thus, if the teacher is designing a drill based upon the agreement of adjectives and nouns, it is a simple matter to leaf through the vocabulary inventories for all previous chapters and to select those nouns, verbs, and adjectives which go well together. The order of listing parts of speech is not of crucial importance, but it is best to follow a consistent pattern from one chapter to the next. A standard dittoed or mimeographed form can facilitate the systematic collection of word inventories. The following form has been used successfully:

TEXT TITLE _____   CHAPTER _____

Nouns   *Pronouns*   *Verbs*   *Adjectives*   *Adverbs*   *Prepositions*

Conjunctions   *Interjections*   *Idioms*   *Grammar*   *Syntax*

The second step is to identify grammatical topics in each chapter toward which the drills will be directed. Then, as vocabulary permits, each point should be covered thoroughly. Also, each drill should focus upon one *new* language structure; never more than one. The number of student responses called for in each drill will be determined partly by the availability of vocabulary in the early chapters. Later in the year, the more difficult structure can be drilled again more thoroughly, as additional vocabulary is acquired. One must constantly bear in mind that genuine pattern drills must contain only vocabulary that is completely familiar to the student, and, except for the grammatical point around which the drill is built, the drill should contain only prelearned structure. This constant reentry through pattern practices of structures and vocabulary items can, in theory, gradually eliminate the interference which the native language habit system exerts upon the acquisition of a second language.

The final step in producing a pattern-drill script for subsequent adaptation to the classroom or laboratory is the selection of that type of drill which best meets the demands of the structure to be learned. However, the type of drill which one selects will tend to reflect the drill writer's beliefs with regard to whether or not

The pattern drill

language learning is a cognitive process or a process of stimulus-response conditioning (see Chapter 6). Adherents of the conditioning school will tend to produce simple substitution drills that do not require the student to make any significant changes in the pattern sentence throughout the entire drill. The following is an example of a single-slot substitution drill:

Teacher's cue	Student's response
John is here.	John is here.
at home.	John is at home.
in school.	John is in school.
downstairs.	John is downstairs.
on the roof.	John is on the roof.

In this type of drill the student is required only to remember the model sentence and to combine the new element with it. However, the new element is furnished by the teacher (or the tape), so that the student is required only to imitate what he has just heard. Such a drill could be used in Spanish, for example, to teach the verb *estar* which would be required in this sequence rather than the verb *ser*. As the student proceeds through the drill, his attention is focussed upon the new elements (at home, in school, etc.). According to the conditioning theorists, it is best to draw the student's attention away from the critical element in the drill (i.e., away from the verb *estar*) because, by so doing, the structure becomes subconsciously implanted in the student's mind as a new language habit. Thus, when future situations require the student to tell where something is, he will automatically use the verb *estar* rather than the conflict word *ser* because he will not have to stop and reflect on the matter. The conflict structure will have become a matter of habit rather than a matter of intellectual choice if enough of this sort of drill is provided. At least this is what the advocates of this type of drill claim.

However, there are others who feel that language learning is a more complex process than this, and that it does actually involve some form of extremely rapid cognition. This group tends to favor drills which require the student to make changes in the model sentence. The student's mental involvement may be simple and sharply focussed, but it must be included throughout the pattern. The following is an example of a drill which requires the student to transform the cue given by the teacher:

Teacher's cue	Student's response
John did the work.	The work was done by John.
John set the table.	The table was set by John.
John started the car.	The car was started by John.
John ate the apple.	The apple was eaten by John.

In this case, all the vocabulary is still supplied in advance by the teacher. However, a greater degree of intellectual activity is involved here than in the substitution drill, because the student must be able to instantly transform the active voice to the passive and to make all necessary morphological and syntactical modifications.

The format of the pattern drill

Drills which are recorded for laboratory use will usually follow the familiar programming format. At the very minimum they will contain the following:

1. Stimulus or cue.
2. Unrecorded space for the student to respond.
3. The reward in the form of the correct response.
1. A new stimulus.

This is the so-called "three-phase" drill. There are many who believe that this format is inadequate because it tends to frustrate the student by compelling him to jump ahead to a new response before he has fully assimilated the old one. Thus, some of the newer materials have included four- and five-phase drills which include the following steps:

1. Stimulus.
2. Space for student response.
3. Reward in the form of correct response.
4. Space to repeat the correct response.
5. Repetition of the correct response.

The pattern drill

213

The fourth step allows the student to doubly reinforce a correct response by repeating it or to reshape an incorrect response if he has erred. The fifth step allows him a further opportunity to confirm the responses made in steps two and four.

In the classroom situation the teacher can provide as many (or as few) reinforcements as the students appear to need. When a drill is being done en masse, the three-phase format is generally considered to be minimal. However, with individual responses, it may not always be necessary to confirm a correct answer. If a student answers correctly and clearly, the teacher may occasionally move on to another student. However, if a student falters or gives an indistinct response, it is considered good practice to supply the correct answer for him before proceeding to another student. Later the teacher will return to the student who responded incorrectly and elicit a correct response from him.

In either classroom or laboratory it is important for the teacher (or the tape) to provide a clear explanation before the students undertake a given drill. In class the teacher can have the students run through perhaps a half-dozen responses chorally until he is certain that they know how they are supposed to respond. If a commercially produced tape contains inadequate instructions, the teacher may record his own directions onto tape and splice the revised instructions into the laboratory lesson. Also, the laboratory drill is often best preceded by classroom drill on the identical material, perhaps a day or two ahead of time. The rapidity and accuracy of student response is the final determination of whether or not the students have been adequately prepared for a given drill.

However, assuming the student has been adequately prepared to manipulate all the vocabulary and structural elements contained in a drill, there is still a great need for overexplanation. Even the very bright student can misconstrue the intent of a drill. Those who are less well endowed mentally are almost certain to flounder unless the teacher takes extra precautions in introducing each new type of exercise. Misunderstood drill work leads to confusion, frustration, lack of classroom control, and loss of student respect for the teacher, the course, and the language itself. Thus, an extra minute or two spent on explaining the nature of the drill is generally time well spent. A rule of thumb would be, "Better to overexplain than to suffer the consequences of underexplaining." Thus, the following type of explanation is recommended for introducing all pattern drills, both in the classroom and in the laboratory.

INTRODUCTORY EXPLANATION

In the following exercises you will hear a question and you will reply by saying that you have not seen the person or object which is mentioned. To speak English, it is essential for you to learn to use the pronouns *him, her, it,* and *them,* and to put them in the right place in the sentence. For speaking, you must be able to do this instantly, without taking a lot of time to figure things out. This drill will help you develop fluency with these important pronouns. Now, each time you hear the question, you can begin your response by saying, "I haven't seen. . . ." Before you reach the end of the sentence, you must know which pronoun, *him, her, it,* or *them,* is the correct response. When you are able to supply all the correct pronouns in this drill without a moment's hesitation, then you have achieved good control of the material.

SAMPLE OF EACH TYPE OF RESPONSE EXPECTED

In this drill you will hear a question such as, "Where's mother?"
And you will answer by saying, "I haven't seen her."
Then you may hear, "Where's my book?"
And you will answer, "I haven't seen it."
Or you may hear, "Where are the chairs?"
And you will answer, "I haven't seen them."
Or, finally, you may hear, "Where's John?"
And you will answer, "I haven't seen him."

MODELING THE DESIRED RESPONSE

This is done to "set" the pattern and to reexpose the student to the proper pronunciation and intonation of the utterance.

Now listen to the question and the answer, and repeat only the answer.

Stimulus provided by teacher or tape	Student response follows immediately	Reinforcement supplied immediately
Where's mother? I haven't seen her.	I haven't seen her.	I haven't seen her.
Where's my book? I haven't seen it.	I haven't seen it.	I haven't seen it.

The pattern drill

215

Stimulus provided by teacher or tape	Student response follows immediately	Reinforcement supplied immediately
Where are the chairs?		
I haven't seen them.	I haven't seen them.	I haven't seen them.
Where's John?		
I haven't seen him.	I haven't seen him.	I haven't seen him.

THE DRILL

From this point on the student must supply the response and listen for the reinforcement of the correct response.

Listen to the question and then supply the answer.

Stimulus	Response	Reward
Where's mother?	I haven't seen her.	I haven't seen her.
Where's my book?	I haven't seen it.	I haven't seen it.
Where are the boys?	I haven't seen them.	I haven't seen them.
Where are the girls?	I haven't seen them.	I haven't seen them.
Where is the chalk?	I haven't seen it.	I haven't seen it.
Where is my pencil?	I haven't seen it.	I haven't seen it.
Where is my brother?	I haven't seen him.	I haven't seen him.
Where are my books?	I haven't seen them.	I haven't seen them.

Similar procedures would be followed for the three commonly taught languages. Naturally, the explanations would be different because the structures are different in each language. However, there is just as much need for thoroughness of explanation in introducing French, German, and Spanish pronoun drills as there is in introducing English pronouns.

Below are samples of German, Spanish, and French pronoun drills based upon the English drill presented above. They illustrate the unique learning problems encountered by the language student who speaks English natively. Note that both grammar and word order present significant learning problems in each language. Thus the drills, as they appear here, could only serve as the culminating exercise to determine whether mastery had been achieved. They would necessarily be preceded by exhaustive practice on the individual pronouns and upon all the verb forms used in the drill. Only the stimulus and response are given in the examples below. Also, to highlight the position and form of the direct object pronouns, the

216

repetitive sentence elements have been omitted in the response. In actual practice, of course, the drill would include reinforcement with the correct response and would contain only complete utterances.

German

Wo ist meine Mutter?	Ich habe sie nicht gesehen.
Wo ist mein Buch?	Ich habe es nicht gesehen.
Wo sind die Jungen?	sie
Wo sind die Mädchen?	sie
Wo ist die Kreide?	sie
Wo ist mein Bleistift?	ihn
Wo ist mein Bruder?	ihn
Wo sind meine Bücher?	sie

Spanish

¿Dónde está mi madre?	No la he visto.
¿Dónde está mi libro?	No lo he visto.
¿Dónde están los muchachos?	los
¿Dónde están las muchachas?	las
¿Dónde está la tiza?	la
¿Dónde está el lapiz?	lo
¿Dónde está mi hermano?	le (lo)
¿Dónde están mis libros?	los

French

Où est maman?	Je ne l'ai pas vue.	
Où est mon livre?	Je ne l'ai pas vu.	
Où sont les garcons?	les	vus.
Où sont les filles?	les	vues.
Où est la craie?	l'	vue.
Où est mon crayon?	l'	vu.
Où est mon frère?	l'	vu.
Où sont mes livres?	les	vus.

Types of pattern drills

Potentially there is no limit to the number of pattern-drill types. Human ingenuity can certainly discover an endless variety of ways to elicit the desired responses from students of language. Thus, the following list does not pretend to be definitive. It is hoped, however, that the list represents the main types of drills which have evolved during the relatively short history of pattern practice as a distinct teaching technique. Clearly, space does not permit a comprehensive matching of drill types for all conflict points in all three of the commonly taught languages. Indeed to do this in any one language would be to write a book of considerable length. Thus, the drill formats will be given in English on the theory that the reader will be able to perceive for himself how each format applies to various structural problems in the foreign language in which he has an interest. (In the following drills the stimulus is designated by "S," the student response by "R.")

Substitution drills

1. *Simple substitution (possessive adjectives)*

   MODEL:

That gets on <u>my</u> nerves.	That gets on <u>my</u> nerves.
That gets on <u>his</u> nerves.	That gets on <u>his</u> nerves.

S:		R:	
	her		That gets on her nerves.
	their		That gets on their nerves.
	our		That gets on our nerves.
	my		That gets on my nerves.
	his		That gets on his nerves.
	father's		That gets on father's nerves.
	mother's		That gets on mother's nerves.

2. *Substitution with mutation (direct object pronoun)*

   MODEL:

I lost my book.	I lost <u>it</u>.
I lost my girl.	I lost <u>her</u>.

S:		R:	
	I lost my pencil.		I lost it.
	I lost my book.		I lost it.
	I lost my boy friend.		I lost him.
	I lost my girl.		I lost her.
	I lost my tom cat.		I lost him.
	I lost my books.		I lost them.

(Note: It is clear that drill 2 would present different types of problems in each of the three languages. In French and Spanish, word order would

be a serious conflict point. In German, the use of masculine and feminine pronouns to refer to inanimate objects would cause the most severe problems of interference.)

3. *Substitution with choices (use of* some *or* any *in negative and affirmative sentences)*

MODEL:

| Do you have some money? (Yes) | Yes, I have <u>some</u>. |
| Do you have some money? (No) | No, I don't have <u>any</u>. |

S: Do you have some books? (Yes)	R: Yes, I have some.
Do you some some money? (No)	No, I don't have any.
Do you have some examples? (No)	No, I don't have any.
Do you have some cash? (Yes)	Yes, I have some.
Do you have some money? (Yes)	Yes, I have some.

4. *Substitution with pictorial cues (prepositions with objects)*

Pictures are projected onto a screen or are drawn on large cards which the teacher can set in the chalk rail and point to rapidly.

MODEL:

(Picture of a book in a box.) Where it it?	It's <u>in</u> the box.
S: (Picture of book under the box.) Where it is now?	R: It's under the box.
(Picture of book beside the box.) Where is it now?	It's beside the box.
(Picture of book on top of box.) Where is it now?	It's on top of the box.

5. *Substitution with changing slot (ability to perceive various structural elements and to use them appropriately)*

The pattern drill

219

Bring him the book.
Bring her the book.
Bring us the book.

S:		R:	
Bring him the book.		Bring him the book.	
_____ her _____.		Bring her the book.	
_____ us _____.		Bring us the book.	
_____ table.		Bring us the table.	
_____ chair.		Bring us the chair.	
Sell _____.		Sell us the chair.	
_____ car.		Sell us the car.	
_____ them _____.		Sell them the car.	

6. *Substitution through choice (infinitive with conditional)*

MODEL:

Would you prefer to walk or ride?	I would prefer to ride.
Would you prefer to go or stay?	I would prefer to stay.
Would you prefer to read or write?	I would prefer to write.

S:	R:
Would you prefer to walk or ride?	I would prefer to ride.
Would you prefer to go or stay?	I would prefer to stay.
Would you prefer to read or write?	I would prefer to write.
Would you prefer to sing or listen?	I would prefer to listen.
Would you prefer to sit or stand?	I would prefer to stand.

Combination and Conversion Drills

1. *Combination (adjective with noun)*

MODEL:

There's a boy. He's smart.	He's a smart boy.
There's a girl. She's smart.	She's a smart girl.

S:	R:
There's a man. He's clever.	He's a clever man.
There's a girl. She's pretty.	She's a pretty girl.

There's a student. He's shy.   He's a shy student.
There's a building. It's tall.   It's a tall building.

(Note: In Spanish and French this drill can be used for teaching either word order or adjective-noun agreement. In German, the drill is applicable to the teaching of adjective endings. Masculine, feminine, and (in German) neuter forms can first be drilled separately, then presented as mixed, random stimuli. When the students have achieved a high level of control over the singular noun-adjective combinations, then the plurals can be drilled in a similar manner. Finally, singulars and plurals can all be drilled as mixed random examples.)

2. *Combination (word order in a dependent clause or, for those learning English as a foreign language, conversion from past emphatic to simple past tense)*

MODEL:

What <u>did</u> he <u>say</u>? I don't know.   I don't know what he <u>said</u>.

Why <u>did</u> he <u>go</u>? I don't know.   I don't know why he <u>went</u>.

S: When did he come? I don't know.   R: I don't know when he came.

What did she see? I don't know.   I don't know what she saw.

How did they sing? I don't know.   I don't know how they sang.

What did they do? I don't know.   I don't know what they did.

3. *Combination (relative pronoun antecedent)*

MODEL:

I have something. It's new.   I have something <u>that's</u> new.

The student was here yesterday. He knows you.   The student who <u>was</u> here yesterday knows you.

S: It was the older man. He bought the car.   R: It was the older man who bought the car.

It was the blond waitress. She brought you the check.   It was the blond waitress who brought you the check.

I saw the boy. He took the money.   I saw the boy who took the money.

The pattern drill

4. *Conversion (present emphatic to simple present)*

Where <u>does</u> he <u>live</u>? (in town)	He <u>lives</u> in town.
Where <u>does</u> he <u>work</u>? (at the new factory)	He <u>works</u> at the new factory.

S: Where does he stay? (with his folks)

R: He stays with his folks.

Where does he eat? (at home)

He eats at home.

Where does she live? (in the dorm)

She lives in the dorm.

Where does she practice? (in school)

She practices in school.

Where does it start? (at the beginning)

It starts at the beginning.

(Note: After the students have been drilled thoroughly on the third person singular forms, "Where does he . . . ," "Where does she . . . ," and "Where does it . . . ," then the drill is presented in the plural. Sentences such as, "Where do the boys stay?" and "Where do they eat?" are used to elicit the plural verb forms. Then a third drill introduces mixed singular and plural cues. When the students are able to cope with both verb types without hesitation, then the first and second person forms are introduced in separate drills. Final mastery of the pattern has been achieved when the student can respond instantly and correctly to all persons both singular and plural—"Why does he . . . ?" "Why does she . . . ?" "Why does it . . . ?" "Why do they . . . ?" "Why do I . . . ?" "Why do you . . . ?" etc.).

5. *Conversion (change of verb tense)*

Mary <u>is buying</u> a new dress today.	Mary <u>bought</u> a new dress yesterday.
He's <u>leaving</u> early today.	He <u>left</u> early yesterday.

S: He's having trouble today. She's singing today. We're having beans today. The bookstore is closed today.

R: He had trouble yesterday. She sang yesterday. We had beans yesterday. The bookstore was closed yesterday.

6. *Conversion through substitution (person-number changes)*

MODEL:

I <u>am</u> in the library. (we)	We <u>are</u> in the library.
He <u>is</u> in the library. (they)	They <u>are</u> in the library.

S: We are in the library. (I)	R: I am in the library.
You	You are in the library.
I	I am in the library.
Howard	Howard is in the library.
Howard and Mary	Howard and Mary are in the library.
They	They are in the library.

(Note: This type of drill differs from the old chanting of conjugations in that the forms are drilled in random order.)

7. *Conversion through addition (subjunctive drill—French and Spanish —use of conjunction* dass *in German)*

MODEL:

I want to read the book.	I want <u>you</u> to read the book.
I want to buy the book.	I want <u>you</u> to buy the book.

S: I want to see the book.	R: I want you to see the book.
I want to sell the book.	I want you to sell the book.
I want to carry the book.	I want you to carry the book.
I want to bring the book.	I want you to bring the book.
I want to read the book.	I want you to read the book.

8. *Conversion through substitution (position and form of direct object pronouns)*

MODEL:

I gave him <u>the book</u>.	I gave <u>it</u> to him.
I gave him <u>the fork</u>.	I gave <u>it</u> to him.
I gave him <u>the spoon</u>.	I gave <u>it</u> to him.

S: I gave him the car.	R: I gave it to him.
I gave him the soap.	I gave it to him.
I gave him the hat.	I gave it to him.
I gave him the coat.	I gave it to him.
I gave him the knife.	I gave it to him.
I gave him the cars.	I gave them to him.
I gave him the keys.	I gave them to him.

The pattern drill

223

(Note: The above responses, which look so simple in English, present serious problems to the English-speaking student of French, German, or Spanish who is attempting to master the comparable structures in those languages. In German, for instance, the student has a difficult time accepting the fact that it can be a masculine or feminine form. French and Spanish present serious morphological and syntactical problems.)

9. *Conversion (declarative to interrogative)*

MODEL:

He <u>lives</u> here.	<u>Does</u> he <u>live</u> here?
He <u>works</u> here.	<u>Does</u> he <u>work</u> here?
We <u>eat</u> here.	<u>Do</u> we <u>eat</u> here?

S: He lives here.	R: Does he live here?
He works here.	Does he work here?
We eat here.	Do we eat here?
They live here.	Do they live here?
She stays here.	Does she stay here?
We stop here.	Do we stop here?
It ends here.	Does it end here?

10. *Conversion through change of grammatical function (transitive versus intransitive)*

MODEL:

The prices <u>have risen</u>.	Yes, he <u>raised</u> them.
The book <u>has lain</u> there.	Yes, he <u>laid</u> it there.

S: The prices have risen.	R: Yes, he raised them.
The book has lain there.	Yes, he laid it there.
The tree has fallen.	Yes, he felled it.
It has sat there.	Yes, he set it there.

(Note: This type of drill is particularly valuable for contrasting two structures which the student is likely to confuse. Thus, it is appropriate for such problems as the difference between ser and estar in Spanish and the function of the dative and accusative in German. If the student learns to contrast the structures in a drill situation, he may have a better chance of producing the correct forms later than if he drilled on each form in isolation.) Note the following examples:

S: ¿<u>Es</u> Juan su amigo?	R: Sí, pero ahora <u>está</u> en casa.
¿<u>Es</u> Maria' su amiga?	Sí, pero ahora <u>está</u> en casa.
Jetzt geht er in <u>die</u> Stadt.	Jetzt ist er in <u>der</u> Stadt.
Jetzt geht er <u>ins</u> Dorf.	Jetzt ist er <u>im</u> Dorf.

224

Chain Drills

1. *One stimulus with two responses (comparative and superlative with the -er and -st endings)*

MODEL:

Tom is <u>tall</u>. (Bill)	Bill is <u>taller</u> than Tom.
(John)	John is the <u>tallest</u> in the class.
Tom is <u>smart</u>. (Bill)	Bill is <u>smarter</u> than Tom.
(John)	John is the <u>smartest</u> in the class.

S₁: Tom is funny. (Bill) R: Bill is funnier than Tom.
S₂: John. R: John is the funniest in the class.

S₁: Tom is clever. (Bill) R: Bill is cleverer than Tom.
S₂: John. R: John is the cleverest in the class.

S₁: Tom is lazy. (Bill) R: Bill is lazier than Tom.
S₂: John. R: John is the laziest in the class.

(Comparative and superlative with the more-most structures)

S₁: Tom is intelligent. (Bill) R: Bill is more intelligent.
S₂: John. R: John is the most intelligent in the class.

S₁: Tom is incredible. (Bill) R: Bill is more incredible than Tom.
S₂: John. R: John is the most incredible in the class.

2. *Initial stimulus by teacher: students supply additional stimuli*

S₁: My name is Miss Smith; what's your name? (Teacher points to Paul Conner)

R: My name is Paul Conner; (turning to designated student behind him) what's your name?

S₂: (Teacher points to student across the row from Cathy)

R: My name is Cathy Brent; (turning to designated student across the row) what's your name?

The pattern drill

225

S₃: (Teacher points to student two rows from Mary)	R: My name is Mary Calder; (turning to designated student two rows away) what's your name?

3. *Directed dialog or restatement drill (interrogatives)*

S: Mary, ask Frank where he is going. Frank, ask Mildred what she is doing. Mildred, ask Henry why he is sleeping. Henry, ask Paul when he is going to wake up.	R: Where are you going, Frank? What are you doing, Mildred? Why are you sleeping, Henry? When are you going to wake up, Paul?

4. *Restatement drill (imperatives)*

S: Mary, tell Frank to go home. Frank, tell Mildred to pay attention. Mildred, tell Henry to wake up. Henry, tell Paul to hurry up.	R: Frank, go home! Mildred, pay attention! Henry, wake up! Paul, hurry up!

Pyramid Drills

1. *Cumulative substitution (word order of time and place)*

MODEL:

I was born.	I was born.
S: I was born. (in Bonn) on the Rhine June fifth 1938	R: I was born in Bonn. I was born in Bonn on the Rhine. I was born June fifth in Bonn on the Rhine. I was born June fifth, 1938, in Bonn on the Rhine.

2. *Cumulative substitution (adjectives: position and endings)*

MODEL:

I have a car.	I have a car.

S: I have a car. (new)	R: I have a new car.
red	I have a new red car.
with spoked wheels	I have a new red car with spoked wheels.
wire	I have a new red car with wire spoked wheels.
sports	I have a new red sports car with wire spoked wheels.
chromium	I have a new red sports car with chromium wire spoked wheels.

3. *Expansion through replacement (syntax)*

S: She lives there.	R: She lives there.
in Boston	She lives in Boston.
the city of	She lives in the city of Boston.
my sister	My sister lives in the city of Boston.
my older sister	My older sister lives in the city of Boston.

Translation Drills

Some language educators feel that English should never be used in drills of any kind. Others are of the opinion that English can be used to good advantage as stimuli for certain types of responses. One concern is that the English cue will create interference and will block fluency of response as the student struggles to find suitable equivalents from the native to the target language. The interference of English, however, can be strongly counteracted by using only a highly consistent pattern of responses in the foreign language. Also, if problem lexical items are avoided, the student can focus his attention exclusively upon the pattern which is being drilled. In this way, the English cues can lead regularly to fluent, accurate responses in the foreign language. They have the added advantage of impressing upon the student the nature of foreign language structures which do not exist in English. Thus, for example, the student translating the verb in drill 1 below, becomes acutely aware that the subjunctive is required to express meaning in Spanish whereas the indicative is called for in English.

The pattern drill

1. *Translation drill (subjunctive in adjective clause)*

MODEL:

I'm looking for a man who eats a lot.	Busco un hombre que coma mucho.
I'm looking for a man who is crazy.	Busco un hombre que esté loco.

S:	I'm looking for a man who is intelligent.	R:	Busco un hombre que sea inteligente.
	I'm looking for a man who has money.		Busco un hombre que tenga dinero.
	I'm looking for a man who reads a lot.		Busco un hombre que lea mucho.
	I'm looking for a man who writes.		Busco un hombre que escriba.
	I'm looking for a man who sings.		Busco un hombre que cante.

2. *Translation drill (personal pronouns in the dative)*

MODEL:

How thoughtless of me.	Wie unüberlegt von mir.
How thoughtless of him.	Wie unüberlegt von ihm.

S:	How thoughtless of her.	R:	Wie unüberlegt von ihr.
	How thoughtless of them.		Wie unüberlegt von ihnen.
	How thoughtless of us.		Wie unüberlegt von uns.
	How thoughtless of you. (familiar singular)		Wie unüberlegt von dir.
	How thoughtless of you. (familiar plural)		Wie unüberlegt von euch.

Using pattern drills in the classroom

Pattern practice is based upon linguistic science and psychological theory. But, however sound the underlying principles may be, the success or failure of pattern practice appears to relate as much to the skill and sensitivity of the teacher as to the pedagogical soundness of the drills themselves. The enthusiasm in the teacher's voice, the energetic way he moves around the room, the emotional bond he has established between himself and the class; these, along with many other factors, determine to a significant (if unknown) degree the ultimate success of the drill work. Thus, since teaching appears to be as much an art as it is a science, no list of logically planned techniques is likely to solve all the problems of the foreign language instructor who supposes that good teaching results purely from following the steps in a cookbook-like manual. The apprentice teacher can perhaps gain some important insights from a list of practices which are often identified with successful teachers of foreign language. The following guidelines are based upon classroom observation of such teachers.

PREPARING THE CLASS FOR PATTERN PRACTICE

1. Every student is informed of what he is expected to do when he is called on to respond. Also, the purpose of the drill is made clear.
2. There are no tricks; the student knows exactly what types of morphological and syntactical changes will occur in the drill. He also knows which part of the pattern sentence will remain unchanged during the entire drill. (Making one or two structural changes and pronouncing the sentence correctly at near-native speed is sufficient challenge in itself. Trick questions presented during oral drills tend to be demoralizing.)
3. The student has been taught all the phonology which occurs in the drill.
4. The students have been taught the meaning of the structures which they are called on to manipulate so that they are not merely mouthing patterns of sounds which carry no message to the brain. (With some justification, critics have labeled noncognizant oral drills "pitter patter practice.")
5. The teacher has selected a drill which covers all the important aspects of the structure toward which the drill is directed. (However, it is not necessary, for example, to have 30 different problems merely because they are 30 students in the class. Ten well-devised cues will often suffice. Each cue can be used over again several times.)
6. Several pattern sentences are done chorally to insure that students know how to respond.

The pattern drill

7. The teacher checks to make sure that all books are closed and out of sight.

1. The teacher gives the cue *first*, then *points* suddenly to a student. (Using the student's name wastes time. Also, it is customary to start with a student who is likely to give a correct response. This gets the drill launched in the right direction and allows the slower students to develop confidence regarding the nature of the expected response.)
2. The teacher repeats the correct response, gives the next cue, and quickly points to another student.
3. The teacher moves rapidly about the room saying the cue and then pointing unexpectedly to the student who is to recite. (With most drills it is best to avoid going up one row and down the other calling on the students in sequence. Otherwise, the only student who is likely to be fully awake is the one who is due to recite.)
4. If a student fails to respond almost immediately, the teacher supplies the correct response and goes on to another student. Later, the teacher returns to the nonresponding student after he has heard a dozen or more correct responses from other students and from the teacher. (It is considered bad practice to stop and discuss a wrong response or to discuss grammatical principles in the middle of a drill session.)
5. The teacher demands universal attention. By moving constantly around the rows and delivering the cues in totally random order the teacher can unexpectedly designate any student who shows the slightest inattention. (Some teachers develop special techniques which fit their unique personalities and which keep the students both amused and alert. For example, one teacher will look to the left and then point to a student on his right, or vice versa. Another teacher will begin raising his right hand, and then point suddenly with his left. If properly executed, techniques of this sort can give youngsters great satisfaction in not being caught off guard. Psychologically, the purpose of such theatrics is to get the students into the spirit of the drill so that they feel the need to be attentive and to react instantly and respond rapidly.)

6. Because pattern practice requires intense concentration, teachers normally limit drill time to twenty minutes or less. In this amount of time, the competent teacher can provide rather thorough drill work on three or four basic language structures with all students in a class of (say) twenty-five responding several times on each structure being drilled.

7. If a majority of students are faltering, groping for words, giving wrong responses, and are showing general unpreparedness, it is best to abandon that particular drill, at least temporarily. Assuming that the drill was properly designed, such failure indicates the need for reteaching the basic material.

Pattern practice in the language laboratory

Many high schools are equipped with language laboratories or electronic classrooms which allow all the students in a class to hear the drill material from a central console. Minimal equipment usually includes a headset through which the student hears the master program and a microphone which enables the student to hear his responses. The same amplifier which makes the student's voice audible to his own ear also carries his utterances back to the console where the teacher can monitor them. In this situation the teacher's role changes drastically where pattern practice is concerned. For, in the laboratory, students do not have to wait to be called on; they are all responding at the same time. Both the stimulus and the reward are supplied by the tape, with a pause for student response. The main function of the teacher is to determine whether the students' responses are generally satisfactory, and to make note of students who are having difficulty with the drill material. If only a few students are unable to perform acceptably, the teacher can prescribe remedial drill work for later laboratory sessions. If most of the students are having difficulties, then it is usually advisable to stop and spend additional time upon the structures which are causing the difficulties.

If each student position is equipped with a dual-channel tape recorder, then a more sophisticated set of procedures is possible. In fact, total individualization is possible because, theoretically at least, each student can be working on a different tape and can be learning at his own rate with that tape. In practice, however, few teachers have found it possible to cope with more than two or three levels of progress at one time. Many high-school teachers are even bewildered by the thought of having any students engage in work which is separate from the lock-step activities of the total class. Thus, even in situations where each student position is equipped with a tape recorder, the following procedures are most often followed:

1. The student records the cue, his own responses, and the reward onto the student track of the tape in the booth recorder.
2. At the end of the drill he rewinds the tape and listens to his own responses as compared to the master cues and responses.
3. The teacher monitors the students throughout both of these steps in much the same manner as she does in a laboratory which has no tape recorders.

The value of the student playback-compare activities is often questioned. Those who are against the practice contend that students merely tend to reinforce errors and that, for the most part, adolescents are not able to hear their own mistakes sufficiently well to make the playback feature worthwhile. Those who favor student tape recorders insist that the student will learn best if he is able to hear himself on tape with his own voice placed in juxtaposition to a native speaker's voice articulating the same material. The question is largely academic at present. For various reasons, high schools have tended to install the electronic classroom or the laboratory without booths. Thus, the new teacher of foreign language is most likely to encounter the listen-respond type of equipment if, indeed, the school has a language laboratory at all.

Either type of laboratory can serve as a library installation to which students come before school, after school, or during free hours. Because of their self-correcting feature, pattern drills are excellent for such self-study work. Students who have not mastered a given language structure can request a specific tape from the laboratory assistant or from the teacher who is on duty in the laboratory. The student can then continue going through the drill until he is able to provide a correct response to every stimulus within the space allowed on the tape. If the laboratory is equipped with student recorders, the students have the advantage of being able to stop and start the tape and to play difficult passages over and over. In the electronic classroom the tape is played at the console, and the student has no control over its progress. Thus, he must listen to it through to the end and request a replay of the entire drill when he wishes to hear certain difficult parts over a second time.

Evaluating commercially produced pattern-drill tapes

Many publishers of modern language textbooks include mention of tapes in their promotional materials. In some cases these "tape programs" are nothing but a recorded version of the contents of the book which have been read into a microphone by an uninspirational native speaker. In other cases, the tapes follow a programming format, but are deficient in psychological and linguistic sophistication. Therefore, it is seldom advisable to purchase tapes without having examined a representative sampling of the contents of the tape program. As a general practice, foreign language teachers might do well to refuse consideration of any text series which by policy does not permit prior examination of the tape program (or at least of a broad sampling of that program). The criteria listed in Table 7 are suggested for evaluating any recorded material which is represented as "pattern drill" or "structural exercises."

7

Pattern drill evaluation sheet

Name of Tape Producer _____

Accompanying Text (if any) _____ *Language* _____ *Level* _____

I. Instructions on Tape
    A. *Language Used—Instructions Are—*
        1. *In English* ( )
        2. *In foreign language* ( )
        3. *In both* ( )
    B. *Clarity of Instructions*
        1. *Purpose made clear* ( )
        2. *Purpose not clear* ( )
        3. *Highly confusing* ( )

The pattern drill

C. *Examples Used to Set the Pattern*
    1. *0–3 examples* ( )
    2. *3–5 examples* ( )
    3. *More than 5* ( )

II. Voice, Quality of
A. *Overall Impression*
    1. *Good* ( )
    2. *Fair* ( )
    3. *Poor* ( )
B. *Specific Qualities*
    1. *Monotonous* ( ) *or lively* ( )
    2. *Stilted* ( ) *or natural* ( )
    3. *Too slow* ( ) *or normal rate* ( )
    4. *Hesitant* ( ) *or smooth* ( )
    5. *Reading intonation* ( ) *or speaking intonation* ( )

III. Recording, Quality of
A. *Overall Impression*
    1. *Good* ( )
    2. *Fair* ( )
    3. *Poor* ( )
B. *Specific Flaws*
    1. *Background noise* ( )
    2. *Hum* ( )
    3. *Volume varies* ( )
    4. *Hiss* ( )

IV. Type of Drill
A. *Format*
    1. *Two-phase (<u>cue-pause</u>-next cue)* ( ) *(Not acceptable for laboratory use.)*
    2. *Three-phase (<u>cue-pause-correct response</u>-next cue)* ( )
    3. *Four-phase (<u>cue-pause-correct response-pause</u>-next cue)* ( )
    4. *Other* ( ) _____
B. *Pauses*
    1. *Too long* ( )
    2. *Too short* ( )
    3. *Appropriate for near-normal response* ( )
C. *Content and Structure*
    1. *There is—*
        a. *Sufficient drill on the grammatical point* ( )
        b. *Insufficient drill to fix the pattern* ( )
        c. *Excessive number of problems* ( )

2. *Length of master utterance is—*
   a. *Short enough to retain* ( )
   b. *Too long to retain* ( )
3. *The response required by the cue is—*
   a. *Unmistakable* ( )
   b. *Ambiguous* ( )
   c. *Usually clear* ( )
4. *How many changes must the student make in each cue?*
   a. *One* ( )
   b. *Two* ( )
   c. *More than two* ( )

(Name of Evaluator)   *(School or Department)*

Reading, writing, and pattern practice

In the early years of the post-World War II language-reform move-ment, it was believed that introduction of the written word should be postponed for weeks or even for months in the high-school foreign language course. This belief was apparently based upon the fact that some of the more successful intensive programs in-volving military personnel and adult civilians had required language students to spend 200 hours or more in prereading instruction. The reason for withholding the written word for such long periods in the initial stages of instruction was to develop thoroughly ingrained habits of pronunciation and intonation which were supposedly "contamination proof" when the student was subsequently exposed to the written word. Proper prereading instruction did apparently minimize the number of phonological monstrosities such as the previously mentioned pronunciations of "sheep" for "ship" and "lowly pope" for "lollipop." (The literate person who speaks Spanish will almost invariably equate the written letter *i* in "ship" with the *ee*-sound of his native language and the *o*'s in "lollipop" with the Spanish vowel *o*.)

However, the long prereading period of the intensive programs does not appear to be valid in the regular junior or senior high-school program. The intensive courses typically operated from dawn

The pattern drill

to dark, and therefore a 200-hour prereading period actually represented no more than a few weeks on the calendar. In the high-school program, however, 200 hours constitute more than an entire nine-month school year. Yet experience indicates that even the most competent high-school teacher can seldom sustain a prereading period of more than a few weeks. (This problem is discussed further in Chapter 9.)

There is reason to believe that the graphic symbols, properly introduced, need not be a hindrance, and can actually be a great help in the learning process. The key to the problem may well be the timing and manner of their introduction rather than the length of postponement. Thus, if a student has demonstrated the ability to produce a given series of phonemes, there is no proven reason why he should not immediately learn to articulate those phonemes in association with appropriate graphic symbols. Nor is there any proof that he should be restrained from writing the symbols in response to auditory, graphic, or pictorial stimuli. Thus, once a student has demonstrated good oral control over the phonological elements of a given pattern drill, he may then profitably use the written forms to reinforce his audiolingual learning.

Reading pattern drills aloud can provide oral homework activity which would be unavailable in a purely audiolingual course. Students can be taught to cover the answers while responding orally to the cues on a printed drill sheet. If they then carefully check each oral response immediately, the students will be reproducing some of the learning conditions associated with programmed instruction. When work with phonology has proceeded far enough, the oral reading practice can be sandwiched between purely oral drill sessions on the identical material. It appears that many students cannot distinguish such basic spoken morphological elements as noun, verb, and adjective endings until they have seen them in written form. And it is axiomatic that the ability to distinguish critical sounds is a prerequisite for producing them. Hence, for many "visually dependent" students, the availability of the written word may be an absolute necessity for full success with pattern practice and with other oral-aural aspects of language learning.

Procedures similar to those described above can be used effectively in the area of writing. That is, students can be instructed to write certain sentences contained in the pattern drills in response to the printed cues while again using the correct response for immediate reinforcement. With all such homework the teacher must do a good job of selling the student on the need for responding and then immediately reinforcing his own responses until complete accuracy is achieved. Unless they see the value of this procedure, many students will rely on merely copying the answer directly from the text. A few check tests early in the year can serve to convince the copyists of the usefulness of the stimulus-response-reward technique.

Written responses can also be elicited in response to oral stimuli, although here it is more economical to select only a few responses from the pattern rather than to have students reproduce the entire drill. Also, short dictations involving recombinations of structures and lexical items from several drills can be useful for teaching spelling and for demonstrating the interchangeability of sentence elements. At the more advanced levels, students can be asked to create their own pattern drills based upon rearrangements of prelearned material. To get the students started, the teacher can supply some of the cues and some of the responses and ask the students to complete the pattern. The following is a sample of an assignment that could follow after ten or more verbs had been introduced in the past tense:

S: I lose my books.	R: I lost my books.
S: I find everything.	R: I found everything.
S: I see him today.	R:
S:	R: I hated that story.
S:	R: I spent a lot of money.
S: I have a good time.	R:
S:	R:
S:	R:
S:	R:

Gradually, students can be encouraged to create their own entire drills as part of their written work. Those who produce acceptable drills can be allowed to try them out on the class. Students will tend to produce extremely complex and ambiguous drills if left to their own devices. They must be constantly reminded that the

The pattern drill

rules for construcing pattern drills are: (1) Use only that vocabulary which is contained in earlier chapters, and (2) use only those structures which have been presented previously (or use different forms of those structures).

The limitations of pattern practice

As with any other teaching tool, the pattern drill is subject to the danger of being viewed as a panacea for all the problems related to language instruction. Overenthusiastic proponents of the drill have tended to use it to the exclusion of other techniques which are needed to produce free responses in the new language. The next step after pattern practice is to take the student from the point where he is able to make minimal changes in cues supplied by the teacher and move him to a point where he is able to use the responses to the cues for generating his own utterances both orally and in writing. Thus, the teacher must insist that the students engage in followup work involving the creation of sentences which apply to them personally. In the early stages, it is a great challenge to the student to express things he would like to say while limiting himself to the narrow range of structures he has learned. Pattern drill work has conditioned him to produce, within a specific pattern, the one right response which the stimulus allows, while the world of reality demands that he produce both the pattern and vocabulary which a new and unpredictable situation calls for. For example, a student may have learned various patterned responses such as: "I haven't seen it," "I haven't seem them," etc., and he may have been drilled upon the structure "Have you been to class?" "Have you been to the play?" "Have you been there yet?" etc. Yet the student has been a victim of arrested language development if the method of instruction has left him unable to combine the interrogative structure of the second pattern with the transitive verb and the direct object forms contained in the first pattern. (Thus, if someone mentions that a certain play has been running for several weeks, he should be able to ask, "Have you seen it yet?") Clearly a major function of the teacher, if he is to be anything but a warm-blooded drill device, would seem to lie in the direction of developing in students this ability to produce new combinations of the structural elements and lexical items which have been mastered during the drill sessions.

The step beyond drill practice

When the students have reached the stage where they are able to read aloud with reasonable accuracy of pronunciation, they can be trusted to produce their own drill responses by referring to the written pattern drills of current and past lessons. Ultimately the student must become involved in the process of recombining sentence elements which are capable of recombination and of avoiding combinations which are not interchangeable. One way to approach this goal is to require the student to produce a certain number of original utterances in writing which the teacher then checks for accuracy of form and meaning. The utterances must be based on structures already learned and the vocabulary must be largely that which is contained in the earlier lessons. However, sometimes a few new content words are needed to make the utterances fully adequate. These too must be carefully checked by the teacher. The student finally has to present his sentences orally either as a solo performance or in conjunction with another student. Students working in pairs or in small groups can often produce better results than can be achieved singly. In some cases the teacher will appoint a good student to be the chairman of such a study group, which usually consists of no more than three or four students. The competent student chairman can help minimize the number of errors produced in the written form of the pattern recombinations and can help correct pronunciation errors during the oral stages. During the work periods, the teacher becomes a roving consultant who is available to help when the chairman and his study group get into difficulties. Also, the teacher must be skillful in keeping the students working at the assigned task. Students must not be permitted to engage in social chatter nor can loud, disruptive behavior be tolerated. The author has seen such groups working smoothly, quietly, and efficiently. Some room noise is inevitable during the oral practice sessions, but it can be kept at a reasonable level. The teacher can learn to distinguish between purposeful oral activity in the foreign language and nonproductive noise.

Simple visuals can also be used to elicit free application of pre-learned structures and vocabulary from an assembled class. The teacher must naturally select the content of the pictorial material very carefully. Simple line drawings depicting situations and actions within the range of vocabulary and structural knowledge of the student are generally better than pictures cluttered with a wide range of items. Also, the skill which the teacher exhibits in drawing out questions and comments from the students is a major determiner of how well the students learn to reapply the structures upon which they have drilled. Some teachers have a special aptitude for stimulating free conversation. The author can recall visiting a class of adult students enrolled in a Spanish conversation course. The teacher entered the room and wrote three words on the chalk board, which in Spanish meant "The Great Society." Then he asked the students to express their opinions in Spanish about the significance of the three words. This simple device was enough to keep everyone talking for the rest of the class period. The teacher's main problem was to restrain some of the more opinionated and vocal students so that the meeker members of the class would have a chance to participate. The Spanish was not always perfect, but the students were motivated to dig deeply into their repertoire of words and structures so that they could express their views on the validity of the Great Society slogan and so that they could react to some of the outspoken opinions of other members of the class. In this situation the step beyond pattern practice had been taken to the fullest. The students were now concentrating on a message they wished to express rather than upon the structure of the language per se. Also, the teacher had relinquished his role as chief performer and had assumed a role comparable to that of an orchestra leader. That is, he was indicating who should perform at any given moment, but was not insisting that all conversational exchanges be directed by him.

Naturally, the complexity of material which the students are able to discuss freely will be limited according to how far they have proceeded through the course of study. Consequently, they will be expected to produce utterances which may seem quite childish during the early lessons. Therefore, the teacher must constantly explain to the students the importance of finding ways, however simple, to apply the patterns they have learned to the world of reality. For pattern practice in itself is not reality. In most cases such drills are merely a representative sampling of an infinitely expandable pattern. Learning the specific content of the drill is a first small step. Learning to apply the pattern is the important step.

Bibliography

Delattre, Pierre, "French Prepositional Pattern in Linking a Verb to an Infinitive Object," *Modern Language Journal, XLVIII* (January 1964), 29–35.

Hok, Ruth, "Oral Exercises: Their Type and Form," *Modern Language Journal, XLVIII* (April 1964), 222–226.

Lado, Robert, *Language Teaching,* New York, McGraw-Hill, 1964, pp. 103–113.

Mathieu, Gustav, "Pitfalls of Pattern Practice," *Modern Language Journal, XLVIII* (January 1964), 20–24.

Politzer, Robert L., "Some Reflections on Pattern Practice," *Modern Language Journal, XLVIII* (January 1964), 24–28.

Stack, Edward M., *The Language Laboratory and Modern Language Teaching,* New York, Oxford University Press, 1960, pp. 7–47.

Reading maketh a full man; conference a ready man;
and writing an exact man. . . .

. . . some books are to be read only in parts; others to be read, but cursorily,
and some few to be read wholly, and with diligence and attention.
FRANCIS BACON

To translate is to betray.
ITALIAN PROVERB

Learning the four skills

9

The specific objectives of a foreign language program with regard to the four skills of listening, speaking, reading, and writing have been stated earlier in considerable detail (Chapter 5, Tables 3–6). However, because of the decades of misunderstanding regarding the function of English in relation to the foreign language it might be well to mention a fifth skill at this point; the skill of translation. Many European countries have entire educational institutions or university departments devoted to teaching this skill. In fact, it is a recognized profession in some countries. If one examines the nature of this profession in detail, he will discover that there are various levels of specialization. Some, for example, will become specialists in translating the written material of certain specified professional or business occupations. Often, the specialization will go even further; it may be found, for example, that a given specialist will limit his focus to (1) written material, (2) in the medical field, and (3) from English to French only (not the reverse). The same is true of interpreters. The people who transform oral rather than written material from one language to the other tend to be skilled only in one direction. Thus it is perfectly ordinary for an interpreter to be able to understand everything that is said in a Spanish conference and to be able to give instant American

English equivalents for the comments of each speaker and yet not be able to interpret back the other way without making serious errors which may offend or puzzle the Spanish-speaking audience. It is because of the near impossibility of finding persons skilled in two-way translation that most important conferences involving worldwide political decisions are staffed with specialists who can translate in one direction for each language involved. Despite all precautions, serious mistranslations occur at the highest levels. Former Premier Khrushchev's allusion to his belief that communism would outlast capitalism was sensationalized into headline news when his comment was rendered into English as, "We will bury you." The activist American mentality apparently interpreted this statement as meaning, "We will bulldoze you under." The Russian expression carried a more tranquil connotation. It conjured up the image of people standing around the grave of the deceased; of burying someone who was dead.

The purpose of this discussion is to point out the complete futility of expecting novice language students in the secondary school to translate from one language to the other. Even the professionals, after long years of rigorous training, make serious blunders. The process of rendering an equivalent form of expression from one language to another is so perilous, so exacting, and so tied to the semantics of the native language that its validity as an instructional objective must be seriously challenged by secondary-school teachers of foreign language. By its very nature, active translation from one language to another introduces a great deal of error, confusion, and misunderstanding into the learning process. Thus, if any work is done at all with this skill, it would seem logical to introduce it only after the student has achieved a high degree of competency in the direct use of the four basic skills. All this does not exclude the discriminate use of English in the teaching process as described in Chapter 6. Instead, we refer here to the *active* skill in which the student is expected to translate on daily exercises and on tests and examinations. Each use of translation— either from target language to English or the other way around— is a step away from the development of direct communication skill. In a real sense it is a short-circuiting of the objectives of the

American Method which call for direct use of the four language skills.

Listening comprehension

The necessity for speed in comprehending auditory signals distinguishes this skill from the other three. In a large number of language situations there is no opportunity for slowing down the flow of speech reaching the ear. For example, in listening to a play, a lecture, a movie, a TV program, or a radio broadcast, the listener has but one chance to hear what is spoken and has no control over the rate of delivery. Even in a face-to-face conversation, communication is badly disrupted if the nonnative speaker is forever asking the native to repeat what he has just said. Therefore, the full development of listening skill demands massive exposure to a wide variety of native speakers discussing familiar topics and using a normal conversational delivery. During the beginning stages of learning a new language, tapes, records, films, and live visitors from foreign countries can be used to present such listening exercises. By using rearrangements of familiar lexical items the teacher can expose students to listening experiences of increasing complexity. Any unfamiliar items which appear in such presentations must be taught in advance so that the student's attention is not drawn toward puzzling new vocabulary items and away from the message carried by the exercise. Students tend to become discouraged if they are constantly stopping to ponder the meaning of new words or the function of totally unfamiliar structures. However, new vocabulary items which appear in listening exercises need not be taught for active use. Prior to playing a tape or showing a film, a few minutes will often suffice to develop aural recognition of the half dozen new words which appear on the tape or sound track. Any other aspects of the filmed or recorded material which tend to confuse the student should also be explained in advance. It is considered good practice to follow each listening exercise with a short quiz to determine whether or not the students have actually understood what was said (see Chapter 11).

In the other "passive" skill (reading), considerable effort has been expended to produce a wide variety of high-interest reading selections of graded difficulty. Unfortunately, the producers of commercial tapes and records have not devoted equal time to the development of interesting material for listening. All too often the listening exercises consist of nothing more than a taped version of the identical material which the student is learning to say or which he must subsequently write. Such activities are a necessary part of language learning, but they are no substitute for practice in listening directly to an aural message which one has not previously heard. Ideally, such listening material would consist of highly interesting stories, plays, and poems that are graded in difficulty. Thus, at the early levels, transcriptions from foreign radio programs and foreign films intended for native audiences are of little value. The density of new words, slang expressions, and unfamiliar structures is too high to permit even minimal comprehension. The teacher must either adapt existing materials or must produce his own.

Speaking ability

Speaking is a productive skill which requires the learner to retrieve almost instantaneously the precise sounds, grammatical forms, word-order arrangements, and content vocabulary which will express what he wants to say in an unanticipated situation. The nonnative can be allowed an extra second or two to react to an auditory stimulus and can articulate his sentences more slowly and deliberately than a native speaker without serious loss in communication. However, excessively slow delivery will usually make the native speaker uncomfortable. The resultant emotional tension soon causes the conversation to bog down entirely as the oversolicitous native speaker begins to finish sentences for the nonnative and to correct errors. All too often, conversation between an American and a foreign acquaintance terminates when the latter diplomatically shifts from his native language into English. Each time this happens, another black mark is chalked up against the American foreign language community, and the stereotype of the American as a monolingual simpleton is further reinforced. The trend toward dialog memorization and pattern drill has done much to accelerate the number of syllables a student can articulate in a given number of seconds and has, perhaps, improved pronunciation, intonation, and speed of reaction to specific stimuli. However, unless the teacher deliberately involves the students in the spontaneous creation of utterances which express their own ideas, the newer techniques appear to produce results which show little improvement over older techniques. In short, it appears that one learns to express himself only by being induced to practice self-expression during each step of the learning process. The teacher cannot wait for free conversation to "jell" only after several tedious years of drill work or rule memorization. The attitude that language is a way to communicate the student's own ideas can be established during the first few days of the course. In developing free oral expression, the teacher must allow a wide tolerance for student errors even though he may secretly note errors for the purpose of assigning subsequent remedial drill. The teacher must resist the tendency to break in and correct publicly each student attempt at self-expression. Overcorrection of young children who are learning their first language can produce stuttering. Overcorrection of adolescents who are learning a second language will produce silence.

Ultimately the student must be able to respond intelligently to what someone else has said in the foreign language, if speaking is one of the objectives of the course. Some critics claim that students in audiolingual programs are no better off in this respect than those who are trained traditionally. Wilga Rivers speaks of ". . . students who perform very well in a pattern drill session, and can repeat memorized phrases perfectly in directed dialogue, but are at a loss to find correct ways of expressing their thoughts in a spontaneous conversation."[1] Such students have only learned to produce a specific response to a specific cue (see p. 133). In free conversation, however, the student "must select a response that will convey his meaning, not one that will fit the situation in an automatic sequence."[2] Apparently, free use of the language does not happen accidentally; the teacher must arrange it. The grammarian requires the student to memorize

[1] Wilga M. Rivers, *The Psychologist and the Foreign Language Teacher*, Chicago Press, University of Chicago Press, 1964, p. 68.
[2] *Ibid.*, p. 68.

"rules of correctness" which he is then supposed to apply as he speaks. The direct-method teacher advocates a sink-or-swim approach in which only the foreign language is used in class; the student must speak to survive academically. The audiolingual teacher tries to teach control of structure in advance through pattern practice. Then the student is supposed to apply the patterns to the real world; that is, to use the patterns flexibly to express what he wants to say as the situation demands. The following points reflect the reactions of veteran language teachers to the problems associated with teaching free expression.

THE CLASSROOM ENVIRONMENT AND FREE EXPRESSION

Most students (teenage and older) are somewhat hesitant in speaking *English* in front of a class. It is unrealistic, therefore, to expect flawless, free expression in the foreign language. Overexpectation on the part of the teacher can kill the student's desire to express his own thoughts. Yet the student must learn to recombine what he has learned in a way which is appropriate to a new and unexpected situation. He must be able to do this with each new grammatical structure but within the limits of his active vocabulary. Under present circumstances it seems that this phase of learning must be carried out in the classroom if it is to be done at all. Some of the dangers of teaching free expression are:

1. The tendency to jump in and correct student errors is almost certain to lead to embarrassment, stammering, timidity, and silence. The principle of immediate correction does not apply here. Errors are bound to be numerous; they can be noted secretly for subsequent drill.
2. The free-expression period should be identified in the student's mind as a time when he is trying to express his thoughts in the language rather than being preoccupied with the mechanics of language. This calls for a relaxed, nonpressured atmosphere. Laughter is inevitable as students produce nonstandard French, German, or Spanish utterances. Teacher and students must accept these blunders as an unavoidable part of the trial and error

process. (We must remember that in learning English, children often say things like "I goes" or "He brung it" or "He disappeared it.")

3. The student does not learn free conversation by hearing the teacher; he learns by conversing freely *himself*. (Some teachers do most of the talking themselves, and then wonder why the students are not more fluent. It is an occupational hazard.)

SAMPLE TECHNIQUES FOR TEACHING FREE EXPRESSION

1. It may be that the main value of visuals is not to teach culture or to present new vocabulary but rather to elicit free conversational responses from students. One teacher was observed using slides of the local community to draw Spanish conversation from her students. The following types of responses were elicited by allowing students to respond to a picture of the local drugstore:

> I have a coke there after school.
> Mr. Knight is the owner of the *drogueria*.
> That's not the right word.
> Why not?
> You can't get a coke in a *drogueria*.
> That's right; they only sell. . . .
> Who knows the word for "drugs"?

Such comments are not always rapid-fire; there are many long pauses. But once a few comments have been made, other related remarks tend to build upon them as the students discover that the foreign sounds can actually be related to the real world as they know it.

2. Map work can be used in a fashion similar to the foregoing. In both cases, however, one must guard against excessive and unnatural question-and-answer techniques.

> Where is Spain? Spain is east of Portugal.
> Where is France? France is east of Spain.
> Where is Germany? Germany is east of France.
> Where is Poland? Poland is east of Germany.
> (Etc. for Russia, Alaska, Canada, Greenland.)

This is a chain-type pattern drill; it bears little resemblance to normal conversation.

3. Summer camps and trips abroad can be effective if they are properly managed. (See p. 279.)

Introducing the sounds of language before the graphic symbols

According to proponents of the American Method, prereading instruction is essential to developing sound language habits. It is felt that, if reading is to reinforce the audiolingual skills rather than contaminate them, then thorough drill upon phonology must always precede reading. This does not mean that the entire phonological system must be mastered before the student is allowed to read or write. Indeed, the transition from speaking to reading has been carried off successfully by skilled language teachers with a delay of only a day or two in the introduction of the written word. Yet the prereading phase, however short, is important because of a simple fact of learning psychology, namely, that it is easier to form a new habit directly than to form the same habit by undoing a wrong one. And to introduce students to French, German, and Spanish through the writing system is to guarantee the formation of bad habits. Because the alphabets of these languages are almost identical to that of English, the unwitting student quite naturally assumes that the letters represent English sounds. Thus, for example, students of German will pronounce *Buch* as [buk] and students of Spanish will say something like [pearō] for both *perro* and *pero* unless their prereading training has taught them to cope with these critical phonemes. The result would be garbled communication in both languages. The German native would hear *Bug* (ship's prow) instead of the intended word referring to "book" and the speaker of Spanish would hear a rather unintelligible sound which is neither the word for "dog" nor the conjunction "but."

According to this line of thought, the language student should first learn to produce such troublesome sounds as the French, German, or Spanish *r* without ever hearing these sounds referred to as "*r*-sounds" and without seeing the graphic representations (i.e., *R*, *r*, *rr*, etc.). Linguistically, the teacher is putting the cart before the horse when he teaches students to pronounce letters. (In learning to read the native language it is always the other way around; the student learns to associate letters with sounds he has long known how to produce.) However, this in itself is not the chief reason for beginning with speech rather than with writing. Perhaps the main reason for the rejection of the writing-first approach is the abundant evidence that this system has produced generations of language students with almost irremediably bad pronunciation in various foreign languages. Apparently the initial introduction of foreign language material has a lasting influence upon the learner's pronunciation. Thus, the negative results of allowing beginning students to associate foreign language graphemes with phonemes which they have not mastered orally encourages excessive interference from the native language habit system. It may be that the association is so strong in many learners that the mere sight of a letter of the alphabet triggers the nervous system in such a way that the tongue is prevented from assuming the necessary positions for foreign language articulation. On the other hand, if the student is asked to place his tongue in certain unfamiliar positions without reference to any familiar letters of the alphabet, he may well learn to articulate the problem sounds and to drill them to the point where they become well habituated. At that point, reading the foreign language graphemes aloud becomes not "a funny way to pronounce English letters" but rather a logical representation for newly acquired sounds.

There are other reasons given for preceding the reading phase with oral drill. One reason stems from the belief that even rapid silent reading is accompanied by subvocalization of the sounds for which the graphemes stand. Thus, the development of direct foreign language reading (as opposed to translation back to English) would best be done in association with genuine foreign language sounds. A second reason has to do with the meaning of words. As a student reads he must draw meaning from the lexical items which come into view as he scans each line of the page. If he has drilled upon the basic words in meaningful contexts, he will not have to rely for meaning upon English equivalents (which, as we have seen, are never really "equivalent").

Withholding the written word for excessive periods of time

Children beyond the primary grades are perfectly well aware that French, German, and Spanish appear in written form. By the age of ten, if not earlier, they have already become quite dependent upon the English writing system as a standard memory aid and as a useful learning tool. Therefore, it appears unrealistic to expect students to adjust readily to an approach which forces them to rely solely upon listening and speaking for lessons done in class. For homework, the purely audiolingual assignment becomes an even more questionable practice. In fact, great enthusiasm for the "prolonged period of prereading instruction" appears to have had no substantial body of research to justify it as far as foreign language instruction in the conventional secondary-school environment is concerned. There is even evidence to indicate that the length of the time lag between learning the auditory symbol and introduction of the written symbol is not of major significance as long as the teacher exercises care in the way that the written symbol is introduced.[3] Furthermore, any advantages realized from an excessively long prereading period may be more than neutralized by the tendency of youngsters to surreptitiously invent their own orthography based upon English spelling. Students who secretly devise their own writing system are not only bypassing the entire intent of the prereading period, they are also developing unacceptable spelling habits that will have to be subsequently unlearned. Thus, the ideal system would seem to be one which capitalizes on the student's acquired taste for the written forms of language while minimizing the negative transfer caused by the premature introduction of those forms. One way to accomplish this balance is to introduce only as many of the problem phonemes as the teacher is capable of dealing with. Thus, the students can begin seeing the written forms of French, German, or Spanish during the very first lesson if the teacher introduces only words containing letters which present no serious pronunciation problems. Thus, for example, the French *n*, the German initial *d*, and the Spanish *ch* can be introduced early in certain contexts without serious danger if the stu-

[3] *Ibid.,* pp. 111 ff.

dent has learned them audiolingually a day or two earlier. The same cannot be said of the French *r,* the German *ch,* and the Spanish *d.* These require thorough oral drill and careful introduction of the graphic symbols to be certain that the student is not reverting to the strongly ingrained sound-to-letter association of the English language. Thus, the teacher can find ways to select only a few of the "pitfall" phonemes for reading presentations in each of the early lessons. The other part of the reading task in the early lessons is to learn new orthographic representations for sounds which are similar (if not quite identical) to sounds which exist in the English language. With a little ingenuity, a large number of meaningful utterances can be created using only "nondangerous" letters along with those critical phonemes which have been mastered in earlier lessons. Naturally, with the passage of time (and with constant reintroduction of drill upon the critical phonemes) the number of "safe" letters will grow. When most students have mastered the main problem phonemes in association with the appropriate graphemes, then the writing system can become an extremely useful tool to be used in support of the listening-speaking skills. For, at that point, students can begin to rely on written stimuli for oral reading and for listening to other students read aloud.

Reading ability

True reading means the direct communication of meaning from the printed page to the reader's mind. Rapidity of reading comprehension is not so crucial as is the case with listening. However, word by word plodding through a page is not reading, nor is it truly reading if the student must stop several times on each line to look up English equivalents for new words. The student *is* reading when he is engaged in the process of drawing meaning directly from the black marks which (in the common European languages) run from left to right across the page. As with the other skills, the student's knowledge of English can be both a help and a hindrance in the development of reading skill.

The advantages of having already learned to read English are: (1) The student has already gone through the difficult process of learning to associate graphic symbols with sounds and their meanings in English; in learning the English alphabet, he has mastered most of the alphabetic symbols used to represent French, German, and Spanish in Writing. (2) The habit of scanning sentences from left to right is so well established that he assumes it is the normal way to read a language. (These same habits can have a negative effect upon the learning of languages which are nonalphabetic or which are not read from left to right across the page.)

The disadvantages of having already learned to read English are: (1) The student's English pronunciation habits strongly influence his articulation of foreign language phonemes when he reads aloud; it is quite likely also that the student tends to subvocalize with an English accent. (2) The student is inclined to think that foreign language words are symbols which stand for English words and that the semantic range of any given vocabulary item is roughly identical with an "equivalent" which is given in a bilingual dictionary. Worse yet, he may draw completely false cultural inferences from translated items or from words which look deceptively like English words. This tendency can be counteracted in advance by using visuals and cultural notes to explain, for example, that bread in France is a dark, nourishing, unsliced loaf which forms a more significant part of the Frenchman's diet than the sliced white fluff that the American purchases in a wax or plastic container. Similarly, the German student can be taught that a *Gymnasium* is neither a sports quadrangle nor a comprehensive high school in the American sense. With more difficulty, the American student of Spanish can be taught that the word *corrida* refers neither to "bull" nor to "fight" and that few Spaniards or Latin Americans view the contest as a slaughter of helpless animals. One of the most challenging tasks in the teaching of reading (as well as the other skills) is the establishment of genuine cultural referents. Temporarily, the problem can be sidestepped by having the students use the foreign language to refer only to their own environment. However, if this process is carried too far, the students may never become involved in learning the genuine foreign-culture referents. Until these are introduced, the students are merely learning a sort of secret code in which strange sounds and written symbols are used to refer to American realities.

Because the student comes to the high-school class with the

ability to read English, the teacher of foreign languages need not repeat the process of requiring students to read infantile sentences such as, "Look Jane, look!" "See Spot run." "Run Spot, run!" In fact, the adolescent student is almost certain to rebel against any content which he associates with a period of development tracing back to his early childhood. Conversely, he will tend to reject material which is written too specifically for the college-age student. Thus, if the student is to be induced to stay in the foreign language program and to develop direct-reading ability, he must pass through an intermediate reading stage during which he is exposed to a great deal of material that is sufficiently simplified to fit his reading ability but is also tailored to his level of intellectual sophistication. In short, if he does not find both challenge and pleasure in reading directly in the foreign language, he will either abandon the venture entirely or else he will resort to practices which completely short circuit the entire reading process. Perhaps one of the greatest travesties of foreign language education has resulted from the premature reading of literature. Evidence of the absurdity of this practice can be found in any college or university bookstore. One needs only to examine the shelves containing used literature books in any foreign language and note the vocabulary sections blackened and ragged from over use along with the text sections in which students have scribbled an English equivalent above every third or fourth word. The grinding drudgery of looking up several dozen words per page may be dear to the tradition of the "Grim" Humanist; but the process bears little resemblance to anything which, in the native language, might be called reading. If genuine reading is to take place, the student must take full advantage of the skill he brings to the language class from his native English. Yet, at the same time, he must be insulated against the interference caused by that language.

THE PRIMER STAGE OF READING-SKILL DEVELOPMENT

The American method calls for an early phase of skill development in which reading is based entirely upon *material which the student has learned to say and comprehend aurally.* During the period which typically encompasses the first two years of high-school foreign language study, a series of carefully sequenced steps are supposed to lead to direct-reading ability within the limited vocabulary range of this early level. It is assumed that all elements of phonology, morphology, and syntax which are included in subsequent reading exercises have been thoroughly learned through oral drill work. The very first reading on any given lesson will involve material drawn from the oral drills. The student will first see the identical written representation of utterances which he has mastered audiolingually. During this process of learning to read, the following procedures seem advisable:

1. With books closed, the students hear the teacher read a group of utterances containing the target graphemes. (The teacher checks to make certain that the class understands the meaning of all utterances.)
2. With books open, the students follow each utterance as the teacher reads aloud. (Students do not read aloud.)
3. With books open, students read chorally trying to imitate the oral delivery of the teacher (or tape).
4. The teacher spot checks student performance by calling upon individuals to read aloud. (Again, going up one row and down the other is considered bad practice. The teacher is likely to get better participation by designating students in random order and by taking the sentences out of sequence. Thus, the individual reading might begin by having several students in different parts of the room take turns reading sentence three. Next, three students might be designated in turn to read sentence one, four students sentence two, etc. Then the teacher would move unpredictably about the room having each sentence read three or four times by different students until all sentences have been covered and until all students have participated.) From the oral reading the teacher can get a general impression of how well students are able to associate the difficult graphic symbols with the sounds for which they stand.
5. Throughout steps 3 and 4, the teacher follows each student response by reading the utterance correctly.

After the students have demonstrated their ability to read prelearned material in an acceptable manner, the next step is to learn

Learning the four skills

to read the problem graphemes in *unfamiliar contexts*. The following procedures seem advisable at this juncture:

1. Familiar structures and known lexical items are reorganized to convey an unfamiliar message.
2. Sheets containing the new sentences are passed out to the students or are projected on a screen.
3. Students are allowed reasonable time to read the new passages, after which the steps of choral and individual oral reading described above are repeated.

The other essential ingredient in the "primer phase" of reading development is evaluation. At various points, students are tested upon their ability to read aloud the target graphemes understandably and to draw meaning from recombinations of the vocabulary and grammatical forms which have been presented earlier (see p. 347).

One of the chief objectives of the primer stage of reading development is the unequivocal establishment in the student's mind of the relationship between the sounds of the foreign language and the graphic symbols used to represent those sounds. Such matters are difficult to prove, but there is considerable circumstantial evidence to the effect that effective reading (even silently) requires a strong base of listening and speaking. It appears that reading is actually a slowed-down form of listening in which the reader first receives visual messages through the eyes. Following this step, he converts the graphic symbols to subaudio symbols which he then decodes through the same channels of thought as those which lead from the ear to the brain. Thus, any ambiguity in interpretation of the sound represented by the written symbol may slow the process of drawing meaning from the printed page. To illustrate this we can show what would happen in reading English if the reader suddenly encountered the sentence, "The *fough* is a rare bird living in the *Treaux* region of Africa." The reader is greatly slowed by the two unknown words, not because there is any doubt about their meaning, but because he is unsure of how to pronounce them. Does the first word rhyme with "cow"? Or perhaps it has the same sound as "too" or "tow" or "fluff." What is the vowel sound of the second word? Is the *x* silent? All of these questions can be pondered in a second or two and the reader can decide to settle for a "foo bird" and a "Trucks region" without being concerned about the accuracy of his pronunciation. He is not likely to encounter either word again, and the few seconds of lost time are not significant.

However, in reading a foreign language, every sound can be as difficult as *fough* or *Treaux* if reading is introduced before phonology has been mastered. In this situation the reader has two alternatives; he can assign English sound values to each syllable or he can stop and look up the phonetic representation of each word (assuming that he has a dictionary with phonetic spellings and that he knows how to use it). From the standpoint of modern learning goals, neither alternative is satisfactory. The first encourages unacceptable habits of pronunciation, and the second makes genuine reading an impossibility. Thus, the reasons for heavy emphasis upon listening and speaking drill in the American Method go beyond the mere importance attached to these skills as valid learning objectives. Of equal importance is the belief that an audiolingual command of the language is the indispensable underpinning of reading and writing skills.

THE INTERMEDIATE STATE OF READING-SKILL DEVELOPMENT

Up to this point, the high-school student will often have an active vocabulary of less than a thousand words. His passive, or recognitional, vocabulary may be several hundred words higher, but it is unlikely to exceed 2000 items. However, we know that, if reading ability is to proceed beyond a type of material containing only slight variations of the topics contained in the beginning lessons, then a large recognitional vocabulary will be needed. It has been mentioned earlier that there are between 5,000 and 10,000 high-frequency lexical items that recur constantly when communication takes place in European languages. In the area of reading, the meanings of these high-frequency words must be learned in their most common contexts if the student is ever to be liberated from dependence upon a bilingual dictionary. Low-frequency words (and unusual meanings of common words) can be guessed at or can be looked up in a

Learning the four skills

dictionary. However, research indicates that the density of new items cannot exceed one per thirty-five words of text, if genuine reading by direct association is to take place.[4] Thus the key question is, how does the language student acquire the large recognitional vocabulary necessary for such "liberated" reading? The intermediate stage of reading development (a period covering roughly the third—and much of the fourth—year of high school) is devoted to this expansion of vocabulary. Most of the third year is also devoted to the further mastery of basic language structures. However, long after morphological problems have ceased to trouble the would-be reader, vocabulary deficiencies continue to plague him.

During the last half of the 1960s, a number of proposed solutions to the vocabulary-building problem had already been incorporated into the texts and readers in common use. Implicit in each of these solutions is the total rejection of the practice of memorizing word lists in which a precise English meaning is ascribed to each "matching" word in the target language. The tremendous inefficiency of word-pair memorization had long been recognized, but many teachers had continued to employ this technique simply for lack of a suitable alternative. Also, the perpetuation of the grammar-translation method in colleges and universities may often cause the senior-high-school teacher to continue the use of translation as a means of testing reading ability and to continue with word-list memorization as the method for learning vocabulary. The fear among secondary-school teachers that their students will not do well when they go on to college is often given as a reason for adhering to traditional methods. Nonetheless, a considerable number of teachers at both college and university levels have persevered in their attempts to develop direct-reading ability (as opposed to decoding the foreign language into English). Chief among the techniques used to build a vocabulary sufficient for the development of this ability are the use of inference, the use of programming techniques, the use of graded readers, the use of vocabulary-building exercises in the target language, and the use of visuals. A few texts have incorporated nearly all of these techniques into their overall format. Others, perhaps unfortunately, have relied heavily upon

[4] George Scherer and Michael Wertheimer, A Psycholinguistic Experiment in Foreign Language Teaching, New York, McGraw-Hill, 1964, pp. 93 f.

only one or two of the possible approaches. However, there is nothing to prevent the teacher from going beyond the text and utilizing techniques compatible with the ultimate goals of the instructional program. The following is a discussion of the more commonly used techniques related to the building of vocabulary.

Inference: The Sensible Guess. For purposes of illustration, let us concentrate for a moment upon the third word in the follow ing sentence:

> Suddenly the *flangel* swooped out of the sky and snatched an unsuspecting spider monkey from the midst of his chattering companions.

Assuming that the reader knows the meaning of the other twenty words, is there any doubt about the meaning of the word *flangel*? From the contextual clues one can immediately infer that a *flangel* is a very large predatory bird living in the jungles of Central or South America. It might aid retention to see a picture of a bird with a pointed beak, sharp talons, and colored plumage or to read a marginal note describing the bird either in English or the target language. However, it is questionable whether such obvious items ought ever to be glossed. Not only is it expensive for the publisher to produce the extra references but, also, their inclusion deprives the student of the opportunity to cultivate the art of sensible guessing in the target language; an ability which he has developed to a high degree in his native English. It is a simple fact that growth in vocabulary accompanies the American throughout his lifetime. Yet only a tiny portion of this repertoire of words can be accounted for through systematic word study or through reference to a dictionary. Occasionally he makes wrong guesses (the author has heard a school janitor state that "smoking is strictly *verbatim* here"), but, by and large, the normal American learns to use, with remarkable accuracy, tens of thousands of words which he has never consciously studied.

Naturally, there are greater problems with guessing meaning for the young adult learning a second language than for that same person when he is working with his native tongue. His most obvious problem is vocabulary. Guessing the meaning of *flangel* is no great task when the other words are known. However, let us change a few of the content words and see what happens to the meaning:

Suddenly the *flangel gleeped* out of the *simmel* and snatched an unsuspecting *brill* from the midst of his *fribbeling* companions.

Now, with the number of unknown words increased from one to five, the ability to infer the meaning of the twenty-one word sentence is almost nil. Yet this sort of nonsense unit is precisely what confronts the student who is prematurely thrust into the reading of literary selections. Thus, essential as the skill may be, inference cannot thrive in a situation where the key content words are unknown. Clearly then, the density of unknowns must be reduced to the point where the practice of sensible guessing can begin to operate. (This assumes that the student already has good control over the morphology and syntax of the language he is about to read so that he is not misled by the grammatical forms and word-order sequences of the target language.)

Vocabulary Building Exercises. Many veteran teachers have long used techniques for reducing the number of unknown lexical items to the point where the student can read the next day's assignment without major difficulty. Those texts, both traditional and modern, which supply a cumulative listing of high-frequency vocabulary items, are of particular value in helping the teacher to select items in a reader to which the student has not yet been exposed. Some of the newer readers have gone even further; they have supplied the actual exercises for building vocabulary. The vocabulary exercises consist of items that have not appeared earlier or have not been reentered frequently. Some of the techniques for presenting these items are as follows:

An example of visualization:

The student sees a picture of a medieval street. Under the picture is a caption which states, "The street is narrow." Immediately following is another picture of a slender boy. The caption states that "The boy is thin." With this as a takeoff point, the students develop concepts regarding the thinness of people, paper, pencils, and other applicable items in contrast with the narrowness of streets, buildings, hallways, and the like.

An example of paraphrase:

The word signature refers to writing one's name on a paper.

An example of restatement:

I always put my signature at the end of a letter.

An example of an action followup to the above activities (done completely in the target language):

This is my signature. (The teacher writes his signature on the chalkboard.)

Now, write your signature on a piece of paper and hold it up. (The students sign a sheet of paper and hold it up. Those who have not previously caught on will now understand by following the example of their classmates. The teacher quickly moves up and down the rows to see that all students have correctly followed directions.)

Examples of other ways to convey meaning entirely in the target language, by placing the new word in a context where its meaning is fairly obvious:

building—The Empire State building is the largest building in the world.

forest—A forest is made up of many trees.

went—Went is the past tense of the verb go.

stupid—The word stupid is the opposite of the word intelligent.

songs—Songs are what people sing. We sing songs in music class.

was—Washington was our first president. Kennedy was president until 1963.

discovered—Columbus discovered America.

Note: The number of devices for clarifying meaning is limited only by the imagination of the teacher and the knowledge of the students. On the latter score, the teacher must not assume too much. For example, Napoleon's name might be used in association with the word *emperor.* Nero or Alexander the Great might be less well known to contemporary high-school students. What is considered to be general knowledge for one generation may be highly esoteric information for a later one.

An example of expanding vocabulary through word families. Fill in the blank with the correct item from the list at the bottom of the page:

A school is a place in which we gain knowledge.

A man with great knowledge is a _____.

A _____ piece of work is one into which much study and effort has been put.

Students with good _____ ability should go on to college.

Students who do excellent work in high school often receive a _____
for attending college.

scholastic
scholarship
scholar
scholarly

In working with root words and the prefixes and suffixes which may be attached to them, it is often necessary to point out the identical elements which exist throughout the list. Many students are incredibly timid about guessing word meanings. In Spanish, for example, even such an obvious cognate as *nación* will often stop a student. For this reason, some reading texts will mark true cognates with an asterisk or other mark of identification. Then, once the student has gained confidence in his ability to perceive the meaning of the basic word, the door is opened for instant recognition of related words when they appear. A few examples relating to *nación* are:

nacional*
nacionalidad*
nacionalismo*
nacionalista*
nacionalizacion*
Naciones Unidas*
internacional*

Once the student has developed the knack of perceiving cognates (i.e., words similar in spelling and meaning to English words) and derived words from within the target language, then he has automatically increased his reading vocabulary by hundreds or even thousands of words, depending upon what language he is learning, and how far he has proceeded in the acquisition of vocabulary.

Graded reading materials. A graded reader is a book separate from the regular text which, if used properly, will be given to the student at that point in his study of the language when he is able to read it directly and pleasurably. Further, the graded reader should be so scaled in difficulty that the completion of the first selection develops in the student the ability to cope with the second selection which, in turn, prepares the ground for progress through the slightly more sophisticated third selection, and so on until the end of the book. Ideally, the graded reader would be built upon the specific course content which preceded its introduction. That is, the reader would utilize largely vocabulary and grammatical structures which had been previously introduced. The potential number of lexical items can be increased by utilizing cognates, derived words, and infrequent footnotes or marginal glosses. Indeed, by the latter half of the nineteen-sixties, a number of texts of this type had been produced to be used in conjunction with four-level programs (see Bibliography).

Unfortunately, not all materials labeled as "graded readers" meet the criteria suggested above. Some are based upon such a minimal word count that they are necessarily repetitious and devoid of content which young people can read with pleasure. Others, at the other extreme, are little more than emasculated summaries of literary selections assembled according to apparent order of difficulty and bound together under one cover. If unimaginative editing has not robbed such readers of their style, their content may be interesting enough to justify the time a teacher might devote to the development of special vocabulary-building exercises aimed at reducing the density of unknown lexical items. However, this often becomes a hopeless task; the teacher soon finds that these edited selections contain too many "surprises" in the form of idiomatic expressions and complex grammatical forms. As a result, vocabulary building begins to consume a disproportionate amount of class time. In such cases, the limited pleasure derived from the subsequent reading hardly seems to justify the effort. Thus, all so-called "graded readers" might well be subjected to a thorough analysis before they are purchased in large numbers. Among the suggested criteria for judging such readers are:

1. Level of interest—This aspect can be tested with a cross section of second-year students who are then asked to fill out an interest-inventory sheet.
2. Length and complexity of sentences—Beginning selections might contain an average of ten words per sentence for early intermediate reading. This could increase to a hundred words per sentence at the advanced levels.[5]

[5] For more precise measures of readability see William Bottiglia, *Language Learning*, Ann Arbor, Mich., University Microfilms, 1963.

3. Abstract content is best avoided—Simple story lines and interesting informational discussions referring to concrete, easily grasped situations are best at the intermediate stage. There should be a minimum of elaborate figures of speech and of esoteric allusions. The teen-age mind is more receptive to heavy-handed humor, for example, than to subtle repartees or satyrical discourses.

At this stage, the goal is to develop skill in reading in such a way that the student has an opportunity to develop confidence in his ability to derive pleasure and satisfaction from the pursuit of that skill. He is at this point somewhat comparable to the second- or third-grade elementary-school pupil who has just discovered that he can read simple material on his own. The right kind of graded books and periodicals can build upon the satisfaction which the student derives from this realization. Conversely, the motivational spark which is ignited by independent reading can be permanently extinguished if the wrong kind of reading material is introduced at this point. The most common blunder committed by well-meaning teachers is the introduction of literary material that is beyond the interest and intellectual grasp of the adolescent youngster. Almost no one at that age is ready for the likes of Kleist, Camus, or Calderón in the original. To expect secondary youngsters to read such authors is as sensible as expecting the toddler, who has just learned to walk from the couch to the coffee table, to immediately thereafter compete in the 100-yard dash at the Olympic games. For most high-school students, the analogy is no exaggeration. Generations of non-reading students who have been prematurely thrust into a foreign language "lit" class, attest to the fact that the intermediate student is not ready for undiluted literature. And who would presume to dilute it?

Programmed readers. To a certain extent, every good graded reader is programmed. That is, the material is logically sequenced to lead to the desired terminal behavior, the new lexical items are presented in minimal steps, and the students are provided with the opportunity to check the rightness or wrongness of their reading behavior at each appropriate phase in the development of their reading skill. However, graded readers are not programmed in the full sense of the word (see discussion of programmed material in

Chapter 7). This distinction would not be significant if it were not for the fact that programmed reading materials have been produced and are presently in use in a number of classrooms. Thus, we use the word "programmed" here to refer to materials which are not only logically sequenced into minimal learning increments, but which also contain most of the other characteristics of programmed instruction such as immediate reward, capability for total self-instruction, minimization of error, and eliciting of overt responses from the reader.

The simplest form of programmed reader is the interlineary book in which English equivalents for the unknown words are supplied between the lines of the text. A plastic shield with evenly spaced strips of clear and transparent material fits over each page of the reader in such a manner that the English words cannot be seen. Thus, the student can read an entire page without ever referring to the English section of the text. On each sentence he can attempt to guess the meaning of each new word using contextual clues. At all times he can check the accuracy of his inference by sliding the shield a quarter of an inch downward to reveal the English equivalent. If the materials are carefully graded, the interlinear texts can supply most of the characteristics of programmed instruction without resorting to the standard programming format. One advantage of such texts is that the interlinear vocabulary items stick out clearly on each page, which makes it a simple matter to count them to determine whether or not the density of new lexical items exceeds the suggested minimum of one new word per thirty-five words of running text. Another variation of the interlinear text is to supply the English equivalents in microscopic print so that they are legible only when the reader places a magnifying glass over the needed word. This obviates the need for the plastic shield, which can be easily lost, but replaces it with the more expensive magnifying glass which can be either lost or broken.

Those who are inclined toward the direct method object to this system of programming on the grounds that it tends to perpetuate the myth that English equivalents are the source of meaning for foreign words. Clearly, there is the danger inherent in the interlinear system that the student will be tempted to refer constantly to the English word between the lines, thereby destroying his will to read the foreign language for direct meaning. If this happens, then the programming device has negated the entire intent of the programmed reader.

Completely programmed texts on the Skinnerian format do exist.[6] One problem with those that aim specifically at developing reading ability at the intermediate level is the impossibility of knowing which structures and vocabulary items the student does or does not know. Consequently, the programmer has no alternative but to program everything. Thus, a student who has proceeded far enough through the regular classroom work to have control over the essential phonological problems, will find a large part of the program tedious and repetitive. To compensate for this fact, the student must develop the art of varying his speed of progression through the frames of the programmed reading course. One advantage to having fully programmed readers is that they can provide a rapid review of vocabulary and structure for the student whose retention has been good, while at the same time offering a carefully sequenced course of study for the student whose retention has been less than minimal. A second advantage is that each student can move at his own pace toward the liberating level of vocabulary acquisition, provided only that the steps leading to the desired terminal behavior have been adequately programmed and that the budget of the local school district is adequate to purchase the massive supply of programmed texts needed to carry the student to the desired goal. In reality, programmed texts for the nonoral reading skills appear to stand the best chance of becoming economically feasible in the near future, for they can be used by the student without requiring expensive tapes and equipment. Moreover, since the overt response can be a silent reaction, the use of programmed readers is not physically restricted to a special laboratory room. The readers can be used anywhere—in the library, study hall, or at home. It is somewhat of a paradox, in view of this, that the majority of the early materials were designed to develop the listening-speaking skills. The scant supply of programmed reading materials is also paradoxical when one considers that, of all the language skills, reading is the one which is most individualized and which draws most heavily upon the process of

[6] Alfred Fiks, "Foreign Language Programmed Materials: 1966," *Modern Language Journal, LI* (January 1967), 7 ff.

convergent thinking, two of the alleged strong points of programmed learning. For, once it is printed, the content of a book is static, and the communication bond which is subsequently established is between the fixed graphic symbols and the lone reader. Using the powers of his intellect and imagination, each reader draws a uniquely individual interpretation from the little black marks on the page. The well-devised programmed course will teach the student to infer the meaning of those ink marks and will follow with an immediate confirmation of each inference, thus—in theory at least—building confidence through success. Much research remains to be done to determine whether or not skillfully designed programmed materials can bridge the chasm existing between the primer stage of reading and liberated reading (that is, reading of unedited, contemporary, adult material without recourse to a bilingual dictionary). It appears that no exhaustive study has ever been conducted to determine whether or not any American graduates from the foreign language reading program ever pick up a foreign language book or magazine after completion of their high-school or college "lit" course. However, from the paucity of foreign language novels, plays, periodicals, and other non-English reading matter available in the non-University bookstores and libraries, it appears that almost no one ever reads a complete work in the foreign language after having completed the foreign language "requirement" in school or college. This apparent reluctance of nonimmigrant Americans to read anything but English could be interpreted as an indictment of foreign language instruction for the past half century, particularly when one considers that the only ostensible purpose of that instruction was to develop "reading ability." Again, the ultimate goal of the American Method in the area of reading is to develop a form of coordinate bilingualism of the single-residence variety (see Chapter 5) which will enable the student to read with enjoyment materials from the foreign culture which are comparable to the items he reads in his native English.

THE ADVANCED STAGE: LIBERATED READING

The reader is partially liberated when he can read with relative ease (and with a speed only slightly less than his English reading rate) genuine but especially selected materials from the foreign culture.

The content of such materials is chosen on the basis of proven appeal to the adolescent reader. These reading materials will also contain a dictionary section along with special notes to enable the student to cope with difficult passages without having to refer to a regular dictionary. By this level, it is hoped that the student has learned to program his own vocabulary development. That is, he will begin to note new words that recur often; and will make a special effort to learn these words by himself, thereby progressively reducing the density of unknowns which will confront him in future reading. Ideally, he will begin to make a self-study notebook of recurrent lexical items. The act of writing helps to fix the word in the student's mind, and the existence of the word list provides a convenient memory jogger. In making such a list, students should be encouraged to adopt the best possible techniques for vocabulary building, such as those mentioned earlier in this chapter. If he avoids using English equivalents wherever possible, he will be reinforcing positive attitudes toward developing coordinate bilingual abilities. Also, the programming technique can be used by having the new word appear on the left of the page with the definition appearing on the right. In this way, the student can create his own programmed study of vocabulary by placing a shield over the simpler meaning of the new word and checking his attempts to define it. The following example in English could be adapted to any European language.

Example of new vocabulary presentation

Defeat was <u>inevitable</u>	could not be avoided; unavoidable
A look of <u>consternation</u>	an expression of fear and amazement
A <u>valid</u> reason	a reason with a good basis, well justified
He <u>clung</u> to the ledge	He held on tightly. (cling, has clung)
A <u>penurious</u> landlord	the opposite of generous with money; very stingy
They have three <u>children</u>.	One <u>child</u> plus one <u>child</u> equals two <u>children</u>.

Naturally, the student should not stop repeatedly on each page to make entries in his vocabulary notebook. This practice would destroy any attempts at genuine reading. Instead, he should simply underline any item which has recurred several times (if it is his own book) or jot the item down on a sheet of note paper. Then, when he has finished his intended reading at a fairly normal pace, he is ready to concentrate upon the new lexical items. After he has studied them, he should reread the troublesome passages at a speed which is fairly close to his rate of reading English. The teacher and the student should be satisfied if the students can grasp the essential aspects of the plot, can distinguish the main personality traits of the characters, and are aware of the more obvious facts about the setting of the story. Discussions about the story can be simple and factual and can be, for the most part, in the target language. Attempts at literary criticism may have a highly negative effect upon students who are trying earnestly to develop direct-association reading.

Fully liberated reading in a foreign language—a common phenomenon in Europe—has seldom been achieved in American secondary education. The author has visited hundreds of high schools whose book stores sell English-language paperbacks of best sellers and significant works of literature. Yet, even though the high school may show four or five foreign languages on its course offerings, paperbacks printed in these languages almost never appear on the stands. The reason for this lack of foreign books is probably that they could not be read by enough students to warrant their purchase; although students who have achieved the goal of fully liberated reading would be able to take any book of moderate difficulty and read it pleasurably and with direct association of meaning. We are not suggesting books by avant-garde or esoteric writers, but rather, those short stories, novels, plays, and poems that are read enjoyably by people now living in the target culture. These might well include the popular fad books as well as the classics-for-young-people. If any great number of liberated readers are to be produced within the framework of the American comprehensive high school, then this diversity of reading materials is a clear necessity. The same wide spectrum of reading tastes which exists among American students in their English-language reading is likely to appear where foreign-language reading is concerned. This implies the need for a vastly expanded selection of readers available either in the regular school library or in a departmental library. To expect a single anthology—however good—to carry the entire reading load for the fourth-level course is no more realistic in the foreign-language course than it is in the English class. Once the student has proceeded beyond the intermediate level in reading skill, the key to further progress (either in English or in a foreign language) is to put into his hands books which he will read because he enjoys reading them. The reasons most commonly given to justify this lock-step progression through a given reading selection are:

1. It is necessary for the purpose of assigning grades on a competitive basis.
2. It is necessary for the class to have some common knowledge for the purpose of discussion.
3. It is not possible to keep track of student progress when they are all reading different material.

The first of these arguments is easily countered; if competitive grading is a necessity, then individualized reading will produce a greater disparity of progress among students, thus adding the factor of quantity of reading accomplishment to that of quality. The second argument has little real validity; there are plenty of other matters which can serve as a common ground for classroom discussion. Further, the assignment of extensive reading does not preclude the use of common reading assignments for classroom discussion. As is the case with reading in the English class, most of the reading in the liberated phase will take place outside of the regular classroom. The third objection is, perhaps most valid of all. It is not uncommon for secondary teachers to meet between 100 and 150 students daily. Clearly, the establishment of individualized instruction for this number of youngsters would be a Herculean task. However, the potential for liberated reading is seldom realized before the third or fourth year of instruction. And, at this level, classes generally consist of a small number of well-motivated, self-directed students. With proper safeguards, such students can be allowed to engage in self-study activities that will facilitate evaluation by the teacher. In the area of reading, for example, they can be asked to submit a weekly progress report including the number of pages read and a brief summary of the plot development during the week's reading. With this sort of assignment, it is a distinct advantage to have no two students reading the same book at the same time. With the lock-step reading program there is always the danger that only a few of the best readers in the class are getting the necessary reading practice on each chapter. The other students rely upon oral summaries of the story supplied in English by the class "brains." A further safeguard against such shortcuts is to convince the students that the chief measure of their reading progress will be the periodic exams which evaluate general achievement in reading rather than knowledge about specific facts (see Chapter 11).

The common practice of having all students read the same book at the same pace, chapter by chapter, is an excellent way to arrest the reading development of all students with potentially superior reading ability. The prevalence of this practice in American schools and colleges may to some degree explain why it is almost impossible to find a graduate of an American foreign language program who does further reading in the foreign language.[7]

Writing ability

At the simplest level, writing in the foreign language involves spelling and word order. Thus, the very first exercises aimed at developing writing skill might logically include such activities as copying, short dictations, sentence transformations, and reordering of scrambled sentences. Naturally, the more complex syntactical exercises will have to be withheld until the various word-order problems have been sufficiently drilled through the other three skills. However, the simpler written exercises can be started in the very early lessons as a followup activity to the work that has been done upon the listening, speaking, and reading skills. At all stages, writing—properly used—can reinforce these skills. As is the case with reading, there

---

[7] Although the evidence is limited, there is one study which suggests that teaching of foreign language reading may be quite ineffective. See, Sam Rosenzweig et al., "Operation Babel: A Survey of the Effectiveness of Foreign Language Requirements for the Ph.D. Degree in Pyschology." *American Psychologist,* 17 (May 1962), 237–243.

is no proof that the written symbol should be withheld for excessive periods with adolescents and young adults. And there is every reason to capitalize on the universal human desire for self-expression by allowing rudimentary writing involving those utterances the student has learned to understand, say, and read. The very first writing will involve material that has been learned via the other three skills several days in advance of the actual act of writing. As the student moves through the course, writing can relate backward to material learned in previous chapters. In a more limited way, it can involve the drill material of the most recent unit of language work. In all cases, the important consideration is the degree of mastery of the critical phonemes. Writing, like reading, must not (according to modern thinking) be allowed to cause a deterioration in the speaking and listening skills. In fact, if the teacher knows how to capitalize upon the body of material that the student has memorized orally, this prelearned knowledge can greatly accelerate the development of writing skill. To illustrate the steps through which one would proceed in developing direct-writing ability, we have used the lyrics of the "Star Spangled Banner." This was chosen in the belief that it is the one set of utterances which American readers are likely to have overlearned to the degree required of students in the contemporary modern foreign language class. (In other respects the example is unsuitable since the words are sung, not spoken, and because they are not in dialog form. However, they are adequate for the limited purpose of demonstrating the learning technique.)

Step One: First writing

The student has already learned to hear, say, and read the material he is about to write. The first writing of this material is done in class with the teacher carefully checking to be certain that each line has been written correctly. All accent marks, punctuation marks, and other orthographic features of the material are double checked.

Step Two: Memory writing

The student is told to prepare for a dictation on the material by teaching himself through a modification of the programming technique. He is taught to place a shield over the dialog utterances and then to write them one at a time from memory after which he carefully checks the spelling of each word in each sentence.

Example:

Student writes from memory, "Oh, say can you see, by the dawn's early light," (Student moves shield down the page to check his written response. He corrects all errors.)

Student writes next line, "What so proudly we hailed at the twilight's last gleaming." (Student reveals correct response and once more corrects his errors.)

In this manner the student continues through the dialog material until he can write the entire passage flawlessly from memory.

Step Three: Spelling

To this point the student has copied the material directly from the page and has "copied" from memory with immediate reinforcement from the printed page. Next he learns to spell certain key words by hearing them read in a dictation either from the teacher or from a tape. The student works with a dittoed or mimeographed sheet from which the key words have been deleted and replaced by a dash. The teacher reads the passage through twice at a reasonably normal rate of delivery. The students fill in the blanks.

Example:

Oh, say can you _____ by the _____ early light,

What so proudly we _____ at the _____ last gleaming?

_____ broad stripes and bright stars, through the _____ fight,

O'er the _____ we watched, were so _____ streaming.

Some teachers make a practice of having students make a carbon copy of the dictation. (Only the answers come through onto a blank sheet of paper.) The carbon copy is then signed and handed in immediately after the dictation. Each student then corrects his own paper (for purposes of immediate reinforcement) as the teacher reveals answers written on the chalk board or projected on a screen from an overhead transparency. The entire process can take less than ten minutes of class time. In some cases the teacher collects the dictations after having instructed the students to make all corrections and to circle those items which are wrong.

Step Four: Limited self-expression

Once the student has established control over the sound-to-letter correspondence by means of copying and dictation exercises, he can begin to move into those types of exercises which allow him a limited degree of self-expression. As with the other productive skill—speaking— he must learn to keep his urge for written self-expression within the

Learning the four skills

limits of the structures and vocabulary items he has learned to manipulate in earlier lessons. The following are but a few examples of the type of exercises suitable to this stage of development. (These sentences would appear only in the target language; English would not be used in any way.)

Completion exercises. In completion exercises the rules are that the student must use only that vocabulary and those grammatical forms that have been thoroughly drilled in the previous chapters.

> In summer I like to _____.
> You didn't tell me that _____.
> Why did you _____.
> He says that the teacher _____.

In no case should the student attempt to look up equivalents of words and expressions which exist in American English. This practice almost invariably leads to disaster because of the different semantic range of words between one language and the other. For example, if he tries to complete the first sentence by saying, "In summer I like to *have a good time*," he will almost certainly go wrong if he has not mastered the expression which conveys the idea of "enjoying oneself." In French, German, and Spanish this idea is generally expressed without using either the common equivalents for "have" or for "time." Thus, the main purpose of the completion drill is to induce the student to produce written recombinations of structures and vocabulary items which he does know how to manipulate and to be as creative as possible within these bounds.

Recombination exercises. The student is instructed to produce complete, sensible sentences by modifying and rearranging a series of words.

> to work / the city / every day

As is the case with completion exercises, the student has some leeway here regarding the sentence he produces. However, the same limitations of vocabulary and structure apply. Thus, the following variety of sentences might appear:

> He goes to work in the city every day.
> I work in the city every day.
> We want to work in the city every day.
> They have to work for the city every day.

If much of this type of exercise is done in a supervised study situation, students are likely to come up with a wide variety of sentence types. The bright student may produce some unexpectedly elaborate sentences without deviating from the rules of the game. Some excessively ambitious youngsters, on the other hand, may produce elaborate but faulty sentences. Both types of written responses should be checked and handed back as soon as possible with congratulations to the successful student and redirection to the one who has gone astray. Thus, for the busy teacher, it is better to assign frequent, regular, short written exercises than to ask for long written assignments which cannot be corrected quickly and handed back immediately. If the student is to be encouraged to engage in divergent thinking, he needs to be informed that he is on the right track whenever he strikes off on his own. For, as we have seen, the cultivation of the ability to do divergent thinking is the one area of language instruction in which the human teacher is demonstrably superior to the machine.

Step Five: Paragraph writing

During the elementary stages of writing, the drill work will have focussed principally upon developing sound-to-letter correspondence and upon producing genuine but isolated sentences. The intermediate stage has arrived when the student has acquired sufficient vocabulary and knowledge of structure to write coherent paragraphs. As with the other stages of learning, this skill must be developed carefully and systemically. Some techniques of long standing include:

Conversion exercises.   The student is given a short paragraph which is complete and correctly written. He is instructed to convert it in some way. For example, he might be expected to change all the conjugated verbs to the present tense, or past tense, or to some other appropriate form. Or perhaps the paragraph is so written that all nouns and pronouns can be changed from singular to plural without changing the essential meaning of the paragraph in other respects. In some languages it might be useful to have the students change a series of direct quotations into indirect discourse. Similarly, a student might take a third-person narration and rewrite it in the first person.

Cued narration.

> *Example:*
>
> MY BEST FRIEND
> What is his/her name? Age? Lives where?
> How long have you known him/her?
> Things you have done together since then. (Note previous lessons: go skiing, swimming, skating, dancing, to movies, to basketball game, to football game; also, play chess, cards, tennis, basketball;

also, listen to music, records, the radio or watch television.)
What do you both want to do after you graduate from high school.
(Get a job? Go to college?)

A paragraph written from a series of cues need not utilize all the cues. Moreover, it is perfectly all right for the student to utilize additional structures over which he has control. Thus, a student who has studied English as a foreign language for several years might produce the following paragraph based upon the cues given above:

MY BEST FRIEND

My best friend's name is Paul Smith. He is 17 years old. For the past eight years he has lived next door to me on Lincoln Avenue. During this time we have often gone swimming together. In winter we have also attended basketball games, gone to movies, and played chess at home. When we graduate from high school next year, we both hope to attend the state university.

Summarization exercises. The student hears a short, simple story read aloud twice. Then, without reference to any resource material whatever, he rewrites the narration in his own words. Similarly, a story can be assigned for outside reading with the explanation that it will have to be summarized in writing later in the week. To facilitate accuracy, the student can be given a series of questions which contain the necessary vocabulary for summarizing the story. The answers to these questions will provide the minimal acceptable summarization of the story and the questions themselves will contain most of the vocabulary needed to write the paragraphs.

Original dialog production. Using the vocabulary and grammar at his command, the student is instructed to adapt a dialog to his own personal experience. For the less imaginative students, some direction in the form of suggested topics may be needed.

Mother (or father) may I _____?

Well, maybe, but first _____.

But mother, (father), I _____.

I have heard that story before. If you expect to _____, then you will have to _____.

All right, I'll _____ _____. Then may I _____?

Free composition. Many students will arrive at the end of a four-year high-school language course without being able to produce spontaneously written compositions in the foreign language. That is, many will still be somewhere in the intermediate stages of composition where they

276

are able to transform narrative material, but are not able to create a coherent series of related paragraphs upon a chosen topic. This should surprise no one. A rather large proportion of incoming freshmen at any college or university campus are unable to produce mature narrations even in English. Writing in any language is a complex art. It consists of much more than the rendering of talk onto paper. Anyone who has attempted to read the transcript of a semiformal conference which has been copied directly from tape to typewriter, can attest to this fact. In speech there is a high tolerance for redundancy, for repetition of the same type and length of sentence, and for simple everyday vocabulary. Remarks which seemed lucid and witty over the conference table, appear as a string of inanities when they are reproduced in print. In any language, good writing calls for conciseness, precision, and variety of sentence structure. However, in learning to write a second language additional problems are introduced. There are certain conventions, levels of style, rules of punctuation, and other aspects which differ sharply from the writing standards of English. These must be acquired along with the acquisition of other more basic aspects of the writing skill. Thus, free composition in written expression is only for those students who have gained excellent control over all the basic language structures and whose vocabulary has reached the stage where they are able to engage in liberated reading. From this background the student can begin to utilize models of good contemporary prose to express what he wants to say at something above a primary-school level. The steps toward something which resembles free composition in the foreign language might be as follows:

1. Using a model of a personal letter to learn form and style, the student writes a personal letter to someone he knows. Hopefully, it will be someone who reads the particular foreign language. An ideal outlet for such compositions is a pen pal in the foreign culture. With a cooperative young person in the target culture, the student can write letters in which the first part is in the foreign language, the second part in English. The pen pal follows the same procedure with his letters. Then each student in each country makes corrections in the foreign language section and mails back the corrected copy. In this way both correspondents profit from writing experience and both have a native tutor available via air mail. (A similar procedure can be followed in developing speaking skill if both correspondents have a tape recorder.)

2. A number of models of business correspondence can be used in a similar manner to teach students to write more formally. Again, the

student will use the model letters only as a guide. The content of the letters produced by the students will have to be different. Possible topics are:

a. Writing to a fictional hotel requesting room reservations for a given period of time.

b. Writing to a bookstore to inquire whether they have certain specific books, what the prices are, if they have cloth-bound volumes as well as paperbacks, etc. (New vocabulary items might be supplied by the teacher in advance.)

c. Write a letter of invitation to another student in the class. (The teacher must exercise great care and tact to see that all students both write and receive an invitation.) Then, each student is required to reply, affirmatively or negatively, to the invitation. (Again, model forms are needed.)

3. Well-motivated and gifted students may be encouraged to attempt a more creative type of composition. Light verse, simple short stories, short skits, and critical essays have been written by high-school students in a foreign language. Some schools have a monthly student newspaper mimeographed in a foreign language and distributed to all students who are enrolled in the language beyond the first year. Some schools produce a literary magazine which includes a foreign language section. Any such positive recognition for achievement is to be encouraged. Also, written work can carry over into the audiolingual areas. For example, the secretary of the language club might read the minutes of the last meeting in the foreign language. For example, the skits which the advanced students have written can be presented before all the students who are enrolled in that language, perhaps in the school's little theatre. Also, brief reports of current news events can be read aloud in class or over the public address system with the switches turned only to those classes in which the appropriate languages are taught. The author has seen a hilarious version of Huntley-Brinkley done in German by an advanced language class. The students had written their own news reports using current German newspapers for resource materials. The same sort of activity can be done in the other commonly taught languages.

Foreign study programs

There is some evidence to indicate that travel to a foreign country and immersion in the foreign language environment of that country can greatly enhance the skills acquired in the academic school program.[8] However, the mere act of traveling abroad will not necessarily produce this result. A striking example of human potential for learning almost nothing from travel and residence abroad is the case of American military personnel and their dependents who frequently spend several years on foreign soil without having developed any significant skill in the language of the host country. This is partly explained by the fact that these individuals never really leave home, but reside in an American ghetto surrounded by fellow Americans and by American institutions such as public schools, supermarkets, liquor stores, and the like. However, a further explanation is the lack of initial contact with the foreign language and culture. Apparently, the most value is received from foreign travel if the traveler has first completed the equivalent of two levels of foreign language instruction as outlined in Chapter 5.[9] Of the dozens of widely publicized overseas study programs which have sprung up in recent years, many have no prerequisites with regard to prior foreign language study. Thus, a student may spend over a thousand dollars to travel to Europe in the hope of becoming fluent in his chosen language only to find that very little learning resulted from the time and expense occasioned by the trip. This becomes doubly unfortunate when one considers that the same amount of time and effort could have produced excellent results with a properly designed, properly timed foreign study program. It is for this reason that the National Council of State Supervisors of Foreign Language in 1966 enlisted the servcies of a nationally recognized authority on foreign study programs, Professor Stephen Freeman of Middlebury College, to set up criteria for evaluating such programs. These published criteria are now available through the State Foreign Language Consultant or Supervisor in the Department of Public Instruction of each state. The criteria are published under the title: *Criteria for Evaluating Foreign Study Programs for Secondary School Students.*

[8] John B. Carroll, "Research on Teaching Foreign Languages," *Handbook of Research on Teaching*, New York, Materials Center, Modern Language Association, 1964, p. 1085.
[9] *Ibid.*

Bibliography

GENERAL

Belasco, Simon, "The Plateau; or the Case for Comprehension: the 'Concept' Approach," *Modern Language Journal, LII* (February 1967), 82–88.

Bottiglia, William F. (ed.), *Language Learning: The Intermediate Phase,* Reports of the Working Committees of the 1963 Northeast Conference on the Teaching of Foreign Languages, Ann Arbor, Michigan, University Microfilms, 313 North First Street, 1963.
This publication presents perhaps the most extensive discussion now available relative to the development of direct use of the four skills.

Cables, Virginia, "How Do We Teach Comprehension?" *Modern Language Journal, L* (March 1966), 141–144.

Dacanay, F. R., *Techniques and Procedures in Second Language Teaching,* Quezon City, Philippines, Phoenix Press, 1963. (Order from: Alemar's, P.O. Box 2119, Manila, Philippines.)

Gage, N. L. (ed.), *Handbook of Research on Teaching,* New York, Rand McNally, 1963, pp. 1060–1100.
A reprint of the foreign language section of this book is available from the Materials Center, Modern Language Association. The language section, written by John Carroll, includes a remarkably complete bibliography of significant research in foreign language education through the year 1961.

Lado, Robert, *et al., Galeria Hispanica,* St. Louis, Webster Div., McGraw-Hill, 1965.
This third-level Spanish text utilizes many modern techniques for developing direct use of the target language including vocabulary-building exercises, writing exercises, oral drill work, cultural content, and the systematic development of reading skill.

Politzer, Robert, "The Macro and Micro Structure of the Foreign Language Curriculum," *Modern Language Journal, XL* (February 1965), 99–102.

Rivers, Wilga M., "Listening Comprehension," *Modern Language Journal, L* (April 1966), 196–204.

Scherer, George (ed.), *French: Reading for Meaning, German: Reading for Meaning,* and *Spanish: Reading for Meaning,* New York, Harcourt, Brace & World, 1966.
These are examples of graded readers in which the density of new vocabulary items is severely controlled to permit ease of reading in

*the direct sense beyond the second level of instruction. A good
audiolingual base is presumed.*

Scherer, George A. C., and Hans-Heinrich Wängler, *Contemporary German*, New York, McGraw-Hill, 1966.
This college text presents a case study of the techniques of the American Method through levels I and II. Among the techniques used here are prereading instruction, graded phonology, application of contrastive grammar, programmed reading, word-building exercises, minimal increment development of language skills, self-instruction, and many others.

Scott, Charles T., "The Linguistic Basis for the Development of Reading Skill," *Modern Language Journal*, L (December 1966), 535–544.

Twaddel, Freeman, *Foreign Language Instruction at the Second Level*, Teacher's manuals for *Español: Hablar Y Leer* and for *Deutsch: Sprechen und Lesen*, New York, Holt, Rinehart & Winston, 1963.

Reference Grammars for use in conjunction with the development of writing skill at the advanced levels.

FRENCH

Fraser, W. H., J. Squair, and Clifford S. Parker, *French Composition and Reference Grammar*, Boston, Heath, 1942.

Gaiffe, F. (ed.), *Grammaire Larousse du XXième siècle*, Paris, Larousse, 1936.

Grévisse, Maurice, *Le Bon Usage*, 7th rev. ed. Gembloux, Belge, Duculot, 1959.

GERMAN

Curme, George O., *A Grammar of the German Language*, 2nd ed., New York, Ungar, 1952.

Grebe, Paul (ed.), *Der Grosse Duden: Grammatik der deutschen Gegenwartssprache*, Mannheim, Bibliographisches Institut, 1959.

SPANISH

Marathon Montrose Ramsey, *A Textbook of Modern Spanish*, New York, Holt, Rinehart & Winston, 1956.

Gramática de la langua española, Real Academia Española, Madrid, Espasa, 1931.

Modern Spanish: A Project of the Modern Language Association, New York, Harcourt, Brace, 1960.

Anyone who can *be replaced by a machine* should *be.*

The language laboratory
and the electronic classroom

Evolution of the high-school language laboratory

The history of the language laboratory began at Louisiana State University in 1947 with the installation of 100 cubicles equipped with disc players, headsets, and microphones.[1] During the following 10 years, the number of college and university installations grew to 240 while the public and private high schools were installing less than 70 laboratories nationwide.[2] The enactment of the National Defense Education Act in 1958 changed this ratio quickly and irreversibly. With the availability of federal funds to match local moneys, public high schools began to expand their facilities by thousands of installations each year. Private and parochial secondary schools found their own sources of funding, and they too joined the language laboratory movement. An unpublished report from the United States Office of Education in 1965 showed a nationwide total of more than 6000 language laboratories at the secondary level. Based upon previous rates of growth, there is good reason to assume that the number of installations in existence by 1967 was over 8000

[1] Joseph C. Hutchinson, *Modern Foreign Languages in High School: The Language Laboratory*, Washington, D.C., U.S. Office of Education Bulletin, no. 23, 1961, p. 1.
[2] *Ibid.*, p. 2.

at the secondary level alone. Thus, within two decades, the concept of the language laboratory, which had begun on a rather modest basis at the university level, became accepted almost unquestioningly by secondary-school leaders throughout the nation. In fact, the image of the language laboratory as an essential part of secondary education became so firmly established that school architects often included as a matter of course a room designated as the "language laboratory" in their preliminary floor plans for a proposed high-school building. However, there is evidence to indicate that the predominance of the university during the first decade of language laboratory development created a stereotype in equipment design which was not fully adaptable to foreign language programs as they exist at the secondary level. It was only natural that the secondary-school people should have turned to the only existing models during the early years of the language laboratory. Thus, a number of college and university figures became prominent in the early 1960s as consultants for laboratory installations. It was quite understandable that these people gave advice based upon their experiences with college-level students. In this process, however, several basic differences between college and secondary education tended to be overlooked. Among the differences most pertinent to this discussion are the following.

THE SCHEDULE

College-level courses may meet two, three, or four times weekly. When the student is not in class he is free to go wherever he wishes. Thus, the college or university student has dozens of open hours each week. In contrast, the high-school student is usually scheduled into academic courses on a five-days-per-week basis. Also, he is typically under adult supervision from the time the tardy bell rings in the morning until the dismissal bell sounds in the afternoon. As a result, the high-school schedule affords little opportunity for open-hour lab work.

RESPONSIBILITY FOR LEARNING

The college student is on his own to a much greater degree than is the case with his high-school counterpart. Thus he can be told, for example, that he will be tested on his ability to perform in certain

The language laboratory and the electronic classroom

aspects of the spoken language and that tapes are provided in the language laboratory which will help him to develop the required skills in some other way. If he fails to achieve what is expected, that is his problem. At the high-school level a much larger share of the responsibility for learning is on the shoulders of the teacher. In most states, students are required by law to be in school well into the late teens. Because of this, they cannot simply be "flunked out" as they are in higher education. There is no place for them to go. The influence of compulsory attendance carries over to all high-school course work including such elective subjects as foreign language. The teacher of a foreign language may insist that one or two of his students are not capable of continuing after the first few weeks of school. But the percentage cannot go very high, simply because teachers in other subject areas have no desire to have their subjects serve as a dumping ground for rejects from the foreign language program. Thus, the secondary-school foreign language teacher is generally charged with the responsibility of moving a hundred or more students through the language program for an entire school year. The students within this group represent an extremely wide range of academic abilities and motivational drives. A substantial number of students will often be from homes where there is no strong incentive for academic achievement. Thus, the high-school teacher is charged, not only with the responsibility to teach, but also with the responsibility for motivating reluctant learners. If a large number of youngsters fail to respond, that is the teacher's problem; and the students know it.

STAFFING

The college concept of language laboratory utilization was based to a large extent upon open-hour use of the equipment. This implies the need for laboratory technicians, laboratory assistants, and a director of language laboratories who is available on a full-time basis to supervise the complex operation of procuring and cataloguing tapes in each language, to produce correlation charts relating each tape to each appropriate chapter in the various texts, to set up a yearly laboratory budget, to arrange for preventive maintenance and for replacement of worn parts, and to perform a thousand other services necessary for the proper functioning of the laboratory facilities. By contrast, the staffing changes permissible in the high-school budget will typically consist of giving one teacher one extra free period per day to serve as director of the language laboratory. In many cases, the local school budget does not even permit this much of a concession to the staffing needs which the college-type of language laboratory creates. Thus it is that, even though high school installations outnumber installations in higher education by many thousands, the newly organized National Association of Language Laboratory Directors (NALLD) was able to enroll only a handful of members below the college level.[3]

In view of all this, it should not seem surprising that the college-oriented concept of language laboratory utilization caused many problems when it was first introduced into the secondary-school program. The first laboratories simply were not designed for the secondary-school curriculum. In the larger high schools, scheduling was a problem from the outset. Lacking the open-hour flexibility of the college schedule, teachers had to take students out of the regularly scheduled classroom sessions and march them down the hall to the laboratory room. And because there were several sections of various modern languages meeting each period of the day, each language teacher might be assigned only one period per week in the language laboratory. This created a situation in which laboratory attendance was dictated by the complexities of the schedule without regard for whether or not the students were at a point where they could profit from laboratory drill work. This fact, coupled with other problems such as lack of teacher familiarity with equipment, a shortage of suitable tapes, and the disruption of class activity occasioned by having to shuttle energetic adolescents back and forth down the hallway, often led to total demoralization of both the teacher and the class. The resultant negative attitudes sometimes led to vandalism as students vented their frustrations against the electronic equipment. Despite these and other problems, many teachers found ways to make the equipment achieve positive results in terms

[3] T. R. Goldsworthy, "Status Report: National Association of Language Laboratory Directors," Madison, December, 1966.

The language laboratory and the electronic classroom

285

of better student performance in the audiolingual skills.[4] However, while some were learning to adapt to the language laboratory as it had developed in the colleges, others were experimenting with equipment which more closely reflected the realities of the secondary-school foreign language program. One result of this experimentation was the development of an electronic teaching system which was contained within the conventional classroom. Through the late 1960s, both the laboratory and the so-called "electronic classroom" were in use. And a different pattern of utilization began to emerge for each type. The utilization of the language laboratory became more closely identified with the Instructional Materials Center Concept (IMC Concept) while the electronic classroom became a device for providing supplementary drill within the regular classroom period. The following discussion will deal with the advantages and limitations of both approaches to the use of electronic teaching systems.

Functions available to the student in various types of electronic installations

Before proceeding into the more technical aspects of electronic teaching systems, it might be well for the reader to review the principal functions that existing installations provide for the student. Item 2 below describes the function of the student position as it is found in most electronic classrooms. Most language laboratories contain at least a few student positions of the type described in item 3. Items 4 and 5 represent more recent approaches to providing one or more of the functions described in the first three items.

1. An *audio-passive* (listen only) installation is one in which a student simply listens to materials recorded by the teacher or by a native speaker. If the student responds during pauses on the recording, he neither hears himself through his headphones nor records his responses. His own voice is partially muffled, producing an effect of semideafness.

[4] Sarah W. Lorge, "Language Laboratory Research Studies in New York City High Schools: A Discussion of the Program and the Findings," *Modern Language Journal*, XLVII (November 1964), 409–419.

2. In an *audio-active* (listen-respond) installation, the student hears himself as he responds to questions posed on the master tape. This is done by a system of interconnected microphone, amplifier, and headphone.

3. The *audio-active-compare* (listen-respond-record) laboratory allows the student not only to listen to the master tape and hear his own responses over the headphones, but also to record both questions and answers on tape by means of a tape recorder installed in his booth or, in the case of a remote-control laboratory, a nearby cabinet. The student can also play back his own responses which he then compares with the correct responses recorded on a different track of the same tape.

4. *Remote-access* (dial-access) systems enable a student to select the program he needs by means of a dial or push button. A central tape library provides many lesson sources in a remote location. These programs are available without tape handling. Remote-access systems can be audio-passive, audio-active, or audio-active-compare.

5. *Wireless systems* can broadcast one or more programs to any number of students. Battery-powered receivers provide portability and are instantly expandable simply through the purchase of additional units. Remote monitoring and intercommunication are not possible.

The electronic classroom and the language laboratory— a comparison

There are several ways in which the electronic classroom differs from the language laboratory. Physically, the electronic classroom is a dual-purpose room serving both as a regular language classroom and also as a device for electronically broadcasting language drill work to an entire class or to individuals or groups within the class. The electronic classroom has no booths to provide physical and acoustic isolation of the student. By contrast, the language laboratory is equipped with acoustically treated student cubicles located in a room separate from the regular language classroom. Both the electronic classroom and the language laboratory include a teacher console from which several programs can be simultaneously transmitted to individual students or to small groups of students within the class. In both systems, the teacher is able to communicate with students and to listen to them individually via the monitor panel. The language laboratory may or may not provide a record-and-playback mechanism in the student booth. The electronic classroom ordinarily has no provision for the student to record and playback his own voice or even to record a program which is broadcast from the console. When a school chooses the electronic-classroom concept, the trend is to put in several installations, one in each room where a modern foreign language is scheduled throughout the day. This is considered neither feasible nor desirable where the language laboratory is concerned. (See Table 8 for a further comparison of the electronic classroom and the language laboratory.)

8

Comparison between electronic classroom and language laboratory

	Electronic classroom	Language laboratory
Cost (1 teacher)	$120 to $170 per student position.	$200 to $500 (and up) per student position.
Cost (3 teachers)	Each full-time language teacher would require an electronic classroom.	Three electronic classrooms are slightly more expensive than one typical booth-type laboratory.
Cost (initial)	No additional room needed regardless of how many electronic classrooms are installed.	One teaching station is "tied up" for each language laboratory.
Transition— classroom to laboratory and back.	Less than a minute with properly installed student positions; confusion is minimized.	Five minutes or more if lab and seating are not in the same room. Confusion often results if large groups of students are required to move long distances or if they have to go up and down stairs.

	Electronic classroom	Language laboratory
Room flexibility	Classroom can be used for other subjects: English, Social Studies, Shorthand, etc.	The language laboratory does not lend itself to regular classroom work in any subject area, including foreign language.
Teaching flexibility	With an electronic classroom, a teacher can go directly from explanation and demonstration to practice. The drill work is given whenever the students are ready for it, not when a schedule dictates.	With a language laboratory shared by several teachers, each teacher is obligated to adhere to a schedule which could mean explanation on one day, no practice until the following day.
Grouping	The teacher has all his students in one room where he can observe all of them while working with small groups for face-to-face oral work. Group work can be carried on while at the same time individual drill work is being transmitted from the console.	The teacher cannot, because of the booths and the distance between students, work effectively with groups in the laboratory. He would normally work with students individually through intercom system.
Electronic intercommunication for individual help	Electronic intercommunication possible from main console.	Electronic intercommunication possible from main console.
Recording facility	Recording facility at console possible. Remote student recorders possible (but expensive to install).	Recording facility at console possible. Individual student recorders more practicable with booths.
Psychological isolation	Provided by earphones only.	Provided by earphones and booths.
Noise level	May be satisfactorily reduced by using quality	A noticeable improvement in noise reduction

The language laboratory and the electronic classroom

Electronic classroom	Language laboratory
earphones padded with material which will adjust to the shape of the wearer's head, by proper use of the microphone, and use of noise-cancelling microphone attached to headset unit.	*may be obtained with booths of good quality sound-absorbing material. These booths must extend well above and in back of the student's head. (The typical commercially produced booth has little acoustic value.)*

Because of the many problems mentioned earlier (i.e., budget deficiencies, scheduling problems, lack of staff, vandalism of equipment, etc.), many schools have elected to install electronic classrooms rather than the more expensive language laboratory. If the concept is fully implemented, each teacher with a full teaching load will have an electronic classroom contained within his room. Thus the problems associated with scheduling and class-to-lab movement are eliminated. The students can shift from classroom work to laboratory drill in seconds without moving outside the room. Moreover, the students can engage in drill work whenever the teacher feels they are ready for it, and the teacher can cut the drill work short whenever he judges that it has reached the point of diminishing returns. The students are never scheduled capriciously into unwanted laboratory attendance. As a result, there are fewer frustrating situations that might cause the students to vent their dissatisfaction against the equipment. Also, unlike the situation which occurs with the booth-type language laboratory, youngsters do not vanish behind cubicle walls. (By definition, the electronic classroom has no booths.) The opportunities for student misbehavior are thereby greatly reduced.

There are other pedagogical reasons for selection of the electronic classroom over any type of equipment which tends toward infrequent, unsupervised utilization. Studies over the past half century have indicated that, where skill development is concerned, it is better to distribute drill work into a large number of short practice sessions rather than to mass the drill work into one long practice session. Twenty minutes of concentrated drill work daily is considered the optimum "dosage" by many practitioners of electronic-assisted instruction. This can be provided easily in a school which has been equipped with a sufficient number of electronic classrooms. Conversely, daily utilization by all students is seldom possible in those schools which have only the one centralized language laboratory. It is true that, in relatively small schools, it is often possible for teachers to approach this optimum daily utilization by having one language class use the laboratory during the first half of a class period while another class moves in during the second half. However, a great deal of precious class and laboratory time can be lost in the process of moving students from one place to another and of getting them to settle back down once they arrive.

Another pedagogical consideration with teen-age youngsters involves their need for professional, adult supervision. While it is true that a paraprofessional aide can hand the student a tape and tell him which cubicle to occupy, many teachers would question whether this is enough. Will the student be attentive while he is listening to the tape if the teacher is not directing the drill session? Or, even if he is attentive, will he be perceptive enough to detect the differences between the sounds which he is producing and the sounds which are coming from the master tape? There is evidence to show that superior achievement *is* possible where the student has an opportunity to hear a recording of his own voice in juxtaposition to the correct response provided this type of exercise is performed daily. Summarizing the results of her study of student performance with various types of equipment (as compared to control groups who had no access to a laboratory), Lorge states:

The recording-playback group generally achieved better results than the audio-active group in the same time pattern, more consistently in the *daily* time pattern. Recording-playback may have greater effect because a variety of activities is more interesting than a single activity and brings various kinds of involvement with the language, or because greater concentration is needed to compare the model speech with the imitation,

The language laboratory and the electronic classroom

or because the student finds it particularly interesting to hear his own voice and listens more attentively.[5]

The implications of Lorge's study are that each student should have the opportunity for *daily* practice with well-designed master tapes. This indicates the superiority of the language laboratory system which permits a student to record his own voice and to play it back in comparison with the master program. However, the simple economics of public-school financing makes it clear that this situation will almost never be feasible if historical budget limitations persist. When one considers that the cost of a teaching station plus the cost of a thirty-position language laboratory represents a total expenditure of between $40,000 and $60,000, then it is not difficult to imagine why school boards are reluctant to approve the installation of more than one fully equipped laboratory per high school. And, for a number of reasons discussed earlier, the single, centralized laboratory tends to be utilized less than the optimum five-time weekly per class. Thus the factor of time appears to be much more significant than the presence or absence of recording facilities. Indeed, Lorge found that using the laboratory only once a week produced learning results that were actually inferior to results achieved by the control group, which used no electronic equipment whatever.[6] Another study involving more than five thousand students in twenty-one school districts of New York State gave strong evidence to support Lorge's suggestion that one laboratory drill session per week may be worse than none.[7] This study reports that most students "spent only one classroom period per week in the laboratory" and that "Significant differences that favored the no-laboratory group predominated and appeared in connection with each language skill tested."[8] (Unfortunately this report is of limited value because it dealt only with students who were scheduled once-per-week in the laboratory, a pattern of utilization which has subsequently been discredited.)

[5] Lorge, *op. cit.*, p. 418.
[6] *Ibid.*
[7] Raymond F. Keating, *A Study of the Effectiveness of Language Laboratories*, New York, Institute of Administrative Research, 1963, p. 13.
[8] *Ibid.*, pp. 38–39.

Thus, it seems that the school systems are often compelled to choose between optimum equipment design and optimum equipment availability. In view of the foregoing discussion, it would appear that the best choice will generally be the one which provides maximum availability of equipment for student drill.

Advantages of electronic teaching systems

There are certain functions which the electronic classroom or the language laboratory can perform better than the unaided teacher. Perhaps no one has defined these more simply and lucidly than Alfred S. Hayes, one of the earliest pioneers in language laboratory installations. Therefore, we have produced the list below in exactly the form in which Hayes presented it in a U.S. Office of Education Publication.[9]

1. In a language laboratory all students present can practice aloud simultaneously, yet individually. In a class of 30 students, 29 are not idle while one is busy.
2. The teacher is free to focus his attention on the individual student's performance without interrupting the work of the group.
3. Certain language laboratory facilities can provide for differences in learning rates.
4. The language laboratory provides authentic, consistent, untiring, models of speech for imitation and drill.
5. The use of headphones gives a sense of isolation, intimate contact with the language, equal clarity of sound to all students; and facilitates complete concentration.
6. Recordings provide many native voices. Without such variety it is common for students to be able to understand only the teacher.
7. The language laboratory facilitates testing of each student for listening comprehension. It has generally been impracticable for the unaided teacher to test this skill.

[9] Alfred S. Hayes, *Language Laboratory Facilities: Technical Guide for the Selection, Purchase, Use, and Maintenance,* Washington, D.C., 1963, U.S. Government Printing Office, Bulletin 1963, No. 37, pp. 16 f.

8. The language laboratory facilitates testing of the speaking ability of each student in a class. It has generally been impracticable for the unaided teacher to test this skill.

9. Some teachers, for reasons beyond their control, do not themselves have sufficient preparation in understanding and speaking the foreign language. The language laboratory provides these teachers with an opportunity to improve their own proficiency.

10. The language laboratory makes it possible to divide the class into teacher-directed and machine-directed groups.

11. Certain language laboratory facilities can enhance the student's potential for evaluating his own performance.

12. Given specially designed instructional materials, the language laboratory can provide technical facilities for efficient self-instruction.

Matching the electronic system with the foreign language program

The only reason for the existence of electronic equipment in the high-school foreign language program is to make learning more effective. The installation is not an end in itself; contrary to popular misconception, there is no language laboratory method. Rather, the equipment is merely a tool or vehicle for delivering a recorded program to the student. If the device does not fit the program of the local school system, then it is not likely to be very effective. Thus, for example, if the school is moving into a program based upon flexible scheduling of students and upon individualized study, then the equipment should be selected accordingly. To be more specific, if individualization takes the form of programmed learning of the linear type, then the language department should select that type of equipment which provides for the maximum number of student record-playback units. For with programmed material on tape, each student must have complete control over the progress of his own tape. That is, he must be able to stop and start the tape playback mechanism according to the instructions given in the programmed text. Clearly, the electronic classroom would be the wrong choice for this sort of programmed instruction. On the other hand, if the usual high-school schedule is in effect, and if a relatively large number of language sections are scheduled for each hour of the day, then the installation of several electronic classrooms may be a better choice. Under certain circumstances, even schools on the so-called "flexible schedule" may find that several electronic classrooms are preferable to one centralized laboratory. Freeing an extra room for dual-purpose scheduling increases the number of alternatives for student activities in the week's schedule. And if self-pacing is not a significant factor in the program, then room flexibility may well be the determiner of equipment choice.

Administering the laboratory as an instructional materials center

In theory, the language laboratory equipped with private cubicles and student tape recorders seems to provide answers to many of the problems associated with foreign language instruction. In the early years of the language laboratory movement, idealistic language educators pictured a type of utilization in which equipment would overcome many of the shortcomings of the lock-step classroom progression. It was not difficult to conjure up visions of the language teacher diagnosing student difficulties with pronunciation and structure, and then immediately—before bad habits could form—programming the student into drill work especially tailored to meet his specific, individual problem. By the mid-nineteen sixties, the equipment people had developed hardware which improved somewhat on this vision when they introduced remote-access equipment onto the school market. With a special arrangement of switches and remotely located tape-playback mechanisms, the student can simply dial a number assigned to him by the teacher and, as if by magic, receive the exact drill he needs to cope with the learning problems his teacher has identified. Again, in theory, the equipment allows the teacher to become a true professional who, like a doctor, diagnoses ills and prescribes treatment. And the preventive medicines for the language learner are all contained in neat, easily retrievable audiovisual packets located in the Instructional Materials Center Laboratory. At least, that is the vision in the mind of audiovisual enthusiasts and venders of language laboratory equipment. Unfortunately, this dream is seldom realized in full, and is often not realized even in part despite the expenditure of many thousands of dollars for equipment and materials. There are many prerequisites for the proper functioning of a language laboratory. The failure of any one aspect in the chain of laboratory administration can lead to ineffective utilization of the equipment. The minimal circumstances that exist in any successfully operating IMC Laboratory follow:

AVAILABILITY OF PROGRAM MATERIALS

A vast number of carefully selected tapes and other materials are necessary if any IMC concept is to function properly. Despite this seemingly obvious fact, the author has found laboratories costing thousands of dollars for which little or no program materials had been provided. A projector without films and a laboratory without tapes are equally useless pieces of hardware.

ACCESSIBILITY OF PROGRAM MATERIALS

Even where tapes have been purchased in abundance, they are often rendered useless simply because they have been locked in a storage cabinet or are otherwise not accessible to the student. There may be an aura of magic about the remote-access system or the less elaborate audio-active-compare laboratory, but that magic can only be conjured up in those circumstances where it has been preceded by hundreds of hours of drudgery. Among the types of work essential to the proper functioning of any IMC installation are the following:

1. Purchasing of tapes for each day's work in each level of each language.
2. Labeling, cataloging, and storing each of these master tapes so that they can be easily located.
3. Dubbing student copies of the master tapes and labeling, cataloging, and storing these.
4. Producing printed correlation charts for each tape in each level of each language so that they are identifiable according to unit

of work, grammatical or phonological topic, chapter of text, etc. If the laboratory is a remote-access system, then there is the additional problem of assigning a number to each tape and to placing each tape on the remote recorder during the period of time when it will be in demand.

5. Having an efficient way of delivering a taped program to the student, either through a broadcast-and-student-record system or by means of a tape check-out system.

SCHEDULING FEASIBILITY

If the IMC laboratory concept is to work, the teacher must be able to assign each student a certain number of out-of-class laboratory periods. If conditions permit (such as in a school system on a flexible schedule), the student may have some choice in the matter. In the more traditional schedule the laboratory may be made available during every period of every day so that the student may sign up for the laboratory during his free periods instead of going to the library or study hall. Students can also be permitted to engage in laboratory work before and after school. In any case, once the schedule is set, the student has the responsibility to attend and to do the assigned work. This work is assigned in addition to the regular classroom sessions in the traditionally scheduled school. It is regarded by the teacher as homework comparable to reading assignments in English or drill exercises in mathematics.

STAFFING

All of the foregoing implies that someone will be available to supervise laboratory sessions. Clearly, a full-time librarian-technician is needed to perform the functions listed above. Further, persons are needed to see that the equipment is kept in proper working order, and that sufficient copies of each taped lesson are available when needed. The person in charge of an IMC-type of installation must also be knowledgeable enough to serve as a liaison person between the various members of the language staff. The taped program received by a student when he enters the laboratory must be precisely the program which the teacher has assigned and which the student recognizes as the one he needs and is able to use. The Instructional Materials Center librarian must be a unique, highly skilled individual.

As we have seen, few schools below the college level have found it possible to staff, equip, and service IMC laboratories for instruction in foreign languages. In staffing, for example, we note that, despite the existence of an estimated 8000 high-school language laboratories, only 134 directors of secondary-school laboratories could be identified throughout the nation in 1966.[10]

The lack of a fully equipped language laboratory does not necessarily completely rule out the IMC concept of utilization. Many high school teachers who perceive the value of out-of-class oral drill have found ways to adapt the electronic classroom to this purpose. Thus, instead of having the student take a tape into a booth (or otherwise receive the program for use on an individual tape player), the teacher or a laboratory assistant may broadcast the tape from the console to where the student receives it via an audio-active (listen-respond) unit. Lacking student recorders, the electronic classroom permits the school to minimize both the initial investment in equipment and the continuing maintenance costs for that equipment. However, the opportunity for individual pacing is lost in the process. The student cannot stop, pause, or rewind his tape. He can only listen and respond to the program as it plays inexorably from the console.

Tapes for the language laboratory and electronic classroom

The laboratory is only as good as the materials used with it. Like all machines, from TV to giant mechanical "brains," the language laboratory is effective only if the human beings in charge of it feed it a good program. A tape recorder can be a means of entertainment, a dictating machine, a toy; it becomes a *teaching machine* only by virtue of its programming. Whether tapes are used in conjunction with a programmed course, or whether they are used *by* the student in the IMC-concept of supplementary drill, or whether they are broadcast *to* the student from the console of the electronic

[10] Goldsworthy, *op. cit.*

classroom, it is generally agreed that they should have certain minimal characteristics. Proponents of the American Method generally feel, for example, that mere repetition is less desirable than the stimulus-response-reward format discussed in previous chapters. Other areas of agreement are that utterances must be kept short, that manipulations should focus upon one structural problem at a time, and that sufficient repetitions of a pattern must be made to ensure the formation of the desired linguistic habits. There is less agreement with regard to whether responses should be evoked purely by audio cues or whether more use should be made of visual stimuli to evoke oral responses.

Unfortunately, many tapes which are attractively boxed and labeled as "programmed tapes" are almost valueless for laboratory drill. In some cases, publishers have merely taped drill material verbatim from old textbooks, apparently as a gesture toward modernization. In other cases, drill material follows a modern format, but has other intolerable disadvantages. Among the problems appearing in commercially produced materials are confusing directions, utterances too long for the student to retain, bad recording techniques, monotonous pronunciation, and absence of correct response to confirm the student's response. Thus, all taped material should be carefully evaluated prior to purchase. (See Chapter 8, Table 7, for criteria for evaluating pattern drills.)

The selection and utilization of tapes will vary considerably with the type of equipment. The language laboratory with student recorders in each position will require drill material of less than ten minutes playing time if students are to engage in a twenty-minute drill session. With student recorders, time must be allowed for rewinding tapes, for playing back the lesson to hear one's own voice in contrast to the master recording, and for stopping periodically to correct mistakes. With the electronic classroom, on the other hand, tapes can be almost twenty minutes in length in a twenty-minute drill session. Inasmuch as the student has no control over the course of the program, tapes should be so utilized as to reduce the chance for error to an absolute minimum. There is more need for elaborate explanations as to how the drill functions and for advance preparation in class. The student must be helped to develop the skill of hearing his own responses in the foreign language and of making objective comparisons with the native speaker's voice which is heard within a second or two after the student response. For some highly nervous youngsters the constant, inexorable flow of stimulus followed by response followed by reward followed by the next stimulus can be emotionally disturbing. The frustration of missing several successive responses or of being interrupted by the next utterance from the console is almost beyond toleration for some students. In extreme cases it might be well to allow certain students to do the drill work independently on an individual tape-playback machine. If a large number of students are experiencing this type of difficulty, the teacher can lengthen the pauses by mechanically holding the tape for a second or two after each stimulus. With technical assistance, the tapes can also be rerecorded with longer pauses. Another possibility is to have tapes recorded with no pauses whatever. Supplied with a foot-control pause switch, the teacher can then stop and start the tape at will. This facility enables him to hold the tape until all students have responded. It also enables him to speed up the pace of the drill work if students are responding faster than anticipated.

Specifications for the electronic classroom and the language laboratory

Experience with electronic equipment used in teaching modern foreign languages clearly indicates that their effectiveness is in direct proportion to the quality of sound they are capable of producing. Whether it is from tape, disk, or film sound track, the signal that comes through to the student's ear must be of sufficient quality to enable him to hear the sounds of the new language distinctly. A signal that is weak, distorted, or obscured by noise can negate the value of audiovisual materials which are pedagogically sound in every other way. Clearly, it would be ideal if all language teaching devices had the fidelity characteristics of the best custom-made high-fi sets. Similarly, it would be well if all films, records, and tapes used in the foreign language classroom were properly amplified and broadcast through full-range speaker systems. However, despite the desirability of such equipment, the high cost of supplying it to every language classroom has necessitated a more realistic approach. Experience has shown that a satisfactory compromise can be reached with medium-fidelity, moderately priced equipment. Studies of student's ability to distinguish minimal differences between two foreign language sounds conducted at the Massachusetts Institute of Technology indicated that "System frequency response of less than 7300 cps, and especially below 5000 cps, prevented a substantial number of American boys and girls from perceiving phonemic contrasts in German and French."[11] Studies conducted at the University of Wisconsin revealed that sound energy registered by a French speaker is very strong up to 8000 cps and beyond.

It may be concluded from all this that the first essential characteristic of electronic equipment used in the teaching of modern languages must be an adequate frequency response. For student headsets and microphones—the weakest links in the component chain—this may be defined as 80 to 8000 cps, plus or minus 3 db. It should be noted here, that the listed frequency response of a component is meaningless unless the db (decibel) tolerance is also given. (The smaller the db tolerance, the better the fidelity.) Also, because of various factors relating to the nature of electronic systems, it is always better to purchase components which exceed the minimum standards. Thus, the reader should bear in mind that the sample specifications given in Table 9 represent minimums below which the bidder should not be permitted to go. It is usually good practice to have a qualified technical consultant review the various bids submitted, for the purpose of determining which bidder is supplying the most for the money. Such scrutiny of components will often reveal that one of the higher bids offers sufficiently more in equipment fidelity and durability as to warrant the additional cost. The consultant who makes such judgments should be a disinterested third party; one cannot, for example, expect sales representatives for language laboratory equipment companies to supply objective data in such matters.

[11] M. Buka, M. Z. Freeman, and W. N. Locke, *International Journal of American Linguistics*, *XXVIII* (January 1962), 70.

The language laboratory and the electronic classroom

Sample procurement specifications for the electronic classroom or language laboratory

The items set forth in the following table are samples drawn from specifications which were used in the procurement of electronic equipment in various colleges and high schools in the midwest. Therefore, they represent the status quo in laboratory equipment rather than the avant-garde movement toward remote-access and computer-assisted systems. The latter types of equipment call for a complexity of specifications beyond the range of possibility for this publication. In any case, it appears that the electronic classroom and the less complex laboratories will predominate in the public schools for at least the next decade. Budgetary factors alone seem to make this inevitable. The following specifications can be useful as a guide to help the prospective purchaser make certain that all functions essential to the electronic classroom or language laboratory are listed in the procurement specifications, along with a technically correct designation of minimal sound quality required to reproduce European languages without undue distortion. In those cases where the school is able to engage the services of a technical consultant, the specifications may prove useful as a checklist of essential features. Perhaps no school would want to use the items exactly as they appear here. The usual bonding and contract clauses would have to be added and, of course, the number and type of components would vary according to local preference. Many of the following paragraphs can be used, with modifications, by those schools that choose to adhere to the general pattern of existing equipment.

9

1.0 *Scope of Work*
The intent of these specifications is to have the successful bidder furnish, deliver, and install one or more   complete and satisfactorily operating   -position language laboratory for School,   , Wisconsin. It is understood that one language laboratory will be installed in

Table 9 (Cont.)

2.0 General

All equipment and furniture (chairs not included) required to provide such systems shall be furnished by the successful bidder whether or not specifically called for herein. In addition, he shall provide all required raceways and wiring to the wall outlets. Each bidder shall submit an itemized list of all equipment he proposes to furnish including technical data and specification sheets on each item. Also included shall be a detail drawing of the console cabinetry showing layout of all components and provision for future expansion. Bidder will submit with the bid a list of recent laboratory installations of equivalent size and scope in the surrounding area, where this equipment can be viewed in operation.

The equipment herein specified shall be the product of a manufacturer of established reputation and in good standing, having plant and organization, and having produced similar systems for at least   years.

3.0 Materials and Workmanship

All materials shall be new and of good quality. All labor shall be performed in a thorough and workmanlike manner by experienced craftsmen versed in the work required. All work at the building shall be performed in a thorough and skillful manner and shall be done at such time as may be for the best interest of the project as a whole and properly correlated with the work of others.

Installation shall be in accordance with all applicable codes. The contractor shall provide a competent superintendent to supervise the installation of the equipment furnished by him and must be ready at all times to give any other trades and contractors information necessary for the completion of the installation.

4.0 Foreign Parts

All foreign parts must be noted, together with a statement of their availability.

5.0 Wiring, Setup, and Installation

All electronic wiring shall be done by qualified technicians under the supervision of factory-trained engineers. The equipment should be set up and checked in order that the laboratory can function as a whole unit. All components must match electronically and

The language laboratory and the electronic classroom

Table 9 (Cont.)

mechanically with each other to form a properly functioning language laboratory.

All necessary wires, terminal points, etc., for the installation are to be included in the laboratory cost figures. All 110V AC wiring to the language laboratory room will be done by others. Bidder shall be responsible for 110V wiring within the system.

5.1 *All audio-circuit wires shall be 22 gauge or larger with 80% electrostatic shielding or better. All cables shall be continuous and free of splices. All wires shall be checked for shorts to shields before shields are grounded.*

5.2 *In a laboratory equipped with 20 tape recorders or more, 40 ampere service will normally be required.*

5.3 *The installation will be guaranteed against "crosstalk," "hum," and "noise." Crosstalk, hum, and noise can result from poor cable characteristics, poor or improper shield grounding, or by placing the audio cabling close to AC power cabling. Good design requires AC power cabling and audio cabling in separate conduits.*

5.4 *All student equipment and console components shall be quick-disconnect. Soldered connections shall not be used to connect components. This shall make it possible for a nontechnical person to remove a nonfunctioning unit and replace it with a usable spare.*

5.5 *The installation shall be in accordance with all applicable codes. Applicable codes require care in cabling and classroom codes are generally rigid. To avoid ground loops and trouble due to differences in potential among various available grounding points, shielding should be grounded at one point only, preferably at the control-console amplifier grounding point.*

5.6 *Expansion of laboratory*

A. *Installations which include student booths shall be so wired as to accommodate tape recorders without necessitating rebuilding of booths or removal of existing wiring or insertion of additional wiring.*

B. *Installations which do not include student booths shall be expandable as follows:*

(1) *All headsets, microphones, student amplifiers, and console components shall be adaptable to an expanded installation which includes booths.*

Table 9 (Cont.)

(2) *Only the wiring from console to the student position shall be made.*

C. *Each bidder shall list any provisions for trading in listen-respond amplifiers in the event that the purchaser should choose to add recording facilities to the student position.*

D. *Expansion without obsoleting equipment shall be guaranteed in all other instances.*

6.0 Consultant Services

Successful bidder shall provide complete sets of operating instructions including circuit diagrams and other information necessary for proper operation and service maintenance. In addition, a full wiring diagram of said language laboratory shall be provided including complete interconnections of all components. All wires shall be coded for future identification.

Successful bidder shall furnish free consultation service on all matters pertaining to the laboratory layout, electrical and audio details, functional setups, etc. This service is to be provided free of charge.

Successful bidder shall provide a competent supervisor to demonstrate and instruct all language teachers and supervisors in the operations and use of the above equipment prior to the month of _____, 19___.

7.0 Modern Systems Guarantee

Should any basic developments occur within one year from date of installation regarding improvement of equipment, design, or application which would enhance the teaching process, such changes are to be made available at cost if desired by the school.

8.0 Service and Maintenance

8.1 *Successful bidder shall assure (48) hour service and sooner if possible.*

(Explanatory note—do not include in written specifications.) Experience over the past four years has shown that some laboratories have deteriorated badly since the date of installation. One of the chief reasons for this loss of quality sound reproduction is lack of proper attention to certain simple maintenance procedures. Hence, the statements below.)

The language laboratory and the electronic classroom

305

Table 9 (Cont.)

8.2 *Service beyond the warranty period*
   A. *Each bidder shall furnish a statement regarding the following:*
      (1) *The service organization or person who will be available to provide the services and repairs listed under B below.*
      (2) *The yearly cost of a service contract if the purchaser desires to contract for the services listed under B.*
   B. *The following maintenance procedures are essential to the continued usability of the language laboratory beyond the first year of installation. The services listed below should be performed annually. This maintenance may best be accomplished during the summer when classes are not in session.*
      (1) *Head demagnetization*
      (2) *Head cleaning*
      (3) *Head alignment*
      (4) *Pressure-pad adjustments and replacement*
      (5) *Brake and tension adjustments*
      (6) *Lubrication of motors, bearings, idlers, sliding parts, and operating controls (avoid overlubrication)*
      (7) *Replacement of rubber drives which have developed bumps or flat spots*
      (8) *Belt adjustments and replacement*
      (9) *Adjustment of erase bias and recording bias for best signal-to-noise ratio*
      (10) *Adjustment of tape lifters and breakage controls*
      (11) *Checks of wiring, switching, plugs, sockets, and grounding*
      (12) *Cut-offs in case of tape breakage should be carefully checked and adjusted to avoid the introduction of flutter and wow by the cut-off during normal operation.*
      (13) *If heads are replaced, alignments and bias adjustments should be made according to manufacturer's instructions. In case separate bias oscillators are used on a dual-track unit, oscillator synchronization is required to avoid beat notes.*
      (14) *Dual-track portable tape units for instructor use or for making master tapes may be included in a laboratory. In electrically braked and tensioned tape units, switches should be cleaned and adjusted and any rectifier outputs*

Table 9 (Cont.)

should be checked to assure sufficient voltage for braking action.

9.0 Warranty

All equipment and component parts shall be guaranteed free of defects in material and workmanship for a period of one year after the installation has been completed. Guarantee shall include all parts, tubes, transistors, and labor required. Also, the equipment supplier shall make available to the owner at owner's option, a service contract for continued maintenance of equipment after expiration of original warranty.

The bidder shall designate the person or organization that will provide service and maintenance during the warranty period. (See 8.0 above.)

10.0 Equipment Specifications

10.1 Complete 6- (or more) channel desk console with 3 tape decks, 1 record player, 2 nonamplified auxiliary inputs, and adequate switching for all   student positions.

10.2 Intercommunication system with monitoring and "all call" provisions.

10.3   student positions each wtih microphone, headset, and storage for headset at each student position.

The microphone shall be:

A. Attached to headset.

B. Permanently mounted to student booth.

    (Choose A or B for language laboratory. Choose A only for electronic classroom.)

10.4   Student positions are to be listen-respond, and listen-respond-compare (with tape recorders).

10.5 No AC-DC amplifiers will be acceptable. Chassis shall be isolated to prevent student contact with AC potentials.

10.6 All operating controls and switches shall be as follows:

A. No decals or stick-ons shall be used.

B. Custom labels shall be engraved plastic or silk screen with transparent protection of labels.

10.7 Additional console equipment shall include (1) master microphone and (2) headsets. There shall be a minimum of 2 outputs for headsets.

The language laboratory and the electronic classroom

Table 9 (Cont.)

10.8   There shall be a master switch, with pilot light, which turns off the power to all components in the student position and console.

10.9   Microphones
Microphones shall be dynamic, variable reluctance, with frequency response of 80–8000, plus or minus 3 db.

10.10 Headphones
Headphones shall be at least equal to Brush ED–300, and with frequency response of 80–9000 plus or minus 3 db or better with volume control.

10.11 Component parts
The completed laboratory including all wiring and all component parts (amplifiers, recorders, etc.) shall have a frequency response comparable to the above specifications. Impedance should match throughout the entire range of operation.

10.12 Tape recorders—console
A. At least one tape deck shall allow for the recording of student's voice at the console in accordance with 11.11 below. Other console transport mechanisms may have playback function only if so specified by the bidder.
B. Specifications: Tape speeds shall be 7½ ips (recommended for normal use) and 3¾. The frequency response of this unit shall be from 50–1200 cps plus or minus 2 db at 7½ ips; it shall have a signal-to-noise ratio of at least 45 db, preferably 50 db; flutter and wow shall not exceed 0.3% preferably 0.2%. Harmonic distortion shall not exceed 2.0% preferably 1.0% at the normal operating level. Recording shall be standard on 2 (or 4) track. Fast forward and fast reverse shall be provided, as well as positive braking action. The unit shall also:
(1) Permit monitoring during recording
(2) Be equipped with a VU-meter for determining volume
(3) Have a tape-index counter of at least 3 digits
All controls shall be clearly labeled as to function.
C. Input impedances and levels shall be consistent with other components of the system. Output impedances should provide for either headphones or power amplifiers, as required by the particular installation.
D. Each recorder shall be equipped with a silent-pause button.

10.13 Record player (One required for each console)
A. Specifications: It shall be of the manual, monaural type and

Table 9 (Cont.)

provide for use of standard and microgroove recordings, including the speeds of 78, 45, and 33⅓ rpm; provisions of 16⅔ rpm is optional. It should accommodate disks up to 12 inches in diameter. A diamond stylus of 0.003-inch radius should be provided for standard recordings and a diamond stylus of 0.0007–0.001-inch radius should be provided for microgroove recordings. The tracking force (stylus pressure) should not exceed 8 g. The player should have an overall frequency response of 80–10,000 cps plus or minus 2 db. The player shall have a 45 rpm adapter and have a 4-pole or 2-pole motor.

B. Turntable assembly shall have spring mounting, or other suitable means of isolation from external vibration.

C. Flutter and wow shall not exceed 0.2% RMS. Rumble shall not be more than 1.8%.

D. Cartridge type shall be magnetic or ceramic (each requires proper preamplification).

E. Stylus (needle) shall be 1-mil (or less) diamond for 33⅓ and 45 rpm disks; 3-mil sapphire for 78 rpm disks.

11.0 Operation Specifications

11.1 The system shall be capable of transmitting simultaneously as many as 6 programs from the console to the student positions.

(Explanatory note—do not include in written specifications.)

On Section 11.2 the school may wish to allow only one of the options A, B, or C. B is the most flexible. C does not permit *individual* student positions to receive a given program. The program must be sent to an entire row thus making it impossible for the remaining positions to receive any other program. To clarify these functions in a rough manner, we could say that C is similar to a four-party telephone line; A, to a private line; B, to a private line that can be converted to a party line at the flick of a switch. C is less expensive and is acceptable where students work in groups or as a total class.

11.2 Each bidder shall list the following three programming arrangements along with the cost difference for each:

A. Programming distribution with one switch for each student position. This allows any student or group of students to receive any one program from the console regardless of seating arrangement.

B. Row distribution combined with individualization. This allows

The language laboratory and the electronic classroom

Table 9 (Cont.)

the instructor to distribute the program by rows (or banks) or to individual positions.

C. *Row distribution only. This permits programs to be sent to rows (or banks) of student positions. All students in a given row (or bank) receive the same program.*

D. *(Optional) A master program switch which simultaneously changes all students to one program.*

11.3 *Program transmission (choose one)*

A. *Teacher assigns the program from the console.*

B. *Student selects the program from the booth.*

11.4 *Monitoring of individual students must be silent and undetectable by the monitored student, who must not hear any clicks, pops, or change of volume. The instructor shall be able to monitor each student position from the console.*

11.5 *The instructor shall be able to carry on private simultaneous two-way communication with any student without interference from the master programs. Interference would constitute "intercom crosstalk." (See 5.5 above.) In addition, the intercommunication function shall enable the teacher to select any group of students with whom he wishes to communicate.*

11.6 *The system shall provide immediate hearback for each student during his own transmission, whether or not the student is recording the transmission.*

11.7 *The teacher shall have the facility to record at the console from any individual student position (or group of positions).*

11.8 *Additional specifications*

A. *All items in Section 3, pp. 109–111 of* Hayes's Language Laboratory Facilities *shall apply here (see Section 12.1). A copy of this publication should be in the hands of each bidder.*

B. *The following items from Section 4, pp. 112–113 shall also apply: 4.3.2, 4.3.3, 4.3.5, 4.3.13.*

C. *Sections 6 and 7 are considered desirable and should be included as bid alternates.*

11.9 *The student position (electronic classroom)*

A. *A combination headphone-microphone shall be used.*

B. *Wiring from console to headphone-microphone output* shall be in ducts and be permanently installed as *follows: (Choose one of the following possibilities.)*

Table 9 (Cont.)

---

(1) *Perimeter, in which the student moves from conventional desk to wall position.*

(2) *Overhead, in which the student stands up at conventional desk, obtains the headphone-microphone from an overhead location, and sits back down at the conventional desk.*

(3) *Student tables without dividers, in which the student obtains the headphone-microphone without moving from his seat.*

(Explanatory Note—do not include in written specifications.)

BOOTH SELECTION: Recent technological developments in microphones have prompted changes in attitude toward the semi-isolated booth. If a combination microphone-headset is used, the booth may be omitted providing all other specifications are met.

There are still a number of advantages in having dividing partitions between students. However, research indicates that these advantages are often negated by infrequent use of the installation (i.e., once a week or less). Therefore, if enrollments do not allow more than once-a-week attendance in the lab by each language class, then it may be better to omit the booths and apply the savings in furniture cost to the purchase of a second or third installation without booths.

Such installations carry the added advantages of not removing a classroom from regular use and of providing the students with ready access to the equipment. This permits the students to engage in language drills whenever they are ready for them rather than when the schedule dictates.

11.10 *The student position (language laboratory)*

A. *Booths (student position; enclosed on sides and in front). Choose one of the following. Front shall:*

(1) *Fold forward on piano hinge.*

(2) *Fold backward to form desk top.*

(3) *Be of safety plate glass on the top half of front panel above the desk top.*

(4) *Be of acoustical material on the top half of the front panel above the desk top.*

The language laboratory and the electronic classroom

Table 9 (Cont.)

B. *Other booth specifications:*
   (1) *Panels shall be of rigid construction.*
   (2) *Panels shall contain tightly packed fiber glass or comparable acoustical material.*
   (3) *Exposed sections of panels shall be of durable materials.*
   (4) *Wiring and electronic components shall be protected.*
   (5) *Booths shall be of wood or metal construction.*
   (6) *Booths must be guaranteed against vibrations.*

11.11 *Students whose booths are equipped with recorders shall be able to record transmissions from the teacher's console. This recording shall produce a master tape suitable for library use.*

11.12 *Pupils authorized to do so shall be able to use their recorders independently even while the remainder of the laboratory machines are being used for other programs.*

11.13 *Tape recorders (student)*

   A. *Specifications for all types: Tape speeds shall be 7½ and 3¾ ips. With a tape speed of 7½ ips (recommended for normal use), the frequency response of this unit shall be 75–9000 cps plus or minus 2 db; it shall have a signal-to-noise ratio of at least 45 db; flutter and wow shall not exceed 0.2%. Harmonic distortion shall not exceed 3.0% at the normal operating level.*

   B. *Recorders shall be standard 2 track (or 4 track). Fast forward and fast rewind shall be provided, as well as positive braking action. Controls should be kept to a minimum, and shall be clearly labeled as to function.*

   Recorder shall be equipped with VU-meter for determining sound level. Master track erasure shall be controlled by the teacher either from the console (this is preferred) or at the booth by locking mechanism which is not available to the student. Each recorder should have a tape-index counter of at least 3 digits.

   C. *Additional recorder specifications (where applicable)*
      (1) *Tape disengages from play and record heads on fast rewind and forward. Tape lifters should preferably be of stainless steel rather than brass.*
      (2) *There shall be a digital tape counter on all decks (console and booth) of at least 3 digits.*
      (3) *Each recorder shall have a silent-pause button.*

   D. *Hub-to-hub cartridge recorders (student position only) shall*

Table 9 (Cont.)

comply with student recorder specifications with the following permitted omissions:

(1) Single-tape speed

(2) Tape lifters

(3) Three-digital tape counter

Any such omissions shall be listed by the bidder.

11.14 Student tape recorders shall be:

Dual-channel capable of recording a master program on master track from the console while simultaneously recording student responses on student track. This shall make possible subsequent erasure and rerecording of student track without erasure of master track. Recorders must be dual-channel or provide comparable function.

11.15 Student units with listen-respond equipment will be capable of listening to any of (6) channels as selected at the console. These positions can respond and listen to their response, objectively, as it would sound if recorded. They shall be able to communicate with the instructor. Wiring for these positions should be such that they can be converted to student recorders. In addition, all booths shall be uniformly designed to accept either listen-respond or listen-respond-compare equipment.

11.16 Console platform and location (for labs which include student booths)

   A. Location of console shall be in (front, rear) of the lab. (Choose one.)

   B. Bidder shall supply a suitable-size raised platform for console. (15 inches or more is considered desirable.) All necessary steps shall be supplied by the bidder.

   C. Audio line for sound track of projection equipment shall be provided if location of console requires it.

   D. Glassed-in console room. (See Hayes; Bibliography)

11.17 Glassed-in console room

   (Explanatory note—do not include in written specifications.)

   This arrangement has much to commend it in laboratories which include booths. A few advantages are:

   1. Ambient noise is greatly reduced by keeping the instructor's comments, machine noises, and the like contained in the enclosed space.

   2. An area for equipment and materials storage can be estab-

The language laboratory and the electronic classroom

lished to which only teachers and other qualified persons have access.

Some rooms have small adjacent rooms which may with slight modification be converted into console rooms. In other cases, major construction is involved. Therefore, since the console room will vary in size, shape, and location with each building, blanket specifications can be written only by those who are familiar with the local situation. Thus, the following is merely *suggestive of what might be included.*

The console equipment shall be housed in an enclosure _____ by _____. The instructor shall have unobstructed view of all student positions through glass partitions in the enclosure while operating the controls at the console. The floor of the console room shall be elevated _____ feet above the floor level of the laboratory room.

11.18 *Annunciator light*
The student shall have the facility to call the instructor at the console by means of an annunciator light which remains lighted until the instructor responds.

11.19 *Acoustic tile*
Acoustic tile shall be furnished and installed on the ceiling and to the top of the moulding on the three inside walls. The tile shall be ¾″ × 12″ × 12″, wood fiber acoustical tile, white paint finish; to be applied with adhesive, centered with the panels on ceiling.

The tile shall be applied with adhesive; the adhesive shall be a type expressly for this purpose. It shall not be water soluble, and shall not contain ingredients which react chemically with oil paint, or will not contain a solvent which has a stronger solvent action on oil paint than naphtha, and shall not contain alcohol.

12.0 **Other Specifications**
All previous specifications for language laboratory equipment are superseded by the present document. Where questions arise between bidder and purchaser, both parties shall be held to the definitions contained in the following publications:

12.1 Newer Media for Instruction 4: Language Laboratory Facilities, Technical Guide for the Selection, Purchase, Use, and Maintenance, *Bulletin OE–21024, no. 37, 1963, U.S. Office of Education, U.S. Government Printing Office, Washington 25, D.C. For sale* by the Superintendent of Documents, U.S. Government Printing Office, Washington 25, D.C. Price 50¢.

12.2 The Purchase Guide and Supplement to Purchase Guide, *Ginn*, 205 West Wacker Drive, Chicago 6, Illinois. Price $3.95 and $1.25.

13.0 Tests
(The local school system may request such tests if a field check indicates that the above specifications have not been met.)
Upon the resquest of the _____ Public Schools, the bidder must submit his equipment to be examined and tested to see if the specifications are met. These tests are to be made at the bidder's expense. Test shall be made prior to final payment. If the bidder or his service agency is unable to meet specifications within the warranty period, qualified technicians must be employed to complete proper installation at no additional cost to the purchaser.

14.0 Installation Completion Date
The installation shall be fully completed 60–90 days after contract is awarded. Specify day. A penalty of $ _____ per day shall be assessed for failure to install as specified above.

15.0 Bids
Address all bids to: _____ . Bids are due in the office of above address on or before _____ . Public opening shall be at _____ .

16.0 Judgment Reservation
The _____ Board of Education reserves the right to accept or reject any or all bids or let the contract to the bidder offering a language laboratory deemed most advantageous to the purchaser.

17.0 Layout of Laboratory Room
The bidder shall include at least one diagram of the proposed room layout for the language laboratory installation, including location of student positions, placement of the console and storage areas, and location of windows and doorways. A scale drawing ¼″ or ½″ to the foot shall indicate position and relationship of console, student positions, and all other items of equipment and furniture.

18.0 Additional Features
18.1 The bidder shall attached a list of additional functions provided as standard features of the bidder's laboratory system.
18.2 The bidder may attach a list of optional features along with the cost of each.

The language laboratory and the electronic classroom

315

19.0 Exceptions to the Specifications

19.1 *Any departure from the above specifications shall be noted by each bidder. Failure to do so obligates the bidder to comply with all specifications above.*

1. *Maintenance Items, Tools, and Supplies*
   A. *Suggested list of basic tools and equipment.*
      (1) *Set of small Allen wrenches*
      (2) *Set of standard and Phillips screwdrivers*
      (3) *Set of nut drivers*
      (4) *Pliers and wire cutters*
      (5) *Small-tip soldering iron*
      (6) *Head demagnetizer*
      (7) *Tube tester*
      (8) *Volt-ohm meter*
      (9) *Spare equipment and accessories*
   B. *Suggested list of supplies.*
      (1) *Head cleaning fluid*
      (2) *Cotton swabs*
      (3) *Alignment test tape*
      (4) *Solder*
      (5) *Spare parts: vacuum tubes, record and erase heads, switches, fuses, pilot lights, capacitors, pads, belts, and other small working parts subject to wear and deterioration.*
2. *Production and Storage*
   A. *Essential equipment.*
      (1) *Tape splicer ($10 to $12 for splicer with tape dispenser attached).*
      (2) *Bulk eraser shall reduce background noise levels to tape from 3–6 decibels below normal erase head levels. Bulk tape erasers shall be equal to or better than the Robins ME–99. (Price range: $25 to $50).*
   B. *Essential materials and furniture.*
      (1) *Blank tapes—quality and price.*
         Polyester or mylar base tapes 1½ mil thick are recommended for laboratory use. They have great tensile strength, do not get

brittle under dry conditions, do not stick together, and leave very little residue on recorder heads. They can usually be purchased for $2.55 or less (7" reel) in lots over 12.

(2) Tape-reels with boxes.

Reels of 5" and 7" may be used. (However, for uniformity of storage many schools with laboratories have found it convenient to put shorter amounts of tape on the 7" reel.) Also, many teachers have found it convenient to use colored reels; a different color for each language. (Reels in boxes can usually be purchased for 50¢ each, 7" size.)

(3) Tape-storage cabinets.

These may be with or without doors, but should be specialized to accommodate tapes 7 inches and smaller.

(4) Leader tape.

(5) Gummed labels.

(6) Card file on index of tapes.

Bibliography

Allen, Edward D., "The Effects of the Language Laboratory on the Development of Skill in a Foreign Language," *Modern Language Journal*, XLIV (December, 1960), 355–358.

Goldsworthy, Thomas R. (ed.), *Newsletter*, 1, No. 3, National Association of Language Laboratory Directors, University of Wisconsin, (February 1967).

This issue lists dozens of publications covering many aspects of language laboratory utilization which are available free from the National Association of Language Laboratory Directors (NALLD). Article titles and mailing instructions are included.

Hayes, Alfred S., *Technical Guide for the Selection, Purchase, Use, and Maintenance, Language Laboratory Facilities*, Washington, D.C., 1963, U.S. Government Printing Office, Bulletin 1963, no. 37, pp. 16ff.

This 119-page publication is an excellent technical guide to electronic teaching systems in the field of foreign languages. It is written clearly and simply and contains excellent line drawings of equipment functions, room layouts, etc. Cost: 50¢ from the Superintendent of Documents.

Hocking, Elton, *Language Laboratory and Language Learning*, Mono-

The language laboratory and the electronic classroom

graph No. 2, Washington, D.C., Department of Audiovisual Instruction, National Education Association, 1964.

Hutchinson, Joseph C., *Modern Foreign Languages in High School: The Language Laboratory*, U.S. Office of Education Bulletin no. 23, OE-27013, Washington, D.C., U.S. Government Printing Office, 1961.

In addition to excellent material relative to the selection and operation of electronic teaching equipment, this bulletin features glossaries of language laboratory expressions in French, German, Italian, Russian, and Spanish. Included are the most practical of expressions such as "Put on your headphones," and "Turn off your tape recorder."

Hyer, Anna L. (ed.), *Audiovisual Instruction, 11,* no. 8, Washington, D.C., Department of Audiovisual Instruction National Education Association, October, 1966.

This entire issue is devoted to the language laboratory. Included are articles on maintenance, the IMC type of utilization, and the latest in language teaching devices both audio and visual. There are excellent photographs of the latest remote retrieval systems.

Lorge, Sarah W., "Language Laboratory Research Studies in New York City High Schools: A Discussion of the Program and the Findings," *Modern Language Journal, XLVIII* (November 1964), 409–419.

Stack, Edward M., *The Language Laboratory and Modern Language Teaching,* New York, Oxford University Press, 1960.

Evaluation of the foreign language program

11   Among the many ways of evaluating the success of a contemporary foreign language program we have chosen three for discussion in this section. The first of these involves a tabulation of characteristics relevant to foreign language instruction. With this approach, evaluators look at such things as the quality of the staff, the availability of audiovisual equipment and materials, the breadth and depth of foreign language offerings, and similar evidence. From this it is assumed that a given school has a quality program if, for example, it has four years or more of course offerings in several languages; it has a high percentage of teachers with Masters degrees; and if students have available an adequate supply of books, tapes, and electronic equipment. The limitation of this method of evaluation is that it reveals only that the program is potentially good or bad. There is no guarantee that the potential will be realized. For example, the teacher with the Masters degree may be performing badly in the classroom, the language laboratory may go unused day after day, and the audiolingual texts with last year's copyright may be used in a manner reminiscent of the nineteenth century. Clearly, by itself, the listing of external program characteristics does not provide sufficient data for program evaluation.

319

A second approach to evaluation of the foreign language program involves a careful analysis of teacher and student activities to determine whether or not these activities are consistent with stated course objectives. If listening, speaking, reading, and writing are listed as course objectives, then a major portion of class and laboratory time must involve active student use of the language in the pursuit of these skills. Evaluators will thus make a study of all classroom activities showing how much time the teacher spends talking in English versus the time spent talking in the target language. A similar count will be taken of student use of the native and target languages. A further breakdown of student-teacher interaction will reveal how much of the use of the target language involves mere rote imitation and how much involves more creative use of the language. After a broad sampling of classroom activities has been taken, it might be found, for example, that 30 percent of class time is devoted to teacher talk in English, 30 percent to teacher talk in the target language, 10 percent to rote student responses in the target language, 15 percent to student discussions in English, and 15 percent to nonlearning activities such as silence, confusion, moving back and forth to the chalk board, etc. It may be discovered through further analysis that the students are largely passive listeners who are seldom given the opportunity to recombine expressions which they have been asked to memorize and who are almost never asked to create utterances of their own in the target language either orally or in writing. This type of evaluation can indicate the activities which will need to be changed if classroom work is to be made consistent with course objectives. One of the major difficulties of this means of evaluation is the establishment of evaluative criteria upon which all teacher and supervisory personnel can agree. The staff must agree that a causal relationship exists between student-teacher interaction and the stated course objectives. Also, the evaluator must be a trained observer with a fairly good command of the languages used by those teachers he is called upon to evaluate. Perhaps the best solution to the latter problem is to train each language teacher to evaluate tape recordings of his own teaching behavior.

Ideally, evaluation would also involve a third approach; the direct measurement of student achievement. The ultimate question is, after all, "Are the language students actually learning to comprehend, speak, read, and write the new language?" To answer this question some high schools use standardized proficiency tests for each level of progress through the language program. The norms which are provided with such tests give some indication as to whether or not the local youngsters are progressing as well as the average language student in the nationwide sample upon which the test was standardized. Another approach is to develop local achievement tests based upon the actual course objectives set by the local staff. Assuming that local objectives have been stated in a form which is of use to the test maker and that the achievement test is then well designed, this type of testing would seem to offer the most advantages. The student who has conscientiously done his assignments throughout the year will encounter on this test the same type of material with which he has been working during the year. Standardized proficiency tests, on the other hand, will often contain vocabulary items and language structures to which the student has not yet been exposed, while omitting many of the things he has mastered. Yet, proficiency tests of proven reliability offer some advantages seldom available in locally devised testing programs. They permit a broader perspective of student achievement, they are printed in a high-quality, professional manner, and they provide native voices on tape along with other aids such as machine-scored answer sheets, directions for administering and scoring, and many other conveniences that are difficult to provide locally. In view of all this, it may be advisable for schools to combine achievement testing with proficiency testing for a comprehensive evaluation of student performance.

Evaluative criteria for the foreign language program

One evaluative technique commonly used by educational agencies at the local, state, and regional levels involves the presentation of a series of questions to members of the school staff. Questions that are answered affirmatively will indicate areas in which the program is strong; questions receiving negative responses reveal areas in which improvement is needed. Theoretically, great benefit will be derived from the very act of having the foreign language staff discuss such a list of criteria for the purpose of assessing the extent to which the local program measures up to the standards implicit in the questions. In some instances, the self-evaluation is followed by a team of language specialists from outside the school district who observe classroom teaching and who examine other aspects of the language program. After the visit, the evaluators may write a report indicating the degree to which their observations coincide with the self-evaluation responses. The following criteria are samples of the types of items often used by state and regional evaluators during the 1960s to evaluate public- and nonpublic-school foreign language programs in many parts of the United States.

CRITERIA PERTAINING TO THE FOREIGN LANGUAGE STAFF

1. How many modern language teachers have taken the MLA Proficiency Test for Teachers and Advanced Students?
2. If any language skills fall below the 50 percentile, are teachers engaged in further education to upgrade their basic language skills?
3. Do all members of the foreign language staff meet the minimum state foreign language certification requirements?
4. How many staff members have 30 semester hours or more in the foreign language they are teaching?
5. How many staff members have a Masters degree in the language they are teaching?
6. How many staff members have studied or traveled in a country where the language they are teaching is spoken?
7. How many staff members have attended an NDEA foreign language institute?
8. Does the local school have any standard screening process to assure that all language teachers are competent to teach the foreign language course as defined by the local curriculum guide?
9. How many foreign language teachers have had a regular credit

course in foreign language teaching methods within the last five years?

10. How many staff members have attended at least one foreign language workshop, meeting, or conference (other than department meetings) during the current school year?

11. How many foreign language teachers have engaged in interclass visitations within the school or have traveled to other schools in or out of the district to observe foreign language instruction?

12. Does the staff include paraprofessional personnel with non-language backgrounds to perform the more routine noninstructional tasks?

13. Does the staff include paraprofessional personnel who are native speakers of the foreign language to perform certain routine instructional tasks under the direction of the certified teacher?

CRITERIA PERTAINING TO THE ORGANIZATION OF THE PROGRAM

1. Is a four-year sequence of study offered in at least one foreign language at the senior high-school level?

2. Does the minimum justification for offering an advanced course exceed eight students?

3. Does the program offer only as many different languages as the school can support as evidenced by the number of third- or fourth-year courses?

4. Is a reasonable portion of the total school population enrolled in foreign language study? (Approximately 35 percent of all 9–12 grade students are currently enrolled in one or more foreign language courses.)

5. Is there evidence of a strong program, good guidance procedures, and flexible scheduling practices in the form of sustained enrollments?

Level I FL course: 50 percent of all eligible youngsters.
Level II FL course: 35 percent of all eligible youngsters.
Level III FL course: 25 percent of all eligible youngsters.
Level IV FL course: 15 percent of all eligible youngsters.

6. Is the school's foreign language department organized with one

person responsible for the effective working of the department regardless of the number of buildings in which foreign language instruction is carried on?

7. Is foreign language instruction offered below grade 9?

8. Is instruction in grades 7 and 8 offered five times weekly for not less than 30 minutes per class meeting?

9. Are students who successfully complete Level I course work in grades 7 and 8 offered a suitable Level II course in grade 9?

10. Are continuing foreign language students from the junior high school kept separate from beginning students of foreign language when they enter senior high school?

11. In schools with two or more teachers in the same language, is the possibility of team teaching or back-to-back scheduling being explored?

12. Does each teacher's schedule of classes and other duties include a reasonable amount of preparation time?

13. Is the district foreign language program, elementary through senior high school, coordinated by one person?

14. Do all language teachers of the district meet at least monthly to plan the effective articulation of the language program?

15. Is the language program designed to meet the needs of all students rather than being designed only for the college-bound?

16. Are usable curriculum guides available in each language?

CRITERIA PERTAINING TO METHODS OF INSTRUCTION

1. In the introductory courses is the primary emphasis upon the learning of new speech habits rather than upon the memorization of formal rules of grammar?

2. Is the use of grammatical generalizations subordinated to functional use of language structures for direct communication?

3. Is the introduction of reading and writing skills not unduly prolonged?

4. Are the reading and writing skills given proper attention along with the listening and speaking skills?

5. Are students required to learn vocabulary in complete meaningful contexts rather than as isolated lists of words?

324

6. Is at least 50 percent of class time devoted to student use of the foreign language as opposed to discussions about the language carried on in English?
7. Does the study of each foreign language include the development of understanding about the customs, beliefs, and traditions of the people who speak the foreign language?
8. Do the advanced courses include the broad cultural view rather than emphasizing American stereotypes of the foreign cultures?
9. Do the advanced courses provide for the maintenance of skills acquired in the beginning courses?

CRITERIA PEPTAINING TO PHYSICAL FACILITIES AND THEIR UTILIZATION

1. Does each modern foreign language classroom contain a tape recorder, overhead projector, record player, and other necessary equipment for use at all times?
2. Is other instructional equipment readily available as needed?
3. Is adequate storage space provided for tapes, books, filmstrips, slides, and supplies?
4. Is it possible to provide near total darkness in all language classrooms?
5. Is adequate chalkboard space available?
6. Are there as many positions in each language laboratory and electronic classroom as there are foreign language students in the largest foreign language class?
7. Was there adequate preservice and/or inservice training for all foreign language staff members with regard to the utilization of electronic teaching devices?
8. Are the materials used in the laboratory or electronic classroom an integral part of the regular classroom work?
9. Do first- and second-year students use the language laboratory or electronic classroom at least four times weekly?
10. How many language laboratories have been installed in the district's schools? (Language laboratory refers to equipment with booths.)
11. How many electronic classrooms have been installed in the district's schools? (Electronic classroom refers to boothless equip-

Evaluation of the foreign language program

325

ment installed in a classroom which has conventional seating. Students have a headset and microphone, and the equipment has provisions for the teacher to monitor and intercommunicate with all students.)

12. Is there sufficient laboratory or electronic classroom equipment to enable all foreign language students to engage in daily oral drill for 20 minutes or more?

13. Are programmed self-instructional materials used to allow the gifted student to proceed at a rate commensurate with his ability?

14. Are programmed self-instructional materials used to allow the academically deprived student to proceed at a rate commensurate with his ability?

15. Do third- and fourth-year students have regular access to the laboratory equipment?

16. Is a skilled paraprofessional available in the language laboratory to relieve teachers of routine duties?

17. Are skilled technical personnel available to perform routine maintenance and repair duties?

18. Are native-born paraprofessionals used to perform routine functions under the direction of a certified instructor?

19. Are special language tables available in the cafeteria so that students in each language can practice using the foreign language during the noon hour?

CRITERIA PERTAINING TO THE MATERIALS OF INSTRUCTION

1. Do all students have the necessary course materials?

2. Are the course materials consistent with the instructional goals listed in the curriculum guide?

3. Are course materials readily adaptable to a varied presentation of lessons?

4. Does the library contain a wide selection of books in each foreign language taught which are appropriate for the various levels of instruction?

5. Does the library have an extensive selection of books in English dealing with the countries where the languages are spoken?

6. Are other reading materials available, such as newspapers and magazines in the foreign language?
7. Do the foreign language classrooms have large foreign language text maps?
8. Do the language laboratories contain an extensive library of tapes and records which are systematically cataloged and correlated with the other instructional materials?
9. Are appropriate professional journals available for each language taught?

Evaluating the instructional process through interaction analysis

One point upon which most foreign language supervisors appear to agree is that the classroom teacher of foreign languages has a badly distorted view of what he is actually accomplishing with his classroom activities. The author has visited many schools where the staff proudly claimed to have a modern audiolingual course of study. However, after visiting all teachers at all levels of instruction it was revealed that 80 percent of the classroom work involved teacher talk, most of which was in English, and that, on those rare occasions when the students were allowed to speak, their responses were either repetitions of what the teacher had said or were responses elicited with reference to written material. It is not unusual to find that all functional communication between students and teacher is carried on in English. Teachers are often astonished when a tape recording of their classroom procedures is played back and systematically analyzed, to find that their use of the target language was both minimal and uncreative and that actual student use of the language was almost nil. It should be obvious to the teacher that the complex sets of skills, which are listed as objectives in the local curriculum guide, cannot possibly be developed unless the students have an opportunity to engage actively in the acquisition of those skills. Yet in all too many cases, the teacher continues to be the active performer, the students the passive listeners. Because of this lack of consistency between goal and method, a number of foreign language educators have developed a system of interaction analysis aimed at allowing the teacher to study his own behavior and that of his students in a systematic and objective manner. The insights gained by this analysis can serve as a guide to changing teacher behavior. The system of interaction analysis described here is an adaptation of the process developed by Ned Flanders.[1]

THE FLANDERS SYSTEM OF INTERACTION ANALYSIS

The Flanders system of interaction analysis is particularly appropriate for the foreign language field because it is concerned primarily with verbal behavior. The assumption is that the verbal behavior of an individual, both in English and in the target language, provides a relevant sample of his total behavior vis a vis the foreign language instructional process. The various patterns of observable verbal behavior are broken down into categories. The first major division is between talk by the teacher and talk by the students. Each of these divisions can then be divided further on the basis of whether the talk involves the native or the target language. And finally, the quality of the talk can be described both with regard to the oral behavior of the teacher and of the students. Through the systematic observation of dozens of different foreign language teachers, Nearhoof has devised ten interaction categories which include all the major verbal activities commonly occurring in the foreign language classroom.[2]

INTERACTION CATEGORIES FOR CLASSROOM OBSERVATION

With these ten categories clearly in mind, the trained observer is then able to provide a quantitative evaluation of the teaching process by assigning a number to every 3 seconds of elapsed classroom time. At the end of the observation period, these numbers can then be tabulated to determine what proportion of class time has been devoted to each category of verbal behavior. In the Nearhoof project,

[1] N. A. Flanders and E. J. Amidon, "The Role of the Teacher in the Classroom," Philadelphia, Temple University, January, 1962.
[2] Orrin Nearhoof, "Teacher-Pupil Interaction in the Foreign Language Classroom: A Technique for Self-Evaluation," from an unpublished research paper.

each teacher in the study had volunteered to record all classroom activities onto audio tape. These actual classroom activities then served as the basis for establishing and refining the interaction categories. However, this same use of audio-tape recordings (or better still, video-tape recordings) can permit the teacher to evaluate with a high degree of objectivity his own classroom performance.

For the teacher or supervisor who wishes to make use of this interaction-analysis technique, the first step is the memorization of the ten categories in association with the appropriate number. Time simply does not permit the observer to refer back to the categories while he is engaged in the process of observing and recording his observations. The categories are as follows:

1. Teacher use of the foreign language for *communication.*
    FL used by teacher to give directions which then elicit desired pupil action.
    FL used by teacher to discuss ideas relating to cultural contrasts, geography, history, literature, etc.
    FL used by teacher to explain problems of structure, of sound system, of written system, or other pertinent concepts.
    FL used by teacher to answer pupil questions.
2. Teacher use of the foreign language for *reinforcement.*
    FL used by teacher to correct pupil errors (provides correct response or causes correct response to be elicited).
    FL used by teacher to let student know immediately that his response has been successful.
    FL used by teacher to shape new responses or to reshape unsuccessful responses (i.e., response is broken into smaller parts, the smaller parts are drilled, and then the full response is attempted); FL also used to give hints (i.e., paraphrase, restatement, etc.), to help pupils produce new response.
    FL used by teacher to provide model for drills.
    FL used by teacher to elicit rote response in pattern practice.
3. Teacher uses English to *clarify meaning* or provide a cue. (A few words of English used quickly and briefly by the teacher.)

Evaluation of the foreign language program

329

4. Teacher uses English as the *functional classroom language.* (This includes the use of English by the teacher for the items of communication and reinforcement described in 1 and 2 above.)
5. Student uses foreign language for *rote response.*
> FL used by student in mimicry-memorization drill and pattern practice.
>
> FL used by one student to elicit rote response from another student.
>
> FL used by students in any type of repetitive drill exercises (i.e., class repetition of a dialog, sentence, conjugation, etc.).
>
> FL used by students to read from text, chalkboard, etc.
>
> FL used by students for any type of exercise which requires only an automatic response.
6. Student uses foreign language *to recombine* prelearned material.
> FL used by student to answer questions.
>
> FL used by student in which he is required to recall and recombine structures (oral or written) to form an acceptable reply.
7. Student uses the foreign language *to ask a question* which he himself has originated.
8. Student (or students) uses the foreign language *spontaneously.*
> FL used by students to discuss a topic of common interest (not rote recitation of prelearned material).
>
> FL used by students to react freely to pictorial or other situational presentation.
9. Students use *English* for classroom communication.
10. *Noninteraction* activities (e.g., silence; confusion; organization; other language activities such as language laboratory, singing, silent reading, etc.). For specialized language-related activities which are not easily categorized, these symbols are used to identify the time interval of the activities:
> O–S—singing
>
> O–R—reading (silent)
>
> O–W—writing
>
> O–L—laboratory

Best results are obtained when the observer spends several minutes orienting himself to the situation before he actually begins to categorize. He will thus develop a feeling for the total atmosphere of teacher-pupil interaction.

The observer records a category number every 3 seconds or with each change of activity. However, often during rapid question-answer sessions or when the teacher interrupts a pupil's response to correct or shape the correct response, more than one notation is required during the 3-second period. This follows the above statement regarding change of activity.

TEACHER: Tiene Ud. un libro rojo? (2)
PUPIL: No tiene . . . (5)
TEACHER: Tengo. (2)
PUPIL: No tengo un libro rojo. (5)

Thus, if more than one category occurs during the 3-second interval, then all categories used in that interval are recorded. Conversely, each change in category is recorded. If no change occurs within 3 seconds, repeat the category number.

However, if a silence is long enough for a break in the interaction to be discernible, and if it occurs at a 3-second recording time, it is recorded as 0. If no change occurs within 3 seconds, repeat that category number. See description of categories for other uses of 0.

These numbers are recorded in sequence in a column, and at the end of the observation period the observer will have several long columns of numbers. It is important to keep the tempo as steady as possible, but it is even more important to be accurate. He may also wish to write down marginal notes from time to time which can be used to explain what has been happening in the classroom.

The observer stops classifying whenever the classroom activity is changed so that observing is inappropriate as, for instance, when there are various groups working on a written assignment or doing silent reading. He will usually draw a line under the recorded number, make a note of the new activity, and resume categorizing when

Evaluation of the foreign language program

teacher-pupil interaction continues. At all times the observer notes the kind of class activity he is observing. A shift to a new activity should also be noted.

AIDS FOR CATEGORIZING

1. Always begin and end each observation by recording a o.
2. If a teacher calls on a pupil for a desired response, and if this action plus an ensuing silence constitute a 3-second interval, this should be recorded as o.
3. As stated before, during an interval when interaction observation is inappropriate (when the group is reading silently or singing in the foreign language), the observer should draw a line under the last recorded category number and indicate the time. When positive interaction recommences, again indicate the time and begin with o. Thus, by using 20 numbers per minute, it is possible to include all classroom activity for the observation period.
4. If the teacher intermingles English and the foreign language, this should be recorded as 4.

> TEACHER: Take out your books and open them *a la page deux cents trois.*

5. Drill and practice on a group basis falls in category 5, and when the drill is on an individual teacher-pupil basis, categories 2 and 5 are also used.

> TEACHER: J'ai deux frères.   (2)
> CLASS: J'ai deux frères.   (5)
> TEACHER: trois frères.   (2)
> PUPIL 1: J'ai trois frères.   (5)
> TEACHER: Nous.   (2)
> PUPIL 2: Nous avons trois frères.   (5)
> TEACHER: voitures.   (2)
> PUPIL 3: Nous avons trois voitures.   (5)

RECORDING DATA IN A MATRIX

There is a method of recording the sequence of events in the classroom in such a way that certain facts become readily apparent. This method consists of entering the sequence of numbers into a 10-row by 10-column table which is called a *matrix* (see Table 11). The generalized sequence of the teacher-pupil interaction can be examined readily in this matrix. The following example shows how an observer would classify what happens in the classroom and how the observations are recorded in the matrix. The observer has been sitting in the classroom for several minutes and has begun to get some idea of the general climate before he begins to record. The teacher begins, Alors, Pierre, comment allez-vous aujourd'hui?" (Observer classifies this as a 2.) Pierre responds, "Très bien, merci. Et vous?" (Observer records a 6.) Teacher, "Très bien, merci. . . . . . . Jacques, quel temps fait-il?" (Observer records a sequence of two 2's.) Pupil, "Il fait beau." (6). Teacher, "Marie, faites-vous du russe?" (2). Pupil, "Non, je fais du français." (6). Teacher, "Today we are going to complete our examination of the irregular verb *faire*. In our various structure drills and dialogues we have used only two basic sound forms of *faire: fais* (fait, same sound) and *faites*. Using our basic frame, *je fais du français,* we shall develop this important verb." (Observer records a series of five 4's followed by a o because of a period of silence during which the teacher picks up several 3 by 5 cards for the drill session.)

TEACHER: Répetez, Je fais du français. (2)
PUPILS: Je fais du français. (5)
TEACHER: Vous faites du français. (2)
PUPILS: Vous faites du français. (5)
TEACHER: Tu fais du français. (2)
PUPILS: Tu fais du français. (5)
TEACHER: Ils font du français. (2)
PUPILS: Ils font du français. (5)

(Observer records the sequence of 2, 5 followed by a final o.)

The observer has now classified the following sequence of numbers in this fashion:

0
2
6
2
2
6
2

Evaluation of the foreign language program

6

4   in matrix sequence

4   (0,2) (2,6) (6,2) (2,2) (2,6) (6,2) (2,6)

4   (6,4) (4,4) (4,4) (4,4) (4,4) (4,0) (0,2)

4   (2,5) (5,2) (2,5) (5,2) (2,5) (5,2) (2,5) (5,0)

4   (The rapid recording of the sequence 2 and 5 results

0   from the change of activity occurring in the three-

2   second-interval.)

5

2

5

2

5

2

5

0

Tabulations are now made in the matrix to represent pairs of numbers. Notice in the listing of matrix sequence that the numbers have been marked off in pairs. This first pair is 0,2; the second pair is 2,6, etc. The particular cell (see Table 11) in which the tabulation of the pair of numbers is made is determined by using the first number in the pair to indicate the *row*, and the second number in the pair for the *column*. Thus, 0,2 would be shown by a tally in the cell formed by row 0 and column 2. The second pair, 2,6, would be shown in the cell formed by row 2 and column 6, etc. Notice that each pair of numbers overlaps with the previous pair, and each number, except the first and the last, is used twice. It is for this reason that a 0 is entered as the first number and the last number in the record. Zero was chosen because it is convenient to assume that each record begins and ends with silence. This procedure also permits the total of each column to equal the total of the corresponding row.

It is convenient to check the tabulations in the matrix for accuracy by noting that there should be one less tally in the matrix than there were numbers entered in the original observation record.

In the example, we have 23 numbers and the total number of tallies in the matrix is 22. This is shown in Table 11.

334

	1	2	3	4	5	6	7	8	9	0	
1											0
2		|			||||	|||					8
3											0
4				||||						|	5
5		|||								|	4
6		||		|							3
7											0
8											0
9											0
0		||									2
Total	0	8	0	5	4	3	0	0	0	2	22

USING THE MATRIX TO DETERMINE
GENERAL ASPECTS OF CLASSROOM INTERACTION

After the observer tabulates a matrix, he then has the job of developing a description of the classroom interaction. He has several ways of describing the interaction but begins by reporting the different kinds of statements in terms of percentages. The first step is computing the percentage of tallies in each of the columns. This is done by dividing each of the column totals, 1 through 0, by the total number of tallies in the matrix. This computation gives each category as a proportion of the total interaction in the observed class-

12

Sample matrix summary

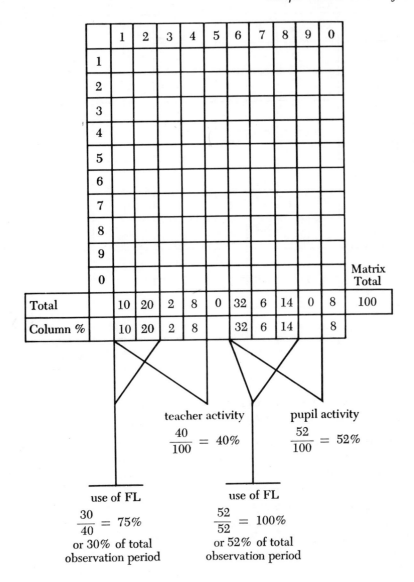

room situation. A similar procedure is used to determine the percentage of teacher activity, teacher use of FL, pupil activity, and pupil use of FL. To determine the percentage of teacher activity, divide the total of categories 1 through 4 by the matrix total. For example, in Table 12, teacher activity (columns 1–4) totals 40. Then 40 is divided by the matrix total, 100; and we find that the amount of teacher activity is 40 percent of the total amount of classroom activity. To calculate the percentage of teacher use of the FL in relation to the percentage of teacher activity, divide the total of columns 1 and 2 by the total of columns 1–4. In Table 12, teacher use of FL is 30; and by dividing 30 by the total teacher activity, 40, we find the percentage of teacher use of the FL is 75 percent. In short, teacher activity constituted 40 percent of the observation period, and the teacher used the FL 75 percent of the time he was in direct interaction.

The same procedure is employed to determine total pupil activity and pupil use of the FL. Pupil activity is recorded in columns 6 through 9, with pupil use of the FL located in columns 6, 7, and 8.

Table 13 is an analysis of a Spanish I class. The observation period was 30 minutes.

13

Spanish I matrix summary (30 minutes)

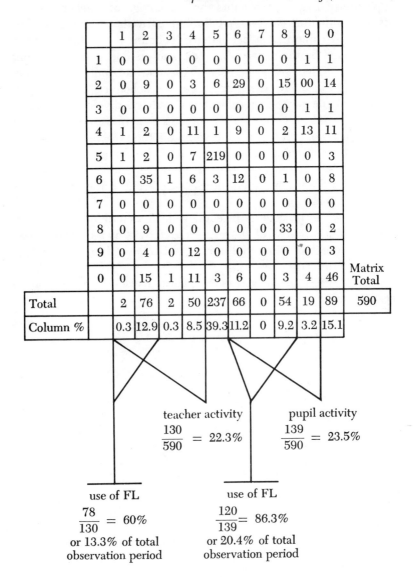

	1	2	3	4	5	6	7	8	9	0	
1	0	0	0	0	0	0	0	0	1	1	
2	0	9	0	3	6	29	0	15	00	14	
3	0	0	0	0	0	0	0	0	1	1	
4	1	2	0	11	1	9	0	2	13	11	
5	1	2	0	7	219	0	0	0	0	3	
6	0	35	1	6	3	12	0	1	0	8	
7	0	0	0	0	0	0	0	0	0	0	
8	0	9	0	0	0	0	0	33	0	2	
9	0	4	0	12	0	0	0	0	0	3	
0	0	15	1	11	3	6	0	3	4	46	Matrix Total
Total		2	76	2	50	237	66	0	54	19	89	590
Column %		0.3	12.9	0.3	8.5	39.3	11.2	0	9.2	3.2	15.1	

teacher activity
$$\frac{130}{590} = 22.3\%$$

pupil activity
$$\frac{139}{590} = 23.5\%$$

use of FL
$$\frac{78}{130} = 60\%$$
or 13.3% of total
observation period

use of FL
$$\frac{120}{139} = 86.3\%$$
or 20.4% of total
observation period

An examination of the matrix summary reveals the following information:

Total teacher activity	22.3% of observation period
Teacher use of FL	60.0% of teacher activity
Teacher use of FL	13.3% of observation period
Total pupil activity	23.5% of observation period
Pupil use of FL	86.3% of pupil activity
Pupil use of FL	20.4% of observation period
Drill and practice sessions	39.3% of observation period
Interaction recorded in category 0	15.1% of observation period

Two activities constituted the major portion of interaction recorded in category o: (1) pupils preparing themselves for language laboratory session and (2) distribution of some printed materials to the class.

Table 14 is a sample interaction form.

14

Sample interaction form[a]

Date _____   Teacher _____
Class _____   Observer _____
School _____   Other notes _____

0	8	4												
2	8	5												
2	2	5												
0	8	5												
0	8	5												
6	8	5												
6	8	5												

Evaluation of the foreign language program

2	2	5													
6	8	5													
2	8	5													
2	2	5													
2	6	5													
6	8	5													
6	8	5													
1	8	5													
1	0	5													
1	0	0													
1	4														
8	4														
8	4														
8	4														

ᵃ The actual length of the form is much longer. It usually provides space for 40 category numbers per column.

Evaluating student achievement in the foreign language classroom

The first step in determining how to measure language skill is, of course, to decide what it means to have achieved that skill. Once this has been determined, testing becomes a matter of taking representative samples of student performance. A good test will consist of items that selectively sample all the significant aspects of the skill being tested. At the same time, a good test will avoid those items which require the student to draw upon unrelated skills or to draw upon knowledge he may not possess. For example, many American youngsters read English very well but would have difficulty in explaining to an Englishman how baseball differs from cricket. The American, not knowing the English game, would be at a loss to supply satisfactory answers simply because he lacks the knowledge needed to translate facts about the American sport into terms that have meaning to the British cricket fan. It would be absurd, of course, to judge the American's English-reading ability upon how successfully he was able to compare the game of cricket with the game of baseball. Yet, to varying degrees, this is somewhat comparable to the process which often passes for testing in the foreign language classroom. For, when we ask a student questions involving literary interpretations, we are testing something other than his skill in using the language. When we ask him to translate from the target language into English, we have—in addition to the situations that are nonequivalent from one culture to the other—vocabulary items, grammatical forms, and word-order sequences which differ in the target language. Translation is the process of decoding linguistic graphic symbols from one language into the nearest cultural equivalents in the other. It can be a fascinating activity, but it is also a very complex process. Because of this, it includes much that has nothing to do with the four basic language skills. And this makes it a very poor device for testing direct student control of those skills. Modern evaluation methods call for testing procedures that measure each skill directly and as a separate entity. Thus, for example, no reading should be involved in the listening test and no writing should be required in the speaking test. In actual practice, such total separation of skills is not always feasible. However, according to modern testing authorities, a high degree of "purity" can be achieved if the persons who construct the tests are constantly aware of the importance of testing each skill separately.

ACHIEVEMENT TESTING AND PROFICIENCY TESTING

It should also be made clear at this point that we are discussing *achievement* testing rather than *proficiency* testing. Proficiency tests can be administered without regard to a specific course of study.

Evaluation of the foreign language program

Achievement tests, as the term is used here, refer to measurements of student achievement in relation to a given course of study. Achievement tests should directly utilize the vocabulary, grammatical structures, and content of the texts and materials which have been used prior to testing. (Standardized proficiency tests aimed at students in fifty different states clearly cannot do this.) As was mentioned earlier, proficiency tests can be useful tools in overall program evaluation. There is also a need for periodic measurement of student achievement; and this, ordinarily, must be done by local staff members. The following is a discussion of the types of tests which might reasonably be devised and constructed by the foreign language teacher. Table 15 provides a checklist of items which pertain to the construction of achievement tests.

15

A checklist of basic principles for constructing achievement tests

---

1. Test that which has been taught. Normally tests can involve:
   a. Simple recall of prelearned material.
   b. Rearrangement of prelearned material.
2. In presenting test items it is considered good practice to:
   a. Begin with the simplest items.
   b. Proceed to the more difficult items.
3. In selecting test items remember to:
   a. Choose problem sounds, structures, and word-order sequences.
   b. Avoid tongue twisters and absurdities.
4. In setting up multiple-choice items it is common practice to:
   a. Include at least one "distractor."
   b. Include two plausible but incorrect items.
   c. Include only one unambiguous item which correctly answers the question.
5. Directions on the test should be in English. However, the questions (multiple-choice items) should be mostly in the target language.

SOURCES OF MATERIAL FOR TEACHER-MADE TESTS

A final but very practical question is: How does a teacher with (say) five classes, a study hall, and lunch-room duty manage to create tests of the type described in this chapter? Some of the newer texts answer this question, at least in part, by providing tests for evaluating each unit of work. Even when such tests are not fully appropriate, they can be adapted to fit the local approach to teaching. Where such tests do not exist, it is advisable to borrow ideas from those who have made a special study of the matter. That is, teachers can model their own tests after the proficiency tests which are commercially available (see Bibliography). It is possible to use the format of these professionally produced tests as models, while adapting the structures and vocabulary from the local curriculum. Where not forbidden by copyright, the visuals in the test booklets can be used directly by making a transparency to be used with the overhead projector. All students can then see the visual without having to have the booklet in their hands. Also, there are other sources of transparency masters which can easily be adapted to testing. The value of visuals is in direct proportion to the teacher's ingenuity in creating suitable test questions to accompany them.[3]

Testing achievement in listening comprehension

In Table 3, Chapter 5, the various aspects of the specified goals for the achievement of listening skill were categorized as follows:

PHONOLOGY: The ability to hear all the meaningful sound contrasts of the foreign language when it is spoken at a normal rate in complete utterances.

MORPHOLOGY: The ability to hear all the changes of meaning caused by modifications of word forms when the language is spoken at a normal rate in complete utterances.

SYNTAX: The ability to hear the foreign language without being confused by syntactical arrangements.

VOCABULARY: The ability to hear and understand words in normal conversational contexts.

CULTURE: The ability to detect nuances of meaning relating to social position, family relationships, customs, national traditions, literary classics, etc.

The ultimate outcome of an ideal program in the area of listening skill was also designated as, "The ability to comprehend aurally new

[3] The bibliography at the end of this section lists sources of tests and visuals which can be used in proficiency testing or which can serve as models for constructing achievement tests.

arrangements of familiar material when spoken at normal tempo and with normal intonation and rhythm."

A *proficiency* test would aim at assessing the degree to which this latter objective had been realized. However, there are many intermediate stages in the learning process which require the teacher to judge the extent of progress toward that ultimate goal. For such measurements of *achievement* it is convenient to focus rather sharply upon the five elements listed above. When this is done, it is then possible to determine with a high degree of accuracy whether or not the student is actually acquiring the potential for comprehending normal native speech. Thus, for example, phonological discrimination can be tested by requiring the student to choose between a series of minimal pairs.

Examples: The student *sees* this:

and he *hears* the following:
It's a clock. It's a cloak.
Or he *sees* this:

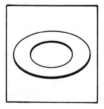

And he *hears*:
It's a ditch. It's a dish.
These are rather "pure" achievement-test items involving listening skill (assuming the student has been duly exposed to all the vocabu-

lary items). Each of these examples require the student to discriminate between two basic phonemes by correctly associating that which he hears with an unequivocal visual. Written material is not used in listening-test items because, if the student is asked to read or write, then his errors may be due to deficiencies in these skills with the result that the purity of measurement is destroyed.

MORPHOLOGY AND LISTENING TESTS

Control of morphology can be tested by compelling the student to select utterances which are appropriate to a given situation. For example, the past tense of certain irregular verbs can be tested as follows:

Step One: The student hears (in the foreign language):

Ralph was at a party. Only a few of his friends were there at the beginning. After they left, Ralph found that the other guests ignored him completely. What did Ralph do?

Step Two: Next the student hears (in English):

You will now hear four answers only one of which uses a fully appropriate verb tense. These are labeled A, B, C, and D. Circle the letter (A, B, C, or D) on your answer sheet according to which best fits the situation.

Step Three: Finally the student hears (in the foreign language):

A. Ralph goes home.
B. Ralph is going home.
C. Ralph went home.
D. Ralph has gone home.

Notice, in the above example, that all choices are potentially correct for *some* situation. However, only the simple past tense (item C) fits the given situation. Note also that all the items in steps one and three are in the simple past. There are no tricks or traps or extraneous details. The item is a straightforward test of the student's ability to recognize the verb tense to which he has been exposed. The danger of this kind of item is that it may become too long and involved so that the student is tested on his ability to recall trivial facts rather than upon his ability to distinguish morphological changes. Thus, a large number of short, clear items, using all **three** steps given above, will serve better than a single lengthy dialog in step one followed by a series of questions in step three. In a similar fashion, items involving syntax, vocabulary, and culture can serve as the focal point of oral choice questions. A simple but effective technique for oral testing is to project on a screen a transparency containing four situational pictures each of which has one common element and one different element. Then the student is asked to match a series of statements with each picture.

Step One: The student sees:

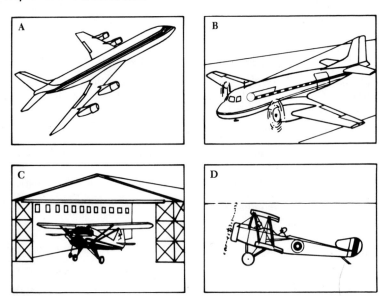

Step Two: The student is instructed to circle the correct response on his answer sheet, which can be set up as follows:

1. A B C D
2. A B C D
3. A B C D
4. A B C D

Step Three: A number of statements are spoken by the teacher, or, better still, are played from a tape recorded by native speakers. Each is spoken twice only with a normal speaking intonation. (A few samples are given below along with an indication of what each item is testing.)

1. This airplane is inside. (Vocabulary test, item C, the word *inside*.)
2. This plane will soon be in the air. (Test on future tense—two planes are in the air—only the one in item D is *about* to take off.)
3. This plane is the most modern. (Test of superlative—item A.)
4. This is the oldest airplane of all. (Test of superlative.)

Testing achievement in reading

Drawing upon objectives listed earlier (see page 82), we can identify five elements which relate to reading skill. They are:

PHONOLOGY: The ability to associate the appropriate graphic symbols with the sounds for which they stand.

MORPHOLOGY: The ability to draw meaning directly from the printed page through recognition of changes in meaning caused by modifications in structure.

SYNTAX: The ability to read directly in the foreign language without being confused by syntactical arrangements.

VOCABULARY: The ability to recognize in context a wide range of vocabulary items with sensitivity to the differences between spoken and written vocabulary and between contemporary and older literary forms, words, and expressions.

CULTURE: The ability to read everything from newspapers to works of literature. This implies a basic knowledge of the history, literature, current world position, etc., of countries in which the target language is spoken.

Obviously, the last category represents the ideal achievement. It will ordinarily be realized only by some of the better students who stay with the language for a period of four years or more. At all levels of instruction, we are involved to a certain degree with the first four; phonology, morphology, syntax, and vocabulary. If we teach these elements systematically throughout the learning process, we have established a basis for sampling. We can further refine the sampling technique by concentrating upon the most serious points of difference between English and the target language. It is axiomatic in modern linguistics that learning the problem sounds and

Evaluation of the foreign language program

structures is the priority task in second-language acquisition. Thus, in testing reading skill with regard to German syntax, the sentence, *Er ist schon hier,* would have little relevance. The transfer from the English word pattern, "He is already here," is so direct, that no learning problem (with regard to word order) is presented. On the other hand, the same sentence when it becomes a subordinate clause does present a problem. For example, the sentence, *Ich weiss, dass er schon hier ist* (literally, "I know that he already here *is*"), will inhibit the unskilled student of German when he tries to read aloud, and will slow him down when he reads silently. Therefore, this is an area which demands extra attention in the teaching process, and which, as a matter of course, must be tested to see if the student has gained sufficient control of the structure.

ORAL VERSUS SILENT READING

In the testing of reading skill we are compelled to identify two areas: (1) reading aloud, and (2) reading silently. Reading aloud requires active manipulation of the speech organs and a measurement of the accuracy of the sounds produced; therefore it relates largely to phonology. Silent reading involves a more passive assimilation of meaning directly from the printed page; therefore it relates mostly to the other four elements mentioned previously (i.e., morphology, syntax, vocabulary, and culture). Testing oral reading carries the implication that the student has been thoroughly drilled on every sound he is expected to reproduce from the printed page. Testing silent reading (particularly at the early levels) presumes that the student has been exposed to all structural and syntactical elements and to most of the vocabulary.

READING AND PHONOLOGY

Many literate people do not read well aloud, even in their native language, particularly when standing in front of an audience. Therefore, it is unrealistic to expect self-conscious youngsters to stand before their classmates and produce perfectly intoned foreign language utterances from the printed page. In the early stages of second-language acquisition, reading aloud is largely a process of using graphic symbols as cues for the production of auditory symbols. Because many of the French, German, and Spanish graphemes are identical to those used to represent English sounds, interference from English is extremely great during oral reading. The student must constantly suppress the inclination to produce the English phonemes associated with the little black marks rather than the sounds of the foreign language. Therefore, during the first few years of instruction, it is a considerable accomplishment if students can read, deliberately and accurately, short sentences containing the segmental phonemes which they have previously mastered in a different context. To expose the student to the problem graphemes before he has learned the phonemes for which they stand is to guarantee that he will mispronounce them. Thus we can predict with near certainty that the American student of Spanish will read *carro* and *caro* the same way (and will read them both unintelligibly) if he has not been thoroughly drilled on the contrasting intervocalic Spanish *r* and *rr* sounds. Lacking such drill, he will naturally revert to his native retroflex *r* and will produce, to the ear of the native speaker of Spanish, a sound somewhat like *cado,* a nonword.

TESTING ORAL READING ABILITY

The most basic aspect of oral reading seems to be an awareness on the part of the student that graphic symbols are merely visual cues used to activate the organs of speech. A written sentence is a series of graphic cues which the student must scan and reinterpret in terms of those tongue, lip, and lung actions needed to produce the appropriate sequence of sounds. If the student dwells too long on the graphemes, he may well produce atypical utterances, even in his native language. Therefore, long before the actual testing is done, the student should have had considerable practice in reading complete sentences aloud, with minimal attention to the pronunciation of individual words. This practice would necessarily include all normal liaisons or pauses characteristic of the target language. To summarize the main aspects of reading aloud it might be said that the student should:

1. Avoid hesitant, word-by-word delivery.
2. Produce all liaisons where appropriate and avoid them where not.

Evaluation of the foreign language program

3. Approximate the stress and intonation patterns nearly enough so that the intended meaning of the sentence is not distorted.

The following techniques would serve to measure the extent to which acceptable oral reading has been achieved:

Work samples. Students are required to read one at a time in the classroom or through the intercommunication panel of the language laboratory.

1. One method is to have students read aloud dialog material that has been memorized as part of the regular lesson. Each word in a sentence can first be read from back to front to prove that the student is not merely reciting from memory. Then the sentence can be reread in the normal way. The backward reading proves whether or not the student can recognize the individual lexical items. The forward reading shows his control of the suprasegmental phonemes (i.e., intonation, stress, juncture, etc.).

2. Another approach calls for the reading aloud of sentences which contain rearrangements of familiar lexical items. This tells more about real reading ability than the reading of memorized dialog material. However, with both of these techniques the teacher's judgment is necessarily rather subjective and arbitrary when work samples are taken under normal classroom conditions. Thus a rather generalized grading notation seems advisable. Below is a rough sample:

GOOD: Fluent delivery with good pronunciation and intonation.
SATISFACTORY: Comprehensible delivery with several mistakes in the above.
UNSATISFACTORY: Hesitant delivery with many mispronounced segmental phonemes and no sense of stress and intonation patterns.

Work samples can serve for a large part of the evaluation of oral reading on each unit or lesson. However, a more formalized testing is called for, perhaps two or three times each semester. Given adequate personnel, testing would be done more regularly to enable the staff to determine the effectiveness of the instructional program and to diagnose student difficulties. Ideally, the program would be modified in accordance with test results.

A formal test. Oral reading ability is tested by having all students read the same material.

1. Provide two or three simple sentences containing the phonological problems to be tested; use familiar but rearranged vocabulary items. (Preferably these should be on a ditto or mimeo sheet rather than copied from the board. Students may copy incorrectly, thus invalidating the test.)
2. Project the sentences on a screen and let everyone practice reading orally for a few minutes. (The test is whether the student can—under any circumstances—produce the problem phonemes in response to a printed stimulus. Thus the element of surprise has no relevance here.)
3. Turn off the projector and have the students come to the tape recorders and record the sentences, along with their names. (In some laboratories this can be done en masse, in others, in small groups. It can be done in the classroom with one tape recorder if the teacher has good control of the class. With a teacher aide or intern, students can be tested separately in an adjoining office. Another possibility is to record from booth to console recorder.)
4. Just before each student reads the test sentences onto the tape, he or she fills out a test sheet containing the questions. (See Table 16.)

16

Oral reading test sheet: English for Germans

Class _____   Hour _____

My name is _____.
1. *Where is the dog?*
2. *He's right behind the house.*
3. *I think he is tangled in the cord.*

On Table 16, 9 different phonemes which would prove difficult for a German have been underscored. Thus, a German learning English would be tested on these conflict points (assuming that these phonemes had been adequate drilled previously). The specific items would not be underlined for the person being tested; the underscoring would appear only on the answer sheet to remind the teacher of the test's focus. Tables 17 and 18 are further illustrations of simple recombination sentences which might be used to test oral reading achievement.

17

Oral reading test sheet: Spanish

Me llamo _____.
1. *El burro es un animal popular.*
2. *Las muchachas son muy bonitas.*
3. *Tenemos que comer ahora.*
4. *¿Dónde está un vaso?*

18

Oral reading test sheet: German

Ich heisse _____.
1. *Holen Sie sofort Ihren Hut.*
2. *Tragen Sie diesen Mantel?*
3. *Das kleine Kind lacht nicht.*
4. *Wo ist mein Zimmer?*

TESTING THE ABILITY TO DO SILENT READING

The ultimate goal of reading is to develop in students the ability to read directly, rapidly, and silently; that is, to draw meaning directly from the printed page without having to look up several words per page in a bilingual dictionary. This presumes that the student has developed the ability to guess the meaning of unfamiliar words from the contextual clues supplied by the more familiar words. It also presumes that he has acquired a considerable repertoire of high-frequency lexical items as a part of his passive or recognitional vocabulary. Further, if the silent reading is not to proceed at a snail's pace, then the recognition of words must be rapid. Therefore, speed of recognition can enter into the testing process, and the administering of timed tests is justified. If too much time is allowed, many students can puzzle out the answers by a slow, deliberate process of elimination. But normal or near-normal reading requires

352

an instantaneous grasp of meaning. Thus the student who can get the most items right in the shortest period of time is likely to be the best reader, assuming the test is well constructed. Table 19 illustrates various formats for testing silent reading. To conserve space the examples are given in English. Points of interference are indicated for each of the commonly-taught European languages.

19

Reading: types of achievement tests

A. Translation—*target language to English. (Maximum interference from English)*
B. *Completion tests with multiple choice*
    1. *Choice of correct structural item.*
    My father _____ in the shoe factory every day until 4:00 o'clock. *(German)*
      a. is working   *c. does work*
      b. works   *d. working*
    2. *Emphasis upon phonology.*
    I could not tell what time it was because I had broken my _____. *(Spanish)*
      a. welch   *c. watch*
      b. wash   *d. wortch*
    3. *Choice of correct vocabulary item.*
    We need an objective appraisal; therefore, we want this material to be read carefully by several _____ persons.
      a. uninterested   *c. distraught*
      b. uninteresting   *d. distinterested*
    4. *Choice of correct idiom.*
    Grandma became furious when she could not get the thread through the _____ of the needle. *(French)*
      a. cat   *c. tick*
      b. eye   *d. cut*
C. *Multiple choice tests.*
    1. *Reading selection with paraphrase answers. (Graded material would be used according to level.)*
    Captain Holt banked his heavily laden transport sharply to the left. The huge jet swept past inches from his upturned wing tip. In a moment Holt knew that he had averted a major air disaster. But his evasive action had cost him air speed, and the turbulence raised by the jetliner threw him into a wingover. His ship and all on board were doomed.

Evaluation of the foreign language program

Which of the following most nearly summarizes what happened?
a. *Two airplanes collided.*
b. *Two airplanes narrowly missed collision and both landed safely.*
c. *Two airplanes narrowly missed collision, but one crashed.*
d. *A transport plane and a passenger plane signaled to each other.*

2. Substituting the correct synonym for the underlined words.
   <u>I'm in a real spot</u>, John; what do you suggest?
   a. *I'm having difficulties.*
   b. *I'm in a significant location.*
   c. *I'm in a position of importance.*
   d. *I'm downtown.*

3. Transformation of morphological or syntactical items.
   I <u>must go</u> there <u>tomorrow</u>.
   (Which of the following refers correctly to the past?)
   a. *I musted to go there yesterday.*
   b. *I should have gone there yesterday.*
   c. *I have gone there yesterday.*
   d. *I had to go there yesterday.*

D. *Timed reading followed by written summarization in the foreign language. (Only at more advanced levels.)*
   1. *The student reads a selection which he can reasonably be expected to understand. (This means a selection which contains very little new vocabulary and practically no new structures or syntactical arrangements.) The student is allowed to read the material over as often as he is able within (say) a 20-minute period. He is not allowed to take notes.*
   2. *After the predetermined period of time has elapsed, the teacher collects the reading selections and distributes the test sheets. The students are then told to summarize the plot of the story using direct, simple language. The target foreign language would be used both in the reading and the summarization of content.*

E. *Timed reading followed by written summarization in English.*
   (Use the same procedures as above except that the student is allowed to write his answers in English.)

Testing achievement in speaking

Among the four skills, the testing of oral production presents the greatest number of practical problems for the classroom teacher. Not only is the teacher confronted with difficulties in eliciting the desired responses, he is also faced with the question of how to evaluate those responses objectively. Listening and reading skills can be evaluated with a high degree of objectivity. The other productive skill (writing) presents some problems in the area of objective scoring, but these are not nearly so severe as is the case with oral production.

The eliciting of written responses is much simpler, both from the standpoint of test design and the mechanics of administering the test. The other three skills can be largely tested with pencil and paper. Only oral *reading* necessitates student recording, and for this the stimuli are the unequivocal graphic symbols. With oral *production*, on the other hand, other stimuli must be used if the test is to retain its purity. And once the appropriate stimuli have been devised as test questions, the teacher must find a means of recording each student's responses and of checking each set of responses as objectively as possible.

THE LANGUAGE LABORATORY AND ORAL TESTING

Ideally, the school would have a language laboratory with tape recorders for every student in the class so that each student's response could be recorded onto tape for subsequent correction. Also, under ideal conditions, the student's tape will be paused while the test questions are playing from the console and will move only when the students are responding. Thus, after all students have been tested, the teacher can play back each tape, on which he will hear only the student's name and his responses to the test stimuli. This technique cuts correction time in half since the teacher does not have to listen to the recorded question as he evaluates the student responses. However, although few schools are likely to have the needed equipment for proceeding in this manner, the testing of oral production need not be abandoned. With two tape recorders and a separate room, it is possible to accomplish the same end if extra personnel are available on the testing days. Students are sent one at a time to the testing room. The questions are played on the one tape recorder and the answers (only) are recorded on a second recorder (along with the student's name). If pictorial stimuli are used, one tape recorder will suffice. Naturally, if an entire class is to be tested in this way, the questions will have to be very brief (less than a minute) and the administration will have to be efficiently organized.

Evaluation of the foreign language program

Also, since all students will be inactive most of the period, it is advisable to have arranged for assignments which students can do on their own during the time that they are not being tested.

TESTING TECHNIQUES FOR ORAL PRODUCTION

Testing phonology in the area of oral production can involve simple mimicry. Utterances are played on one recorder; and the student, speaking into the microphone of a second machine, is required to mimic the native speaker. The utterances will contain, of course, the critical phonemes upon which the student is being tested.

Morphological and syntactical items can be tested by adapting the pattern-drill format to the testing situation. Thus the student will hear a foreign language utterance and will be required to transform or recombine what he hears.

Examples: (Directions in English; stimuli in foreign language)
DIRECTIONS: Answer the following sentences, changing each verb to the past tense.
STIMULUS: Every day I go to the store; what did I do yesterday?"
RESPONSE: Yesterday you went to the store.
STIMULUS: Every day I eat lunch here; what did I do yesterday?
RESPONSE: Yesterday you ate lunch here.
DIRECTIONS: Change each of the following sentences into contrary-to-fact statements.
STIMULUS: If I am early, I do it.
RESPONSE: If I were early, I would do it.
DIRECTIONS: Change the nouns in the following sentences to pronouns and make all necessary word-order changes.
STIMULUS: Give Mary the book.
RESPONSE: Give it to her.
STIMULUS: Bring your father the papers.
RESPONSE: Bring them to him.

The essential difference between the drill format and the test format is that the latter does not include the correct response. In achievement testing, it is presumed that the student has been exposed to all aspects of the test items in the course of studying the language. This includes the directions as well as the stimuli. If the student errs because he is unfamiliar with the instructions, then the test is invalid.

Vocabulary (and phonology) can be tested with the highest degree of purity if pictorial stimuli are used. At the simplest level, a series of objects can be shown each of which is labeled with a number. The student simply reads the number and identifies the object in the picture. At a slightly more complex level, the pictures can portray a series of actions or qualities for which the student must supply an oral comment.

Examples:
DIRECTIONS: Tell what is happening.

STIMULUS:

RESPONSE: The boy is running.

STIMULUS:

RESPONSE: The girl is sleeping.

Evaluation of the foreign language program

Tell what the person or object is like.

RESPONSE: The girl is <u>pretty</u>, *or* She is <u>pretty</u>, *or*
She's a <u>pretty</u> girl, *or* other acceptable response.

STIMULUS:

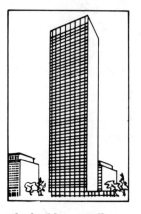

RESPONSE: The building is <u>tall</u>, *or*
That's a <u>tall</u> building, *or* other acceptable response.

TESTING FREE ORAL EXPRESSION

Fluency and free expression are the ultimate goals of oral production. It appears that these can best be tested by means of selected visuals. A series of simple line drawings which tell a story are used as stimuli. The student describes orally what is happening (or what has happened, what will happen, etc.) and, within a time limit, records his description onto tape. In the laboratory, the drawings can be projected onto a screen on the front wall; in individual testing, the same test booklet can be used with each student. Also, the possibility of utilizing motion pictures in the foreign language for oral testing should not be overlooked. With this technique, the students see an action series on the screen which is narrated in simple language. When the film has been played once, it is rewound and replayed silently. On the second showing the students supply their own narrations which are recorded on tape. (Here, of course, special laboratory facilities are required.)

In all cases involving spontaneous oral production, the tapes are graded for fluency, correctness, sophistication of language, and quantity of information. Thus it often is difficult to choose between the cautious student who makes a series of grammatically accurate comments in infantile but precise language and the intrepid student who supplies more information in a more mature manner but with a number of errors. Obviously, a large element of subjective judgment unavoidably enters into the grading of free oral production.

Testing achievement in writing

Many of the techniques used for testing oral production can also be adapted for testing written production. Dictations can serve for testing spelling ability (i.e., the relationship between phonemes and graphemes). Some of the transformation and completion exercises discussed in earlier chapters can also be used to test written command of morphology and syntax. Similarly, a series of pictorial stimuli can be utilized to elicit direct written expression as can motion pictures which are viewed and then summarized briefly in writing. At the more advanced levels, written compositions can follow reading assignments in the form of simple plot summaries or comments upon characters in a story or novel. However, the more difficult the reading assignment is, the more questionable is the purity of the writing test. Similarly, written compositions which ask for even simple literary criticisms are highly impure tests of *either* reading or writing ability. American students who read English perfectly well are often unable to engage in simple literary criticisms involving American and English literature. To expect the same students to read a foreign language and to write perceptive compositions about the relative literary merits of a given selection in the foreign language is highly unrealistic for all but a handful of American high-school youngsters. For these few, perhaps some sort of advanced placement testing is in order. For the vast majority, however, testing would seem most appropriately to focus upon measuring the extent to which a student can write reasonably mature sentences and paragraphs about nonabstract content.

Bibliography

Flanders, N. A., and E. J. Amidon, "The Role of the Teacher in the Classroom," Philadelphia, Temple University, January, 1962.

Lado, Robert, *Language Testing the Construction and Use of Foreign Language Tests,* New York, McGraw-Hill, 1961.
    This text provides a comprehensive introduction to the field of language testing. It demonstrates the relationship between modern linguistics and testing theory.

Moskowitz, Gertrude, "The Effects of Training Foreign Language Teachers in Interaction Analysis," *Foreign Language Annals, I* (March 1968), 218–238.

Valette, Rebecca, *Modern Language Testing,* New York, Harcourt, Brace & World, 1967.
    This is a very useful handbook containing a large number of model test items along with clearly stated directions for constructing FL tests.

PROFICIENCY TESTS AND OTHER MATERIALS

Auditory and Reading Comprehension Tests, New York, College Entrance Book Company.

Common Concepts Foreign Language Tests, Del Monte Research Park, Monterey, California, California Test Bureau.

Fearing, Percy, *Evaluating Foreign Language Speaking Skills,* St. Paul, Minnesota Department of Education, Division of Instruction.

MLA Cooperative Foreign Language Tests, Princeton, Educational Testing Service.

New York Regents Exams, Albany, New York, University of the State of New York, State Education Department.

Pimsleur Modern Foreign Language Proficiency Tests, New York, Harcourt, Brace & World.

Tests for *Voix et Images,* Philadelphia, Chilton.

Test Transparencies, St. Paul, Minnesota, 3M Corporation.

Index

Bilingualism, 59, 64, 72, 77–81
  as an instructional goal, 76–77, 80,
    81, 86
  and reading skill, 59, 267
  and writing skill, 59
Birkmaier, Emma M., xv
Books, *see* Textbook and Reading
    materials
Boyd-Bowman, Peter, 192, 193
Brooks, Nelson, 66, 80, 81
Business needs and FL study, 35, 36,
    37

Camps, foreign language, 248
Careers requiring FL study, 34–37
Carroll, John B., 173
Cartridge, *see* Tapes, magazines for
Children, cognition in first language
    learning and, 136, 137, 138
  first language learning and, 57, 63,
    66, 132–133
  speech recovery after brain dam-
    age, 64
  See also FLES
Chinese, 47
Classical languages, 1–3, 6, 7, 8, 24
Classroom, electronic devices and,
    289
  for encouraging free expression,
    246, 247
  language laboratory and, 325
  limitations of traditional, 67–68,
    178, 327
  pattern practice in, 205, 214–216,
    228–231
Cognates, 253, 262
Cognition, in first language learning,
    136, 137, 138
  pattern practice and, 212–213, 229
  in second language learning, 117,
    118, 133–157
Cognitive-Code-Learning Theory, 117
Coleman Report, 15
College preparation versus general
    education, 324, 360

Colonial period and status of FL
    study, 5–6
Committee of Ten recommendations,
    11, 12
Committee of Twelve Report, 9, 12
Composition, *see* Writing skill
Compound bilingual, *see* Bilingualism
Computers, use in flexible scheduling,
    67, 68, 69, 70
  use in programmed instruction, 180,
    184, 185, 302
Conditioning, 183, 189
  FL learning and, 117, 118, 127,
    189, 133–134
  pattern practice and, 208–209, 212,
    237
  phonology and, 127
  programmed instruction and, 189,
    200, 201
Conflict points, as a basis for drills,
    206–207, 209, 212
  learning priorities and, 48–51, 56,
    211
  phonology and, 50, 51, 52, 128, 132
  spelling and, 205, 251–252
  testing and, 344, 347–348
Content of FL program, 84–87
  French, levels I–IV, 87–96
  German, levels I–IV, 97–106
  Spanish, levels I–IV, 106–116
Context and meaning, 167–170, 209
  in reading skill, 250, 259–260, 265
  in vocabulary acquisition, 55, 167,
    168–170, 324, 352
  See also Vocabulary
Conversation, *see* Free expression
Conversion exercises, 213, 215, 216,
    217, 218, 221–224, 275
Coordinate bilingual, *see* Bilingualism
Correction of error, 246, 247
  See also Error
Cortex, early commitment of to
    speech, 64

Credit system as a block to educational progress, 67, 69, 70, 197–198
Crowder, Norman, 179, 180, 184, 185
Culture, 55, 81, 85, 253, 324, 347
  in basic dialog utterances, 123
  visual presentation of, 79, 81
  vocabulary and, 84, 88, 253–254
    in French, 89, 92, 94, 96, 253
    in German, 98, 101, 103, 105, 253
    in Spanish, 109, 111, 114, 116, 253

Decoding, see Reading skill
Descriptive grammar, 40, 41
Dewey, John, 117, 155
Dial-access laboratories, 69, 295
Dialog, see Basic dialog utterances
Dictations, 271, 273, 359
Dictionaries, 254, 257, 259, 268, 352
Direct method, 9, 10, 160, 163, 247
Discipline problems in the language laboratory, 290
Divergent thinking, 198, 275
Drill work, need for short daily sessions, 290–291
Drills, types of, see Pattern practice

Eclectic school of FL learning, 118
Electronic classroom, 286, 288, 289, 290, 298, 325, 326
  advantages of, 290, 293–294
  compared to language laboratory, 287–293, 325, 326
  limitations of, 233, 298, 300
  specifications for, 300–317
  tapes needed for, 299
English, 5, 6, 7
  cultural topics taught in, 165, 326
  disadvantages of classroom use, 162, 163, 164, 165, 166, 167–170, 171, 172, 250, 253, 254, 332
  effect of FL study upon, 36, 37
  guidelines for classroom use of,

160, 161, 162, 163–166, 342, 354
  in interaction analysis, 327, 329–330
  as a second language, 50, 51, 128, 131
  student use of, 327, 330
  teacher use of, 163–166, 171, 172, 243, 327, 329, 330
  as a universal language, 26
Enrollments in Latin and modern languages, 8, 14
Equipment for FL instruction, 71, 176–177, 186, 195, 325, 326
Error, 165, 300
  free expression and, 165, 246, 247, 300
  prereading instruction and, 249–251
  in programmed instruction, 178, 179, 180, 181, 182, 183, 185, 199
Esperanto used as a shock language, 140–152
Ethnocentricism and FL study, 24, 253
    See also Monolingualism
Evaluation, 319–321
  of FL program, 321–327
  of student achievement, 321, 340–360
  of student-teacher interaction, 320, 327–340

Failure and the FL program, 181, 284
Fallacies of language, 39–40
Federal aid to education, 30, 282
Films, see Visual aids
Flanders, Ned, 327, 328
FLES, 61, 62, 63, 65, 66
  definition of, 61–62
  failures of, 64–65
  history of, 9, 12, 17
  rationale for, 63–66
    See also Age and Children

Flexible scheduling, *see* Scheduling, flexible
Fluency, 156, 189, 209
Foreign language camps, *see* Camps
Foreign Service Institute (FSI), 72
Foreign study, 249, 278–279, 322
Formal speech, 53, 55
Free expression, 84, 330
  failure to develop, 246, 247, 248
  grammar and, 119, 134–136, 143–144, 156, 159
  pattern practice and, 209, 238–241, 247
  programmed instruction and, 191, 197–198
  speaking skill and, 124, 245, 246, 247, 248, 249, 326
  techniques for eliciting, 201, 240, 241, 246, 247, 248, 249, 326
  writing skill and, 273–278
  tests of, 358, 359
Freeman, Stephen, 279
French language, compared to English, 42–43
  course objectives for, 87–96, 188–189
  drill examples in, 217, 218, 221, 223
  history of in U.S.A., 6, 7, 8
  interaction analysis and, 332, 333
  phonology and, 48, 132, 251, 252
  reference grammars for, 281

General education and FL study, 284, 324
General language courses, 25
Generalizations, grammatical, importance of, 117–122, 127, 151, 152, 153, 156, 157, 173, 324
  inductive learning of, 138, 139, 140
  memorization of, 151, 153, 154, 155
  techniques for learning, 139–157
  See also Grammar
German language, compared to English, 42–43
  course objectives for, 97–106

  drill examples in, 217, 219, 221, 223, 224, 228
  history of in U.S.A., 6–8, 13
  phonology and, 48, 132, 251, 252, 348
  programmed instruction and, 193
  reference grammars for, 281
  test items for, 348, 352
Glaude, Paul, 134
Goals, instructional, 76–87, 321, 326
  See also French, German, and Spanish
Gouin series, 161, 173
Graded readers, 258, 262, 263, 264
Grades (marks), 270, 271, 284
Grammar, in first language learning, 136, 137, 138
  in FL learning, 10, 122, 123, 124, 125, 134–136, 151, 152, 153, 156–157, 258, 324
  inductive learning of, 138, 139, 140–146
  misuse of, 23, 24, 49, 73, 137, 156
  modern approaches to, 39, 40, 41, 53
  pattern practice and, 204, 205, 206, 211, 212, 213, 229, 230
  traditional approaches to, 10, 39, 40, 41, 53, 147–151
Grammar-translation method, 7, 9, 10, 267
Grammars, *see* Reference grammars
Graphemes, 185, 186
  in relation to phonemes, 44, 236, 249, 250, 255, 256, 349
  when to introduce, 251–252
Greek, 2, 3, 5, 8
Grim humanism, 23
Grouping students in language laboratory, 289
  See also Small-group work

Habit formation, 200, 201, 324
  See also Conditioning

Hayes, Alfred S., 293
Hindi, 25, 26
  self-instruction and, 193
Homework and pattern practice, 237
Humanism and FL study, 28, 35, 254
  in the modern era, 23, 24, 27
  versus utilitarianism, 33, 34, 35
Huxley, Thomas, 23

IMC concept of the language laboratory, 286, 295–296, 298
Immigrant heritage and anti-FL attitudes, 14, 16
Increments, minimal, *see* Minimal
  increments
Individualized instruction, 70, 85, 86,
  178, 270
  in the language laboratory, 231–
  232, 289, 294, 326
  programmed instruction and, 190,
  191, 197
  reading and, 270, 271
Inductive process in FL learning, 138,
  139, 140–146, 151–153, 154
Industry, influence of on education,
  176, 194–195
Inference and learning of vocabulary,
  256, 257, 258, 259, 260, 267
Inservice education, 322, 323, 325
Institute program, *see* National Defense Education Act
Instructional Materials Center, *see*
  IMC concept
Interaction analysis, 320, 327, 328, 329
  classification techniques for, 330,
  331, 332–334, 336–339
  use of English, 327, 329, 330, 332
  use of FL, 329, 330
  use of matrix, 332–340
  French examples of, 332, 333
  Spanish example of, 331
Interference, *see* Conflict points
Interlineary readers, 265
International understanding and FL
  study, 31, 32, 33

Interpreting as a profession, 242, 243
Intonation, 45, 46, 47, 48, 49, 123,
  130, 167, 215, 350
Isolationism and FL study, 15

Japanese and programmed instruc-
  tion, 193
Journals, professional, 327
Joyaux, Georges J., 28
Junior high school and articulation of
  FL program, 324

Kant, Immanuel, 155
Keating, Raymond, 292

Lado, Robert, 133, 241
Lange, Dale L., xv
Language, nature of, 39–43, 55, 56
  See also Linguistics
Language laboratory, 287–293, 295,
  296, 297, 298, 311, 325
  administration of, 283, 284–285,
  296–298, 327
  advantages of, 291, 293, 294
  history of, 20, 282–283, 284
  maintenance of, 305, 306, 316–317
  problems with, 284, 285–286, 290
  specifications for, 302–315
  staff needs for, 69, 284–285, 291,
  297, 298, 325, 326
  tapes for, 213, 214, 296–297, 299–
  300
  testing in, 330, 350, 351, 355
  utilization of
    by students, 190, 200, 231–232,
    283–284, 289, 294–295, 325,
    326
    by teachers, 205, 231–235, 284,
    289, 291, 292, 293, 295, 297,
    299, 300, 325
Language tables for developing free
  expression, 326
Large-group instruction, 70
Latin, 2, 5, 8, 37, 39, 43
Letter writing in FL, 277–278